John Lennon in Heaven

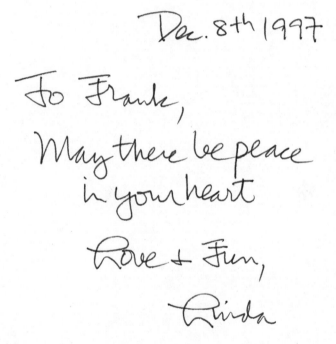

Dec. 8th 1997

To Frank,
May there be peace
in your heart
Love & Fun,
Linda

John Lennon
in Heaven

*Crossing the Borderlines
of Being*

by

Linda Keen

Pan
Publishing
P.O. Box 1286
Ashland, OR 97520

Two extracts from "Skywriting by Word of Mouth" from *IN HIS OWN WRITE* by John Lennon are hereby acknowledged. Appreciation is expressed to the estate of John Lennon, the source, and Jonathan Cape as publisher.

ISBN 0-9636218-5-8

LCCN 93-84161

ATTENTION ORGANIZATIONS, HEALING CENTERS, AND SCHOOLS OF SPIRITUAL DEVELOPMENT: Quantity discounts are available on bulk purchases of this book for educational purposes or fund raising. Special books or book excerpts can also be created to fit specific needs. For information, please contact Pan Publishing, P.O. Box 1286, Ashland, Oregon 97520 or call (503) 488-8001 / fax (503) 488-2115.

Table of Contents

Part IV: Arcadia

Part V: Trip to the Mountain

Introduction

If it wasn't for the dream I had in the Swiss Alps, the whole thing might never have happened. In it I am visiting a woman who is planning to write a book entitled *John Lennon in Heaven*. She is going to converse with John about what it is like to exist after death and, apparently, he is very eager to participate—in fact, he has organized the whole thing himself. I see the intentions of this woman are real and powerful, and what's more, I wish intensely that *I* could write such a book. As I awaken, the quality of it lingers in my whole body and mind, leaving me inspired yet perplexed.

Vacationing in the homeland of Carl Jung, the western world's modern pioneer in dream analysis and what he called the collective unconscious, I had been observing my dreams lately and writing them down. Was that why I had this special one, or was it because I was sleeping a little closer to heaven, being so high in the mountains?

Wandering in the imposing Swiss Alps that same morning, my heart and imagination allowed me to feel closer to the spirit of Carl Jung than ever before. Realizing how the mountain peaks were all connected to the same earth, I started thinking about the collective unconscious, that information which is common to all—the foundation of what the ancients called "the sympathy of all things." One curious element about the collective unconscious is that it can be tapped and communicated with. Was my dream tapping into John Lennon's reality? Was I communicating subconsciously with him?

1

I found the dream impressive, yet the more I reflected upon it, the more I considered it to be a clear message of my ability to write about metaphysical subjects. I'd published a book in the Netherlands about intuitive development, and in it I wrote that essentially everybody is clairvoyant, telepathic, clairaudient and what-have-you. I wanted to demystify the psychic experience because I believe our tapping into the collective unconscious (or as I prefer: the collective awareness) need not be mystifying.

Breathing in the cool mountain air in bright sunshine, I considered my dream about John Lennon to be a metaphor; yet part of me felt intrigued by the possibility of tuning into him as a conscious entity and attempting to communicate. Had my dream been literal—was *I* supposed to do this? Somewhere inside I knew I'd already started writing that book I had dreamed about just a few hours earlier. Suddenly, right before me, I saw the face of John Lennon as it had appeared on his last album. He seemed to be smiling at me wryly. Then it disappeared as quickly as it had come.

Back home in the Netherlands I continued to teach intuitive development at my school. During the next six months I kept setting aside any ideas about the possibility of communicating with the specter of Mr. Lennon and settled for the comfortable habit of communing with my familiar, old, intangible guardian, Basil. He had not only helped me write my first book, but had continued to assist me in many aspects of my professional and private life. I felt totally safe with him and didn't have to think about meddling around in the affairs of a world-famous, deceased Beatle.

I did feel compelled, however, to nose around regularly in record stores and bookstores, trying to discover more about what John Lennon had actually been like. The idea captivated me. I was able to uncover information I had never known, facts I hadn't kept up with when he was alive. There had been more written about John Winston/Ono Lennon—both before and after his death—than I ever supposed. The stories were amusing, sad, absorbing and sometimes deeply moving. I read about his dark side: he had been an extremely difficult person to get along with at times and this had made his life complicated, to say the least. The more I opened up to John Lennon's life through numerous biographies and his own books, recordings and video tapes, the more I began to feel I'd known him personally when he was alive. I realized I wasn't the only one who felt this way, that this was part of John's unusual and powerful charisma. Yet there seemed to be something else going on.

The existence and proximity of John's consciousness—as a nonphysical entity—was steadily growing more real. I began to have more dreams about him. Sometimes we were playing music (I had been a musician before getting into intuitive work), and sometimes it felt as though I was helping him in ways that weren't yet very apparent. A turning point came when I dreamed I found him lying underneath the ground and was helping him to stand up and step into a pair of my denim pants. Intrigued, I decided this had something to do with my ability to give John Lennon new substance.

No matter what my rational convictions may have been, John as a friend and presence, was growing steadily more genuine. I could swear he was taking a strong interest in my daily life activities. For instance, it seemed I could hear him laughing at some witticism; or, I could feel him observing with curiosity the way I would teach a class or help heal my sick daughter simply by laying my hands on her. Sometimes, grinning to myself, I imagined John Lennon was becoming like a spirit guide to me, and I remembered what he had written in his posthumously published book, *Skywriting by Word of Mouth*.

"My spirit guide, a certain Dr. WINSTON O'BOOGIE, was beginning to manifest himself in no uncertain terms. At the drop of a hatcheck girl he would give forth on various subjects, ranging from the ridiculous to Mamie Eisenhower. That summer whilst holding a pet semester in my hands, I had grasped the meaning of life, only to fall flat on my face. Knowing fool *[sic]* well how the majority of people would respond, Dr. Winston began to speak at dinners. A disembodied group of experts had invited me up a flight of fancy . . ."

I discovered John had believed firmly in the existence of spirit and read numerous accounts of his involvement with spiritual phenomena. I grew to learn he had been psychic his whole life and had suffered indeterminately because of it. Yet, paradoxically, his psychic sensitivity had also sustained his ability to be original and creative.

John Lennon understood what spirit was all about, but, as with practically everything, he loved to make outrageous jokes about it. He often had the capacity to not take himself or life too seriously—although his portion of suffering far exceeded what is dished out for most of us in our lives—and this was something I continued to admire about him.

In March of 1987, I reached a decision. Having grown steadily more curious, and somewhat less apprehensive, I knew the time was ripe to meet directly with John Lennon's elusive essence.

Linda Keen
The Netherlands, 1993

"Perhaps life's Karmic Wheel had bent his spokes."

John Lennon
Skywriting by Word of Mouth

PART I

The Meadow

~1~
No Famous Souls

It was Saturday morning, March 21, 1987. I was sitting anxiously alone in my study. Outside my window it was cold and damp, so I reached over to turn up the heater. Every year there seemed to be less and less of a springtime in the Netherlands and, as a native Californian, I often found the Dutch climate hard to get used to.

Luckily I knew I could change anything inside my own mind—even bad weather—and that's exactly what I was planning to do this morning as I sat in my swivel chair, trying to relax and enter a deep trance by means of focused concentration. It had taken me about nine months to find the courage to do this; I think I'd been afraid it wouldn't work out. Or had I been afraid it **would***?*

With the help of a cassette tape of an English meadow with birdsong playing through my headphones and another tape for recording my voice, I slowly permitted myself to travel with full concentration to an imaginary meadow. It was here I was planning to meet my friendly and faithful advisor, Basil, and, hopefully, the specter of John Lennon—if he decided to show up. Since childhood, I was used to hearing inner conversations with various intangible beings. Now I was prepared to repeat everything which might be conveyed to me into the tape recorder.

9

In a state of suspended animation, I projected myself into the meadow. It was a technique I often taught others as a means of coming into contact with deeper layers of reality, especially those relating to the nonphysical world.

It is delightfully warm and sunny and gentle with bird song. A brook is flowing nearby and I can smell the moist, green grass and fresh air. The sky is blue with puffy clouds hanging lazily about, and everywhere around me are beautiful, colorful wild flowers. I am sitting under the partial shade of a large and stately oak and, as I gaze into the distance, I notice an entire group of them which seem to be whispering secrets to one another.

Reclining into my tarpaulin lounge chair, I turn my face slowly upward to catch several delicate yet glorious sunrays. A fly buzzes around my ears, then darts away, and I linger awhile, doing nothing. Slowly, I'm getting the feeling. It is the feeling to begin: to start somewhere, anywhere.

I look to my left, and there is Basil reclining in his lounge chair. His eyes are closed, which gives me the chance to inspect him thoroughly. He is an elderly gentleman, well-dressed in a blue tweed suit, handsome and well-preserved for his age. I stare appreciatively at his gentle face. Basil has been an important teacher and my father-figure for several years, giving me strength and courage to trust more and more in the reality of the immaterial world, in the power of healing and transformation. I wonder now if he is asleep and if he will hear me when I speak to him.

"So—when is the show going to start, Basil?" I ask timidly.

He opens one eye and winks, straightens himself in his chair and beams.

"I was wondering when you were going to ask me that! It looks as if you are having a touch of stage fright, my dear—you need to relax for a moment and not be so nervous about all of this."

"I thought I was doing pretty well so far."

"Connect yourself more with the ground . . . take a few deep breaths . . . there that's it . . . that's much better."

I pause, sigh deeply and immediately feel more at ease.

"Now," he resumes, "it just so happens that you can serve as a reliable medium for particular information. But if you keep taking this project so personally, you're going to prevent the information from coming through! You're aware of this yourself, of course, but it's just going to take some more practice."

"Practice makes perfect," I laugh sarcastically, adjusting my position in the chair and inspecting the folds of my new forest-green dress which I have never seen before.

"You are hung up on all of this, aren't you?" Basil grins. "This desire to be perfect is a problem you often suffer, yet it does have it's positive aspects."

He waits for a moment, then speaks.

"It is so natural sitting here with you—just like a father with his daughter. Don't you think?"

"Yes it is, actually. The same thought was passing through my mind a moment ago when I watched you sleep."

"Well, you know," he says, "it's not meant to be such a serious place here."

He reaches over to a small table I hadn't seen before and I can hear ice cubes clinking in the pitcher as he pours me a glass of what looks like lemonade.

"John is waiting," he says calmly, handing me the glass.

"I know. I just can't see him yet," I answer uneasily. "Am I not suffering from illusions of grandeur? I need you to help me."

"Oh, never mind. Now it's a matter of trust—you haven't made enough contact yet. And, don't be so fearful! Why is it that a famous name can be so incapacitating? We're just who we are in this place, plain and simple. There are no famous souls here! Of course, each soul is unique and has its own singular expression . . ." Basil smiles at me again.

"We think it quite amusing to regard all of you on earth with your silly attitude of 'famous' and 'not famous,' as if it has some bearing on each person's importance—or lack thereof!"

"You must be right, but still, it's just the idea that I even dare. I suppose I need to jump right into deep water and force myself to swim."

I watch the ice cubes floating in my glass, take a sip of cool lemonade and observe Basil swatting at a fly which seems to be just as annoying as its earthly counterpart. Taking a handkerchief out of his breast pocket, he carefully wipes his forehead. A light breeze is rustling the new, bright-green leaves of the oak tree and there is a sweet smell of flowers in the air.

"You could think of it in such a dramatic way . . . but once you get involved, I think you'll see it differently." Basil dabs again at his forehead.

"Okay! Let's get on with it . . . John, I can't see you yet, but I can *feel* that you're here. You're sitting somewhere on my right, aren't you?"

There is a moment of complete silence as I stare tensely at the ground, then look imploringly at Basil.

"Yeah, hallo there! How's it going?" a substantial, friendly voice booms out.

I can now see the figure of John Lennon sitting next to me as distinct as the oak tree. I'm surprised to see how happy he looks. His face is fresh and radiant. He's dressed in brown corduroy pants and a cowboy shirt. He has sunglasses on, so I can't see his eyes. His hair is medium length and tousled, he's got a slight growth of beard with full sideburns and a big smile. My heart pounds.

"You certainly don't have to be afraid of me or anything else in this luv'ly meadow," John utters in his distinctive Liverpudlian voice, "I'm so glad you and Basil asked me to come!"

I'm smiling from ear to ear and begin to chuckle uneasily.

"Well, hello there, John . . . it's great you decided to show up, I mean . . . I wasn't so sure. How exciting that I finally get to meet you face to face! You know how long I've been thinking and wondering . . ."

"Yeah! You sure as hell took your time since that first dream we had together," he says, shaking his head at me. "Linda, it's a pleasure ta be here and you must know that. And don't make me too shy. I'm not used to that anymore."

"Oh, I'm sorry! I didn't realize . . . so it really *is* true! I mean, you really *did* want this yourself . . ."

"My God, kid, yer about as insecure as I used to be," he says shaking his head and chewing on a piece of gum. "Hey, what's that ya got there?"

"Oh this? Well, it's your book. I mean, a book which was published after you, uh, died."

"Oh, yeah, that thing . . . *Skywriting by Word of Mouth.*"

He pauses, chomps on his gum, then continues, "When I look back at my writing and drawing and stuff—however fun and amusing it used ta be—I remember, too, how isolated I used ta get."

John is sitting with legs crossed, tapping his fingers on his wooden armrest. Looking around, he chews enthusiastically as a faint breeze blows lightly through his hair. Basil and I wait in silence for him to carry on.

"Nice place ya got here," he says, continuing to glance around. "Well, when I look at that little book, I can remember how much insight I had then, and how it related to so many things I did . . . but it was as if I couldn't cross over the threshold of my own limitations. D'ya know what I mean?"

"Well, I'm not sure, really."

"It had somethin' to do with pride, with bigheadedness—which most human beings have in their own peculiar way. Although I dared to speak out—and God knows I did!—and even, at a certain point, tried to change the world, I never really dared to take certain steps within my personal life. I just wasn't ready for it yet."

He shifts in his chair and scratches his head.

"I could only see all this, though, after leaving my body and looking from the perspective I have now."

It's not easy for me to get used to this sudden intimacy with John and it's difficult to think of what I'll say next.

"Gee, you really look great, John. I didn't know what to expect. I was so curious what you'd look like!" There is an uncomfortable lapse. "Uh, do you mean you weren't ready to see certain things about yourself?" I ask, glancing at Basil who is looking vaguely amused.

"Lucy in the Scarf with Diabetics," John mumbles as he glares at me.

"What's that?" I answer anxiously.

"Well, ya know, there were certain important aspects to my personal life which I didn't wanna hafta face. And on top of that, it's actually very limited, what a person can say—what I ended up even *wanting* to say—to the public. During my whole life I expressed a lot . . . and eventually ended up not *caring* if I was misunderstood or not. There was more going on inside of me than I could come out with directly . . . and . . . of course . . . my favorite way of letting it all out was to act crazy! It's just that I didn't wanna admit to myself I was tired and fed up with the life I had created for myself . . . who does?"

He peers at me, and I see Basil offering him a frosty bottle of beer which materializes out of nowhere. Obviously, John is thirsty. He takes the wad of gum out of his mouth and sticks it neatly under the armrest of his chair. Then, as he tilts his head back to drink, I watch self-consciously as his Adam's apple bobs up and down with each swallow. He sighs with pleasure and burps nonchalantly.

The meadow remains remarkably real and peaceful, bearing distant memories of idyllic calm and safety—of carefree childhood dreaming—hopeful and free. I sit and gape at John.

"This new perspective you have since you died . . . could you possibly describe it to me?"

"Take a look . . . whadaya see? Whadaya feel? This is really one of the main reasons you're here with me in the first place—ta perceive it for yerself. But it's gonna take some *time*! You're gonna have to be extremely patient, not only with me but with yerself! It's gonna take years . . . and it's gonna ask a certain amount of guts ta keep on believing in us and what we're doing together."

"Oh no . . . my meadow sounds tape just ran out! I didn't rewind it before I came here!" I shoot partially out of trance and look down at a tape recorder sitting on a white formica desk. "Can you wait a few seconds until it turns itself over?" I ask feebly. "I've got this new auto-reverse thing, and I can't seem to concentrate properly without our meadow sounds . . . dammit . . ."

I keep fumbling nervously, fearing John will disappear if my tape recorder stops functioning properly. My concentration is divided equally between the reality of the meadow and that of the stuffy room where I started out.

"There we go—God! This is all so new . . . excuse me . . ."

"By all means . . ." He looks at me tolerantly.

"Okay, here we go." I'm completely in the meadow again and greatly relieved. "I agree with you that this is going to take a lot of patience. But I'm the type who doubts continuously—it's one of my weak points."

"You'd better be happy about it, kid, 'cause that's one reason me and you are gonna be good working together! Your insecurity makes it easier for me to get through . . . it's like you've got more channels tuned into me that way. You know how ta listen well."

"You mean I can listen better to you because I'm unsure of myself?"

"Somethin' like that. I can get through to you with me own ideas . . . 'cause yer not blocking them constantly with yer own plans and opinions. A channel needs ta be empty in order ta function properly."

"That's a nice way of looking at it," I answer, absorbed.

With dazzling sunrays shining through the new leaves, I notice beads of sweat forming on John's forehead. Feeling all of a sudden very warm myself, I start to blush and hope no one will notice. I look over at Basil, who bats his eyes at me and focuses again on his folded hands.

"But John, you were just telling me about your lack of courage. It seems as if you did risk a tremendous amount . . . compared to the rest of us—for instance, when you and Yoko staged your bed-ins for peace after your marriage."

"Oh, that! That was more innocent than most people wanted to think. Yeah, I know what you mean . . . but that's not really what I'm talkin' about. It's all so bloody relative." He shakes his head in frustration.

"Do you mean you felt a need to present yourself to your fans in a way they could relate to? If you began to say too many outrageous things, they would think you had lost it?"

I take a sip out of my glass, feeling my cheeks continue to flush. I'm becoming emotional and don't know why.

"I think that's a bit naive," John answers in his nasal tone. "Many people thought I had gone fuckin' mental long before that! You can't fathom how many people couldn't handle my moods and changes as it was. I stayed busy in my own private world tryin' to discover who I *really* was as this weird person, John Lennon . . . and it often caused awful depression."

He gazes at me solemnly for a moment, as if he's been reminded of certain things which are still painful. I suspect, at this moment, it is taking him just as much nerve to have this encounter with me as the other way around, perhaps more.

"I admire you for your courage," I blurt out. "I've got a faint idea of how it must have been, but you're the only one who knows how it actually felt. I guess this is something you can tell me more about . . . eventually."

He shows a crooked smile and finishes his bottle of beer in a few gulps. I notice he, too, is somewhat flushed.

"Sure, friend, we've got all the time in the universe."

I glance again at Basil, who is enjoying his reclining position in the partial sun.

"Basil," I ask, "what is your purpose, sitting here with us in your outrageously comfortable lounge chair? Is it because you make me feel safe? With my two feet on the ground? Of course I'm much more down-to-earth when you're around. And what about the funny fact that both of you are Englishmen? Is it coincidence that we happen to be sitting here in the English countryside? I mean, both of you *were* British in your last life on earth . . ."

My cheeks seem to be hotter than ever and Basil pats me gently on the knee.

"Linda, my dear," he answers, "it has become a bit obvious to you, perhaps, that John and I are also old friends, just as you and I are, and that's one reason our meeting has been able to take place. John and I have known each other before—just as you and John have. Do you think it a coincidence the names of Lennon and Keen are both derived from the Irish?"

"Oh. Okay. Maybe I'm starting to understand this whole setup a little better." I look solemnly at the ground. "Are we going to talk about all of these things? I mean, will those lives we've all had together be revealed to me through you and John?"

"Yes, eventually," Basil replies, trying to suppress a grin, "but you'll have to let this whole meeting unfold itself naturally . . . without wanting too much, remember? This attitude is essential for our success as a team."

"A team? You make it sound like we're going to play baseball or something . . ."

My serious expression switches into a mischievous smirk. John takes off his sunglasses, rubs his eyes and says, snorting, "By the time we finish, luv, you might feel as if we had!"

For the first time I see his piercing brown eyes, and it's as if I'm looking timidly at a person I have known for a very long time. Basil clears his throat and sits up straight.

"Just to pick up and begin somewhere . . . John and I have a very strong link together from the legendary days of King Arthur. During that period, we had, as men to men, a deep bond of loyalty together. In those days, John and I incorporated a strong code of respect and honor into our human ways. Those were the themes of the day, along with the mystical experience and its accompanying ideals."

I'm puzzled. "What do you mean by the 'mystical experience and its accompanying ideals'?"

"I mean that in those days there was a wonderful connection between the forces of nature and early Christianity in its purest form. The connection we have is a mystical one, and through it came our creative and poetic expression. Not only were we spiritually attuned as brothers, but we had also been able, in earlier lives, to express ourselves through words and music—as poets, as bards. We sang the fabled poetry of the times. That's where we connect, then—at a period on earth when there was more accommodation for this poetry, which in these modern times, I'm sorry to say, is much more obscured."

Basil is looking into the expanse of trees and sky, as if part of him is no longer present and John and I wait quietly for him to continue.

"My friend here, John, has helped—on many diverse occasions, I must say—to bring some of this mystical and poetic inspiration back to earth when it was urgently needed. That is one reason so many people have dearly loved him. John and I were Englishmen in our last lives because we share a common history in the British Isles. If you look closely, you'll see that this is Celtic, and more specifically and more distant in time, Druid."

John has been listening with his eyes closed and head tilted back. At this moment, my attention is seized by a distant grove of oak trees—between my view of the two men. I get a queer sensation in my stomach. The trees look as if they are moving and talking together in an odd, whispering way and making funny, subtle gestures. I want to hurry over and find out what they are doing, but my attention darts back to Basil and his last statement.

"You mean both of you were once Druid priests, as well?"

"As you were, my dear . . . and this is one connection the three of us strongly share. You were, and more than once I might add, a Druid priestess: women were able to serve a powerful function in those days, you realize. It would be worth your further investigation. Why are you so much in awe of the moon's cycles? Why do you worship nature, love magic and adore rituals? Why do you use crystals? Your Druid training was not meant to be limited to one lifetime—not by a long shot! That's what John and I mean when we say you'll have to be patient."

"Yeah! I guess so!" I shake my head and look over at John. "Were you aware of this Druid stuff, too?"

"Aye, that I was," he says with his eyes closed, as if half asleep. "Reviewin' this kinda stuff is part of my regular curriculum since I got here."

"What do you mean, your regular curriculum?"

"Oh, I'm sorry . . ." John sits up, opens his eyes, squints and puts his sunglasses back on. "I really am getting too much ahead of meself. Basil, why don't you finish what you were telling about?"

Basil adjusts the handkerchief in his pocket and fidgets with the large, golden ring on his finger.

"Yes, let me see . . . where were we? John's and my Druid—and later Celtic—background might serve as a good introduction to the concept of western mysticism, or the occult, which simply means 'hidden.' The occult has gotten a pretty bad name for itself in recent years, which is unfortunate since it used to be western man's ultimate connection with the inner God and Goddess and with all of nature. A problem seemed to arise when too many people began to use the occult for their own selfish gains. So many souls have been lost to darkness, pride, fear and loneliness this way! People's silly games, the desire to control others—hard lessons the human race has been forced to learn! The original mysticism on earth had to do with *inspiration*—indeed, of being an instrument, without judgement, for all that is natural and creative."

"And this is the base whereupon we meet, my good friends," John adds gently.

"I've got the distinct feeling my time is up," I say abruptly. "I'm so tired . . . I want to go home." I look at my bare wrist. "I wonder what time it is."

"There isn't any time here, Linda," Basil informs me in a soothing voice.

"You're right, I forgot. Anyway, I want to thank you. This is fantastic . . . I mean, this is so real!"

"*Now* she figures that out . . ." John whispers loudly with his hand to the side of his mouth, leaning towards Basil.

"Thank you! I've got to go! 'Til next time, guys . . ."

I felt myself hunched over, tired, in the swivel chair in my study, dressed once again in my woolen sweater, denim pants and boots—so different from my stylish green dress and delicate shoes in the meadow. The air was stifling and I had the urge to throw the window wide open even though I knew how cold it would be outside. Glancing down at the two tape recorders, I saw that I had recorded about an hour-and-a-half of talking on one, and my birds were still merrily chirping away on the other. I switched everything off and collapsed onto the foldout bed next to my desk.

About an hour later I sat up and tried to comprehend what had happened; I felt strange and giddy, exhilarated and confused. Disarrayed, I left my self-imposed isolation to look for my husband, Aart.

"Well! I see you're still alive . . . how did it go?"

"What a trip! It actually worked—so much happened. It's pretty hard to believe . . ."

"Tell me about it."

*"Maybe it was something like falling down the rabbit hole—into a modern version of Alice in Wonderland. I'm tempted to think it's all pure **fantasy** . . . but how could so many facts get into my head?" I looked at him imploringly.*

"Like what for instance?" he asked, wide-eyed.

"It's too much to tell right now," I said, falling down onto the sofa. "You can listen to the tape—it was just like visiting with real, flesh-and-blood people. But let's get out of here for awhile. Let's go to the woods and walk around—even if it's cold out there."

We drove to the woods near our house and walked silently among the dark and dripping trees. The smell of wet pines cleansed us while the sight of bare birch, beech and oak branches reminded us that spring had not yet arrived in Northern Europe.

As usual, I was contemplating. The recollection of my sunny meadow friends from down the rabbit hole clutched at my heart in a way I could not forget. The memory of their faces and personalities warmed me just like Christmas. I was used to Basil, of course—I didn't question his existence anymore. Why, then, should I question the existence of John? I knew why. It was hard to accept that I should have the privilege and honor to talk to him as easily as I just had. My ego kept getting in the way and I hated myself for it.

*"But, **somebody** has to be able to talk to him," I contended to myself.*

"That's right, you doubting Thomas," a familiar voice boomed inside my head; it was unmistakably Liverpudlian.

I knew that, somewhere, I believed in John and the reality of his presence and this made me exceedingly glad. It was, undoubtedly, a different kind of John than the one who had walked the earth until December 1980—yet, it was clearly "him," and whatever that meant, I was determined to figure out.

~2~
Angels and Things

Teaching classes in the days following, I could feel Basil helping me as usual. But there was something else going on: I was sure John was observing me with increasing interest. In several of the lessons, students were learning how to come into better contact with their own self-guidance—with the "inner teacher," as we called it. I was describing the differences between this part of a person's inner wisdom and that of a spiritual entity separate from one's self, called a "personal guardian." Was John Lennon becoming one of these for me?

The days passed rapidly and I couldn't forget my visit to the meadow. I was resolved to remain practical about it, though; I didn't want to become so preoccupied with that Other World that I would be neglecting this one. I couldn't afford to.

Some people say this world is all illusion, that whatever the physical plane has to offer us is just "maya"—deceptive and unreal. But I maintained that these worldly preoccupations are just as real and precious as what the ethereal world has to offer, that the two cannot be divided nor separated. They must be one, I'd come to affirm. I was convinced my attitude while doing mundane chores at home was ultimately just as significant as my outlook while going into trance in order to teach or visit my celestial friends in the meadow. I considered

23

this a major conviction, although not always an easy one to carry out.

In the meantime, I had been doing research on John Lennon and had uncovered new things about him. For instance, I learned he and Yoko separated in 1973, and he spent 18 months, until they reunited, practically annihilating himself. This was the kind of information I considered essential in my understanding of John's temporal past.

Another week passed. The Dutch weather persisted in expressing the dark side of its nature and I was looking forward to my next visit to the meadow, where the sun shines and the birds sing nonstop, if you want them to.

On Sunday, April 5th, I returned to my study. With tape recorders at my side, I made my second entrance into the rabbit hole.

"Hello! Hi, John, Basil . . . I'm back! How have you both been?" I say this apprehensively, since my focus in my new surroundings is still not totally complete. I'm sitting halfway on my swivel chair while the tarpaulin lounge chair is still materializing.

"Terribly busy . . . yes, I have had a lot to do this past week. Lots of people to help, places to go . . ." Basil snorts.

"Oh, I've been just dandy," John joins in.

This time he looks different—he's wearing a white tee-shirt with a big tree printed on the front of it, a pair of cutoff denims and white tennis shoes. His hair is shorter and his sideburns are missing. He has sunglasses on, though, as usual, for it's as bright here as the last time. Looking around, everything seems exactly the same, or maybe even more beautiful.

"It changed things for me, Linda, to meet with you like we did," John confides. "Good ta see you back! And, I appreciate how you kept in touch. You've done a whole lotta thinking— and dreaming—since then."

I sit and stare for a moment. It's something to see him looking so different, and I've got to get used to him all over again. I've got to get used to myself, too; I'm wearing blue tennis shoes and a blue cotton jumpsuit with short sleeves. On the left breast pocket there is embroidered a tiny tree.

"Did I really?" I say softly, distracted. "I do sort of recall one dream, but it was so vague this time. It had to do with being more open to you." I pause, looking at him. "I know I need to keep on trusting and approaching this whole business with an open heart."

"We will try to help you with that," an elegant-looking Basil interrupts. He is wearing a forest-green cotton suit with a white shirt. A dark green handkerchief is pointing neatly out of his breast pocket and his silvery hair is combed immaculately to the side.

"Your insight is great . . . but your ability to trust us has to stay strong," John adds.

"But I *do* trust you guys . . ."

"I don't mean ya have to trust *us*—I mean you need to keep having faith with the *project*. As soon as you stop believing in yerself or in how real this is, the whole project starts to go off . . ."

John's voice is slightly whining, but then he suddenly makes a very silly face.

"And we don't want that ta happen, do we?"

I can't keep from laughing. "I'll certainly do my best, really."

Basil remains dignified but is obviously fancying John's humor as much as I am.

"Dear Linda, it looks as if you and John could afford to get to know each other a little better."

John smirks and I see his eyebrows raising from behind his sunglasses.

". . . because up to now, you have related to me much easier than John and have grown to have faith in me. But I dare say, the two of you seem to be getting along just fine already! Actually, I should be speaking of the *entity* which we are calling 'John Lennon' at this moment; of course you realize he is not only that person anymore . . . he is much more!"

"Damn right," John mutters.

"Yet it *is* the easiest way to think of him right now—to focus on one aspect of his being, which is the personality called 'John

Lennon.' From here, you may be able to focus more and more upon other levels of his total being, which have infinitely more to say to you than just one man. You could say the personality called 'John Lennon' is your home base . . ."

"And just see if you can make it to third . . ." John quips and raises his eyebrows again in parody.

Basil persists, undaunted, ". . . and, as you explore this path of communication, you will leave the groundwork of the personality and travel to other levels of awareness and knowledge . . . which are, as you might have gathered, very developed and large in scope."

"No wonder I've been scared about all of this!"

"I don't mean it has to be overwhelming and filled with effort," responds Basil. "To the contrary. It takes a specific kind of quietness and receptivity on your part to be able to comprehend the scope of any entity, your own included."

My hands are folded on the soft material of my jumpsuit and I begin inadvertently to twiddle my thumbs.

"Yes," I say, "but it's difficult for me to get away from those typical considerations about why I should take this job on. Why shouldn't someone else do it? It might seem like a classic modesty game I'm playing . . . but I need to hear more about it. I need to become more clear about why *I* should be doing this in the first place."

"You already know the answer, but I'd be happy to recapitulate," he states in his charming, fatherly way. "To begin with, you received the dream message and responded to it with interest. Secondly, you are coming as an old friend—we are all old friends, as I have already told you. And thirdly, as John has aptly expressed, you know how to listen. Real listening is an art and has to be learned by most people."

John has been shaking his head subtly in agreement with everything Basil is saying, no longer clowning, but growing more thoughtful.

"And fourthly," John adds flatly, "she knows how ta write."

"Thank you—I had forgotten that one," Basil says, nodding emphatically at John, then fixing his gaze back on me. "If you are meant to serve as an instrument of communication, it will occur without any worry or effort. And if there is worry or effort, that's a sign that your own ego—however helpful it may be to learn and accomplish specific things—is getting in the way! An ego can often be conceited—it wants everything explained rationally. It wants to grasp the why's and how's! Believe me, dear, you are capable of bringing this material through because you believe in and know us—you can even love us—and there are few people in the world who can hear what we have to say! Don't you see how tragic this is for all concerned? Do you know how painful it can be when we are not heard? It means a great deal to us that you take us as seriously as you do."

John motions dramatically, "Right on . . ."

I am moved and see that John is too. The three of us linger for several moments in silence. In the far meadow, I can see a deer grazing while, nearby, a couple of rabbits are hopping about, oblivious to our abstract discourse.

"Ya know, Linda," John continues earnestly, "when people don't appreciate that there's spirit to communicate with, it gets pretty sad—in this wonderful place we like ta call our Infinite Dwelling. Quite a majority of us are learnin' just as much from you human folks as you're learnin' from us! So you might compare our situation to being accustomed to livin' with your family or other people close to you, and from one day ta the next, having these people start to ignore you completely—all of the time! Or, they are *afraid* of you! Even though you're perfectly willing and wanting ta communicate."

"That's a good way of putting it, son," Basil says, ". . . and Linda, when you do this work for us, you need to leave part of your personality on the sidelines. Empty yourself, don't analyze. Make sure your physical body is comfortable and makes its connection with the ground. Relax your shoulders and your neck. Don't be afraid to speak . . . and to let us speak through you. You are still frightened sometimes that it will turn out to be nothing! Yet I must remind you there have been so many, throughout the ages and cultures, who have done this sort of thing. It is nothing new—indeed it is very old! It takes openness and conviction, which you certainly possess. Go ahead and do it, child. Have some more lemonade?"

"All this talking for three is making me thirsty! I'd love some, thanks . . . thanks, too for your trust. You know I'm willing to try everything you suggest, but I still feel great resistance sometimes."

"Yeah, whadaya expect with characters like us?" John snickers.

"The resistance is natural and healthy," continues Basil. "Look at the conditioning you've had during your lifetime."

"Jes' stick 'em in the looney bin, folks!" John continues. "They's done *gone off* the deep end . . . talkin' ta *ghosts* and *spooky spirits* . . . oooohhhhh!" He yells, making weird faces and writhing in his chair. Then he pretends to be choking himself, and falls over, limp.

"More beer, John?" Basil asks, poker-faced.

"Don't mind if I do." He sits up very straight as if nothing has happened.

"John does have a point, though, Basil, and it's about human fear . . . fear of the dark side of life. Isn't it logical for most human beings to think that, once you begin to communicate with spirits, you can't be sure of who you'll get?"

"I assume you are now referring to dark forces—what many would call 'the devil and his advocates?' "

"Precisely. What is your answer to this problem of people wanting to be careful, then?"

"Well," Basil continues, "using John's depiction of the home in which family and closest friends are desiring to communicate— on whatever level—it is a matter of learning to trust one's own common instincts. If an evil stranger were to be wandering around your own house—would you not know it?"

"Hopefully that's encouragement enough for some," I say. "But, do you believe that, in the future, the average person will learn how to recognize and trust their own spiritual guardians surrounding them?"

"I'm quite sure of it."

"I hope you're right."

There is a short interlude.

"Basil," I say, "there's one thing I don't understand."

"And what is that, my friend?"

"Why do I have to drink lemonade, while John gets beer?"

Basil feigns a frown. "Why, you know you wouldn't last long drinking beer."

"But this is just pretend stuff . . . surely you don't think . . ."

"You might be astonished what can happen to you, even Here! It's imperative you keep your head. And next time we'll all have tea. You can already see the effect one beer had on John!" Basil utters with a laugh.

"But he drank that two weeks ago!"

"Don't forget . . . there's no time nor space here. I suppose in your last incarnation, you learned your lessons the hard way, eh, son? Not that I'm a teetotaller . . . I like to partake of the occasional happy hour with old friends myself."

"Yeah, yer right," John said. "I blew it with alcohol, as well as with a whole lot of other things! I'm still busy with those lessons . . . it's an important matter. And now, where's that other beer ya offered me?"

Basil materializes another frosty bottle and glass and offers it to him politely. Then he picks up my empty glass, fills it with liquid refreshment brimming with ice, and hands it to me.

"Thanks. When I see this, I kind of prefer it anyway. Cheers!"

Basil pours himself a glass and the three of us toast each other, falling again into silent reflection.

Leaning back, I gaze up through the new, delicate, green leaves on the boughs of the immense oak tree next to us and view some patches of lucid blue sky beyond. The air is brisk and scented with spring; a robin inspects us from his perch overhead. I close my eyes now and allow myself to dream—a lovely, timeless dream. I am grateful to come here and grateful, also, for the knowledge of how to accomplish it.

"It's so simple," I muse to myself, glad my friends are also content to be silent.

"By the way," I say, interrupting the calm by sitting straight up in my chair. "I looked up our last names in a book last week, John."

"Oh yeah?" he replies dreamily.

"Yes." I take another sip out of my glass. "Did you realize 'Lennon' is derived from the Irish name 'O'Leannain' and means 'cloak,' and 'Keen' comes from 'O'Cathain' and means 'ancient' and 'beautiful'?"

"Beautiful, ancient cloak, eh? That makes a good watchword when we find ourselves braving the adventures of the unknown! When shall we leave on our journey? This may be a great place, Linda, but we won't be staying here forever."

"Don't start that yet! I'm just getting used to being here. And it's about time I asked you more specifically why we are becoming involved with each other . . . I mean, what is your real intention in creating this story? What is *John Lennon in Heaven* actually going to be about?"

"Hey, it's good you finally asked me that! Do you remember what it's like in heaven, Linda? Everybody's been Here, they just can't recall what it's like. I want to help them to do this. And, actually, heaven and hell are just a state of mind."

"I was wondering about that. I wanted to remind you of your song, 'Imagine.' "

"Literally, there's no such thing as heaven or hell. They're cute ways of saying we live after we die; there are other dimensions where the soul resides which are places we construct ourselves, depending on the kind of reality we believe in. And with this in mind, I'd fancy showing you, and other folks who hear about it, what some of the possibilities *are* in this delightful place of nonphysical existence."

"What makes me wonder, John, is now that I've met you face-to-face, it continues to look so much like earth here. Most people think of heaven as being abstract, or at least filled with clouds and angels and things . . ."

"Each to his own . . . there are a lotta things goin' on here which might surprise the hell outta people."

"Do you mean that literally?"

"You could take it literally, yeah. But we're talking about *creativity* here, Linda—on both sides of Life. We're talking about matter and spirit serving each other like infinite mirrors. As above, so below! This or that consciousness is being conveyed from *being to being*, from thing to thing, from one form of Life to another. It's all *one big act of creation* . . . and we're part of it whether we're alive in a body or alive in spirit! You can't escape the involvement."

"Are you saying life where you are now is similar to life on earth?"

"There are big similarities . . . and big differences, which you'll hear about soon enough. But what you're doin' with me Here is opening up to a certain kind of inspiration, as Basil was mentioning to you earlier, which allows for the free flow of consciousness on both sides—back and forth between physical and nonphysical existence."

Basil nods in agreement.

"It makes it difficult to know what's real—and what's not!" I declare. "It's so easy to think of what we're doing now as all my own fabrication . . . I mean, aren't all writers doing basically the same as I am by using their imaginations freely?"

"Ah-hah! You've just asked another important question," John says, leaning forward in his chair and slapping my knee. "Artists have always been responsible for bridging the gap between the two worlds. They just didn't always know they were doing it. And if you combine spiritual perception with true ingenuity, you get a special kind of thing going on."

"And what is that?"

"Both worlds are able to *converse* . . . there's a natural conveyance of consciousness from one side to the other. Most human beings don't remember this yet, though, or are afraid of it. That's why it can be a pathetic story for those of us Here when we need the rapport and aren't gettin' it . . . sorta like havin' only half the band show up."

"This whole subject baffles me. It's so big and there seem to be no guidelines except to follow your own inner intelligence."

"That is the only guideline," Basil breaks in. "But don't forget that artists—and healers of all kinds—are, and always have been, the messengers in your world. And it's remarkable they have such exceptional access to their imaginations, which are the source of spiritual vision and inspiration."

"And the source of all change," John adds. "The collective awareness on earth is makin' it possible for all kinds of folks to use their original intuition again. And in order to experience what I like ta call *consciousness conveyance*—the two-way path between matter and spirit—a human being's imagination is the key."

He looks over at me, smiling like an adolescent and I have the urge to tease him.

"You look so pleased with yourself. I suppose this is what we are sharing together this very moment—this 'consciousness conveyance' you're telling me about."

John keeps beaming. "You're oh so very right! I wanna experiment with this new-but-very-old concept . . . do you wanna be my first apprentice?"

"How can I do this?"

"Well, you've made one helluva good start already. But, basically, you need ta allow yerself more space to create—with me. Remember I said you needed to keep on believing, not just in me, but in the project?"

"Yeah."

"Well, this is how you'll be able to learn something from me, just as I am learning from you."

"I would enjoy hearing what you are learning from me!" I say, a bit embarrassed.

"Don't be so damned humble, girl . . . keep up with the changes in all of us. What will I be learning from you? I'll be learnin' how to make it easier for myself the next time I come to earth . . . and how to better practice what I preach, among other things! But I'm not going to reel off anymore ideas like this right now."

"Well, anyway, the answer is 'yes,' " I say, looking into John Lennon's shaded eyes.

"Yes—what?" He looks at me quizzically.

"Sign me up as your first apprentice."

~3~
Red Clouds

A few days later, I was obsessed with the idea of returning to the meadow. I waited impatiently through my teaching and household chores that day, until finally it was evening. At home alone with my two daughters, I put them to bed with the attendant rituals and then rushed to my study to prepare for my next exciting escapade. Soon reclining in my lounge chair, it was like switching a movie projector back on. Everything was the same, only Basil was asleep, and there was John, drinking out of his never-empty glass of beer and looking as he had before, only a bit more inebriated.

"Well, well . . . my little pigeon!"

"Hey, gimme that!" I cry, reaching for his glass. "You know this isn't getting you anywhere."

"You're perfectly right! Throw the damn stuff away!"

John makes a sweeping movement with his hand, and I set the extraordinary glass on the ground.

"I had to come back here," I add.

"I appreciate that . . ."

"I didn't know why . . . maybe I do now! And, I missed the quietness—it's always so hectic where I come from."

"Hey, it's good ta see you again, friend. Basil's been snorin' away and I took a few winks myself."

"John, there's something I want to ask you."

"That's what I'm here for, ya know."

"I was hoping you'd tell more about your life on earth. I mean, you left so unexpectedly."

"Aye . . . that's true. My life on earth is a good subject to discuss, but I'm not sure how ta go about it."

"Why not?"

"Fer starters . . . I wasn't honest with meself. I'll agree I inspired a lot of folks and I'm happy with my accomplishments. But, as I said before, there was so much in me which I didn't get the chance to come to terms with."

He crosses his bare legs and scratches his chin. "And, as you might guess, I wasn't prepared to go out so fast—I left so damned abruptly! I didn't even get the chance to say goodbye to my family! Can you imagine how bloody frustratin' that is for any soul?"

John's face looks strangely drawn. Then the robin in our oak tree begins to sing and we glance up to admire it.

"It must have been terrible for you," I said. Looking down, I notice I am still wearing the cotton jumpsuit with a tiny tree embroidered neatly on the left pocket.

"I get the impression, though, you have come a long way since that fateful day . . . you've had enough positive experiences Here to have changed drastically."

"Right you are, and I've definitely got some awesome tales to tell, especially to those who don't believe in Life after death."

He rests, again staring up into the branches of the tree.

"I certainly love being here in our meadow," John digresses in a soft voice. "It's so peaceful and healing for me because I'm making this luv'ly connection with you and my good old buddy, Basil, as you call him. By the way, I've known Basil by other names—among them Aenaed, George, Percival. He's had lotsa other names before—as all of us have—but for now I'll just call him Basil, as you do. Furthermore, since you've become aware of our connection, Linda, there have been interesting changes going on in me, just as there have been in you . . . don't forget that part."

He looks over at me with a faint smile. "Anyway, right after I got shot outta my body, it was literally a livin' hell! It felt like I was in this appalling, negative, heavy—very *sticky*—atmosphere."

"I took a peek at you then," I interrupt. "You were surrounded by red clouds . . ."

My thoughts raced back to December 14, 1980. There was to be a ten-minute vigil given in John Lennon's memory in New York's Central Park. Sitting in my living room at this moment in the Netherlands, I had tuned into the collective awareness of John and all of the people who were thinking about him. The red clouds I had seen surrounding John seemed to be caused not only by his own grief, but by the sorrow and heavy emotions being projected upon him by scores of other people.

"I guess they must have been pretty damned noticeable—those enormous, insufferable clouds of pain and turmoil!" John says, looking anguished.

"I can recall that moment so distinctly. I wished you good luck then."

"Thanks dear. I needed all the help I could get. At first, I didn't even realize I was dead! I kept wondering why I couldn't just go home. And then something amazing happened. I saw me mother and father. They looked just as I remembered them when I was a kid! They embraced me and my mother stared straight into my eyes and said, 'Johnny, you're with us now. You can't go back.' I felt awful remorse then . . . although I was eager to learn more about what was actually goin' on. Then my mother said, 'We can't stay here with you now, John, but we'll be seein' you again. You'll be well-cared for, I promise.' She kissed me and then both my parents disappeared."

"God . . ."

"I was left surrounded by a kinda white luminescence which seemed to be creating the form of another person. This person didn't speak to me in words, but gave me the distinct sensation I wasn't alone, I was deeply loved and cared for. It was a superb feeling! And this person was remarkably familiar, but I couldn't recollect when or where I had known him—or her—before. I was so confused and angry. I could feel the whole world projecting their sorrow and pain onto me! They didn't understand the process of death and that ultimately there are reasons for everything."

I wait in silence.

"Yes, but the fact you were so famous must have made the situation unusually difficult for you to become free," I say, frowning.

"Aye, it was worse than what I had experienced on earth! And for what seemed like forever, I remained overpowered by the dark, heavy emotions being projected upon me *by those millions of people*, in spite of my white-light friend. I was constantly busy tryin' to disentangle meself from those emotions . . . it was exactly like bein' in a bad dream where you can't wake up. It was torment, I tell you."

"What did you end up doing?"

"Some people did comprehend the situation. They tried to let go of me, to let me be free. The vigil Yoko organized in Central Park immediately after my death was an attempt to have people project positive vibes toward me, but most people didn't get it . . . they can't be blamed."

"Were you able to stay spiritually in touch with Yoko?"

"Yeah, sometimes," he answers hesitantly, "and with my sons." John suddenly brightens. "Sean was especially easy to communicate with, being so young. During this period it was the same as dreaming. I kept expecting to wake up. Here I was, in this chaos of emotions and projections from those folks who idolized me and didn't want to accept what had happened. That part was a super drag! The gag was on me 'cause I thought when I died, I would finally get some rest from fans—but shit no! I didn't become 'free' until I could find me way outta those bloody clouds." He stops talking.

"Then what happened?"

"Well, it seems that it took about three years, according to your earth's Time-Mode, to totally escape the influence of the red clouds and go on, gradually—with the help of my white-light buddy—into a new place of learning and tranquility. Funny enough, I found myself as sort of a student, going to some weird kinda school!"

"Huh!" I say, staring wide-eyed at John.

He picks his glass up from the ground again and drinks.

"It's really hard ta describe it in words. That's about as close as I can get to what happened. I found myself existing in a small group of other disembodied souls . . ."

"Ugh . . . that word always sounds so creepy."

I make a face, but John doesn't react because he is so involved in his story now and I'm sorry for interrupting.

". . . participating in all sorts of learning games. Initially I thought it was silly and bizarre and rejected it. I built a barricade of resistance around meself, but that seemed to be alright. *Everything* I did seemed to be *alright*! The folks around me accepted everything I did—with no judgement, only love. What a fuckin' strange period that was, I tell you! At least I could feel untroubled in this new dimension. I had finally accepted the loss of my physical body and—in many ways—the separation from my home and family. When I gained this new freedom, it was a great jump in consciousness as a soul because I was allowed to look at myself—and from a super-expansive viewpoint."

"That must have been encouraging," I say, looking at him supportively. "But before you go any further, I was puzzled why you had to leave the earth when and how you did—none of us were the least bit prepared. Could you explain why it had to happen that way?"

John appears solemn again. "Well, it certainly had ta do with me own past deeds . . . you know everything that happens to us on earth is a reflection of our own inner world, no matter how subconscious it may be. And I always had unresolved personal hangups which weren't peaceful or gentle, to say the least."

"But when Basil told us about your past life as a strolling minstrel . . ."

We both glance over at the serenely-sleeping Basil.

"That's right. A lotta my past was as beautiful and composed as you can get," John replies, "but not all of it. Even in my life as John Lennon, I put myself through a lot of mental violence . . . and *everybody* has gotta experience both sides of the coin on old planet earth. The art of deception is in the eye of the beholder."

"So you left earth when you did because you had created too much mental violence in your lifetime?"

"Yeah, that's one reason. And another was that my time was simply up! It was time to move on to other kinds of learning."

"Was it premonition, then, when you wrote your song, 'Living on Borrowed Time'? Did you know you were going to die young?"

"I had a lotta inner messages about my early death—yeah. I wasn't so deft at knowing what ta do with 'em, though. Sometimes I thought it was due to the early death of me uncle, me Mum and other close friends. It always seemed abstract and irrational, and I never came to terms with it, I guess."

"In hindsight, do you think you could have prevented such an early death . . . if you had taken more precautions?"

"No dear, that wouldn't have been possible. It's not what me soul had in the planning. I'll admit it was a dramatic way to leave the world, and I can speak calmly about it now. 'Cause, then, my lost ego-personality felt sorry for itself and was burdened by a great sense of loss, failure and alienation."

John is staring at me. "What'er ya thinking about?"

"I'm sorry, my mind is wandering. I was recalling the childhood nightmare I often had when I was becoming sick. It started when I was about five years old. It began by my viewing a car drive down a winding, mountainous road—a big, black, thirties sedan—and suddenly the road opened up as if an earthquake had struck. There were horrible sounds of metal on gravel, and huge rocks would roll down the mountain in a gigantic landslide . . ."

"Sounds real cheery . . ."

"Right! Then a horrible fear would come over me—a turmoil of immensity and noise. I would feel a sensation of vastness, as if the parts of my body had grown a thousand-fold. The next thing I knew, I was suffering amid these huge clouds of a thick, enclosing substance which was trapping and suffocating me."

"It sounds a lot like my red clouds."

"You're right!" I stop to reflect.

"Later in my life, I discovered I had been killed in this car. I guess my spirit body was looking around for someone to help, little knowing it had just left the physical world behind."

"Sounds similar to my experiences—not particularly pleasant," John says, frowning.

"It certainly wasn't a pleasant affair, no," I say. "But I began to understand, gradually, when learning to look at my life on earth in new ways—that my higher self—the 'aware part' of my soul—had organized the whole drama."

"Aye . . ."

"Was your soul aware," I ask, "after you died, that your higher self had organized your demise for some purpose?"

"Of course, but I wasn't strong enough for that in the beginning. My acceptance of the responsibility for my changes—even my death—had to grow inside me, and that was the whole point. I had ta learn how ta pull meself out of it—naturally, with a little help from me friends."

I show a corny smile and John does the same, then I start to think.

"And which friends are you referring to now?"

"Friends like your Basil and my white-light chum . . . angels of Light . . . healing beings who were ready to help me but who understood there were specific things I had to do and learn initially *for myself.*"

"We are all space travellers, looking for the purpose of our existence and the source from which we come," Basil says softly from his reclined position, his eyes remaining closed as if talking in his sleep.

John and I grin at each other.

"And what were those things you had to learn?" I ask.

"Put into basic terms . . . I had to learn, again, in new ways, how I was building my own reality. I was quite aware of this already as a body and personality on earth, but it was different after I got killed."

"And how was that?"

"The landmarks were different. I didn't have my family with me anymore. I had ta depend on myself and my inner resources

. . . sorta like returning to L.A. in 1973 when Yoko and I broke up for awhile. Only this time, I did a better job of it."

"How?"

"I found the nonphysical world easier in terms of changing myself—once I *wanted* ta change. Aye, there's the rub! I'm learnin' at my school that only after incarnating again into a physical body can a soul bring this change fully into conscious evidence—something which is gonna last! Apparently the earthly training is essential for a kind of super-glueing of the big changes . . . it molds soul's entire spiritual foundation. Once you've learned something on planet earth, you've *really* learned it."

"That strikes me, somehow, as being very true. And can you tell me how you got in touch with this desire, as you described it, of wanting to change?"

"Right'o." John gazes skyward. "It was an insight I slowly grew to have—that my reality was larger and more promising than I had originally supposed it to be. I needed space within my being to recover from the traumas of my life and the violence of my death . . . to recover from the sudden loss of physical life and all that was dear to me. It became a process in which I had to consider that Life—whether physical or nonphysical—was worth changing for."

"Is it actually true, then, that you have to believe in Life and its changes even when you're physically dead?"

"That's fer sure! Do you realize there are souls who made the choice long ago to not believe in change, and they are the shadowy ones who carouse in and out of church graveyards, haunted houses and whatnot? Where do you think those horror tales come from? They're not just a figment of somebody's rotten imagination! Those are disembodied souls who couldn't let go of earthly planes in order to allow themselves further growth. If they don't make the choice themselves, there's nothing that can be done for them."

"That sounds pretty miserable and creepy."

"Probably because it *is* miserable and creepy! But many times those stuck entities can be helped simply by the fact that someone has sent them love and light, yet has been able to let go of them. They do this because they realize a soul needs ta be free in order to undergo a new state of being."

We stop talking again for a moment and listen to the sounds of birds and a rushing brook nearby. Taking off his sunglasses, John rubs his eyes and I feel a depth of recognition for him which is almost painful.

"I could see the personality of John Lennon as being a small part of the whole *me*," he resumes. "It might sound odd, Linda, but I was allowed to look into my own sort of *book*—it was like a record book of everything I had ever done. Can you fathom this? And I was shown the different moments and events—like endless reels of movie film—representing meself as a soul through time and space."

"Wasn't that a bit tiring?"

John guffaws. "Maybe it sounds that way, but in the dimension I'm in now, it isn't always necessary to feel effort—I think it's something you'll appreciate more and more about this place."

He hesitates a moment and continues, "When on earth, the personality of John Lennon had been aware of other Past Time-Mode Expressions he had experienced."

"Past what?" I interrupt.

"Time-Mode Expressions. I'm sorry, it's another kind of jargon. Since there is no time *Here*, some of us find it easier—when dealin' with the physical plane—to speak in terms of Past, Present and Future Time-Modes. An' since there is *always* Life, it is more logical to speak in terms of this or that *expression* on the physical plane, get it?"

"I guess so."

"I'll explain more about *that* some other time. But what the hell was I talking about?"

"Something about looking into your own book . . . your own movie."

"Oh, right. In spite of the insight and perception which I had on earth, it was just one tiny fraction of the real perception possible now. Those Past Mode Expressions weren't so intelligible to this guy, John Lennon—kind of confusing, to say the least! Once outta his body, lookin' back at his earthly encounters helped him become balanced and harmonized in this new dimension. Here, he found his own essence—which is easier to acknowledge, I might say, when not occupying a physical body. He doesn't have the problem anymore of his bloody intellect wantin' ta ask dumb questions."

"What's wrong with asking dumb questions?" I object.

Beside us are the sounds of soft snickering.

"Basil, stop that—you're laughing at me! And you continue to doze like an impervious Buddha."

Basil sits up straight, amused. "When I have the need to speak up, I will, my child. You don't have to think I'm laughing at you! It's just that I so much admire the naiveté of the human being. You're charming—really, you are."

"Gee, thanks." I smile at him pertly.

"It's not that a person shouldn't ask dumb questions," John says kindly, "when a soul gains a particular awareness, certain questions of the human ego, in hindsight, seem irrelevant."

"I think I understand. But it somehow puts me in the mood to ask an extremely dumb question. How's this for one—you're sitting here next to me, as real as life, in the form of John Lennon. Do people smoke here in heaven? I haven't seen you light up yet."

"Hah! Don't tell me! Actually, a person can do anything he damn well pleases Here . . . but the cigarette trip is something I no longer crave."

"That's undoubtedly because I can't stand them," I say.

"Possibly . . . but we've gotta get one thing straight, dear. There are various levels of heaven in our Infinite Dwelling, and each can give us lessons, when we need them. Where you and I are now resembles earth, 'cause souls need ta keep in practice for their next Expression. As above, so below—remember? Do you think the physical world could exist without something to model it after? Do you believe earth is set apart from its creators? Hell no. Our lower levels of heaven serve as a prototype for everything earth contains."

"That's a new one on me! I hadn't the slightest idea heaven was divided up into levels . . ."

"It doesn't work the way you are trying to envision it, 'cause yer human intellect is gettin' in the way. Heaven isn't divided. But, depending upon the kind of lessons needed and the sort of energy available to a soul, heaven offers diverse possibilities."

"Just how many levels are there, then?"

John sticks up seven fingers.

"Somebody's in seventh heaven . . . that's a well-known saying."

"There's often hidden wisdom in the most mundane phrases. But, actually we're somewhere between the third and fourth right now. As you can see, I still appreciate me drink! As you'll discover, everything we do here is based on creativity and expression. If I needed a cigarette to express a certain aspect of myself to you, then I would, without a doubt, light up!"

"Heaven forbid."

"Am I glad you love ta listen! Yer hangin' out Here with us—thinking this is common—but as Basil and I said earlier, you've no inkling of how few people will sit down, or stand up for that matter, and listen to spirit. For starters, they wouldn't know how, even if they wanted to, and this makes the whole process even more damned difficult."

"I know. Most people would think I'm crazy. I'm definitely not telling anyone about this until it's over! I mean, until I'm sure I've actually got something."

"For Christ's sake, woman, you really *are* crazy! You mean you still aren't sure, after all of this, whether you've *got* something?" He looks disgusted.

"I'm sorry! I didn't mean it that way—it's just my hopelessly uncertain nature . . ."

"Yeah, I know, that's part of yer trip. I've gotta learn to be more patient."

"More lemonade?" Basil leans toward my glass with a large pitcher and pours.

"Oh, yes. Thank you."

"If I may interrupt the two of you for a moment," Basil says, "I do think it would be wise for Linda to keep her silence about this project the three of us are sharing—for an indeterminate period of time—in order to be able to grow with it, unhampered by the reactions and judgements of other people. As you realize, son, this is one of those inevitable human vulnerabilities which must be taken into consideration."

"So you agree I shouldn't tell anyone about my experiences yet?"

"In general, you shouldn't . . . with the exception, of course, of your husband and several other people you will recognize when the time is ripe."

"Oh yes, thanks. I did sense this somehow, already."

I gaze at John with new assurance.

"See? It's really not so bad after all," I say to him. "Now, then . . . you were telling me what it's been like to exist in your new reality."

John looks softer and switches to a low voice.

"Outta the body—we still have a heart and mind as you perceive it. Of course, it's quite another story when they're connected to a physical body. We have no physical heart, but we still possess the same substance of that source of power! It's easiest for you, of course, to envision me as a soul manifesting a body and personality for yer benefit—sitting here and drinking me ale . . . delicious, by the way." He toasts Basil again with his glass.

Basil winks and raises his glass too.

John continues, ". . . a body, made of light or energy perhaps—but you, as a mortal, must have a form—something to relate to. The ale, of course, is a toy, as cigarettes would be . . . a way of havin' fun . . . of playing and expressing myself to you."

"Do you still have chakras?" I ask thoughtfully.

"Ya mean me life-wheels? Yeah, I've got these things in my light body and they correspond quite well with the ones you've got in yer mortal body. Only mine don't relate to the physical world so often anymore, 'cause they're working on other frequency levels. The most vital exception is when I'm experiencing these moments with you—or other mortal folks. We've got this luv'ly convergence goin' between the life-wheels of both worlds simultaneously! It's the medium through which we communicate."

"I certainly didn't expect spiritual entities to have chakras . . . I mean, life-wheels."

"Yeah, well they are a dissimilar vibrational plane than yours, but they are similar. When particular impulses and impressions are registered within the assorted life-wheels in my light body, it's how I learn, feel and communicate. And, as on earth, these wheels are connected to my soul essence—what could most simply be described as me own private little sun."

John looks down at the tree on his tee-shirt as if he hadn't seen it before.

"I'm certainly accustomed," I say, "to feeling my own private little sun, since that's how we refer to it in class."

"Naturally, dear, that's why I described it that way, so you could understand me better."

"How kind of you."

"I've been eavesdropping on you lately, ya know."

"Yes, I noticed that. I like it."

"Gotta learn any way I can," John says. "Now listen, I'm showin' myself here as a body and a personality in order to communicate with you in a way that feels familiar. I don't need ta look this way anymore, although I have to admit it's a real trip. Brings back a lotta good memories."

"I would think so."

"But how would it be for you if I was, instead, a big glowing ball of light sitting here in my chair?"

"I'll have to admit—not as interesting! I like your personality and your body's not bad either . . ."

"Hah! Just listen to her." John looks over at Basil. "Physical charm can work wonders when it comes to communicating, eh?"

"I'm not kidding, John, I'm happy you can still manifest your old personality. It's charming and makes me grateful. Besides, I don't think I'd be inspired by a ball of light drinking beer."

"Shall we try it?"

"Sure. You make me curious."

I'm startled to see John has immediately disappeared, and in his place is a brilliant sphere of light, holding a half-empty glass of yellow liquid. There is total silence for a moment, until John's familiar voice speaks flatly from within this radiating orb.

"What yer tellin' me illustrates an essential point. Human beings need to be constantly reminded of themselves and their human ways. They need ta feel safe, appreciated and loved. How is it to relate to me this way?"

I peer from half-closed eyes, the radiance is so blinding.

"Well, fascinating . . . but unusual. It's as if I'm a visiting with the Wizard of Oz. Are you going to help me stay human, or do you want me to try to identify with how it feels to be a ball of light?"

John's human-like form immediately reappears.

"How about both? We're gonna try to bridge the two worlds—yours and mine. I'm gonna be learning through you, and you through me. This is the nature of Consciousness Conveyance—we need each other."

We glance at Basil, who is asleep again, looking placid and innocent.

"That looks tempting. I'm going to retire to my snug little Dutch home and go to bed. I'm exhausted!"

"Sounds wise. We wouldn't want you ta get wiped out coming here."

"I've sure had a great time talking with you, John."

"The feelin' is mutual, kid."

He motions and smiles, and I'm gone.

~4~
Love and Learn

I felt elated, yet shaken, after this last session. Much of it was gone from memory, making me grateful for tape recorders. Yet, it was one thing to be talking to John Lennon during a trance in my fantasy meadow, and another to revert to my daily state of mind and speculate upon what I'd done. Surely some people would call me crazy, though I knew I wasn't. I did know that I felt as if I was living a double life: one tangible and the other not.

It was strange to be able to teach classes, cuddle my girls, eat meals, play music, go jogging and sleep with my husband in one world—sensing this was entirely real—while knowing the other world of thoughts, imagination, inspiration and communication with spiritual intelligence was just as real, only in a different way. I could be as moved by my experiences in the intangible world as by those in the tangible, and was taking the former, ethereal realm more seriously than before. Spirit was perpetually interacting with matter and somehow I could vaguely follow the processes of this mysterious interaction at work.

There was a problem, however. I had been getting out of balance lately by my love affair with the Other World. This love affair seemed, in some ways, to enhance my daily life on an emotional plane; but it was wreaking havoc on more practical levels. Was this the price I had to pay for new experiences with "Consciousness Conveyance," as John was calling it? I wasn't eating or sleeping as I should; I wasn't able to concentrate when teaching class; and often, I had headaches. It appeared I was growing weaker and more vulnerable—physically and sometimes psychically—and I knew there was something wrong. What was it?

Based on the information I taught others about psychic development, I guessed I hadn't been making enough separation between myself and John Lennon's entity. Though I knew precisely how to do it and why I should, lately, I hadn't taken the trouble to do so.

"Concerning the proper use of your own energy, you should be able to treat spiritual friends as you would physical ones," I could hear the teacher in me saying, "and however pleasant the relationship may be, you need, at any given moment, to know how to disconnect . . ." This was sound advice—was I going to follow it?

Out of zealous curiosity I had begun to venture unchecked into unknown spiritual realms. Did I believe I could handle it? I was starting to admit that my earlier prudent resolutions of staying "uncomplicated" with the John Lennon project had been tossed to the winds. My husband was also reacting about this time.

"I don't appreciate this setup anymore," he told me resolutely one day, "it makes me nervous—you're not the same."

I had to agree with him.

In addition to everything else, as I persisted in doing more research on John Lennon, two conflicting sides of his nature became apparent. Was it good for me to be so psychically receptive to an entity who manifested so many problems as well as successes? Was I being too open to possible negative influences? What did I want and need out of this setup? I was forced to stop in my tracks and put recent events into perspective.

Basically I wanted to stay myself. Fortunately, I was aware of the fact that the forces attracting me to work with John Lennon were not only offering me the chance to experience happiness and fulfillment, but also the chance to face my own doubts and difficult side. I realized I was responsible for making my own reality, just as John had said. The primary consideration was and had to remain: Am I staying myself in this setup?

I began to ask myself this question each morning when I looked into the mirror, and it soon became easier. Thanks to this new attitude and the techniques I could employ involving the use of energy, I managed to reconnect with myself. The results were striking—a healthier state of mind and body. Assuming these challenges were part of my apprenticeship with John, I was beginning to conclude the art of Consciousness Conveyance needed to balance psychic awareness with basic common-sense.

On the earth plane, I remained overwhelmed by the emotional richness in which John Lennon had been able to express himself, not only through music, but in the way he could choose words and use his voice—strikingly honest and direct. As I listened one afternoon to him screaming out his guts in "Mother," I could barely contain myself. How could anyone sing so profoundly about pain? Then, when I heard him singing, gently and whimsically, "Hold on world, world hold on, it's gonna be alright, you're gonna see the light," I was soothed and comforted. How could a person express so aptly the different sides of Life?

Another few weeks had gone by before I felt ready to meet again with Basil and John. On a Sunday in late April, I revelled at my chance to journey anew.

John is waiting Here as usual, as well as Basil, who is wide awake this time. It appears they have been having their own private party in my absence and, as I become accustomed to my position in the lounge chair, their banter and raucous laughter seem inappropriate to such composed surroundings.

"Well, at least I can see you guys aren't getting bored while I'm gone!" I interject. Secretly I'm just a little bit jealous. "Surely you haven't been sitting here by yourselves these last few weeks?"

"Well, hallo there!" John chimes out merrily.

"Why, there you are!" Basil splutters. "We were wondering when you would reappear. We weren't worried of course, but you have been quite a busy woman of late. You must take your rest, my dear. I don't want to see your energy getting depleted."

"I'm going to be more careful about that," I say, "I suppose you've already been helping."

"That's one of the main reasons I'm here, of course . . ."

"You and John haven't been sitting here, though, for the past few weeks waiting for me?"

"You forgot—it doesn't work that way. You see, there is no time in this dimension, and we can be in several places at once. Had you forgotten that?"

"No, I didn't forget, but it seemed as if you hadn't moved since I was here last. Everything looks exactly the same. We've even got on the same clothes."

"God, now that you mention it . . ." John feigns a worried look and sniffs at his armpits, and Basil and I give each other a hopeless-yet-pleased look. The meadow is alive with the sounds and smells of nature. In this place, existence seems eternal.

"You're right, I've just got to keep reminding myself there are no restrictions Here."

"Except for those which you impose yourself," Basil murmurs, handing John and me each a steaming cup of tea. I lean forward to receive it, inspecting the large cup and saucer. They are made of exquisite porcelain and painted with many colors—in the forms of birds, flowers, trees and animals. I'm instantly captivated by their beauty.

"Do go ahead and enjoy your tea."

"Yes . . . of course."

I take a sip. It's delicious and unmistakably jasmine.

"You know something, Basil?" I say after several slurps.

"Yes, my dear?"

"I'm pleased you're able to help us."

"That makes two of us," John adds, sipping his tea. His brown hair is tousled, his face open and honest. He's not wearing his sunglasses this time, but his normal metal-rimmed ones, and again I behold his penetrating eyes.

"Basil, there is so much you can teach us," I continue, "and there are so many things we need to understand."

John beams enthusiastically. "You'd be amazed how much I've learned from him since he and I started comin' here to our meadow. And I'm really looking forward to showing you other places sometime, Linda."

I'm impressed with how happy and innocent John looks this time, and wonder what sort of metamorphosis he's been going through.

"Yep, I'm terribly curious what's in store for me, that's for sure!" I utter bravely, heaving a sigh.

"Don't look so worried," Basil reacts. "You understand we are helping each other in every way we can. But for this moment, I'm going to leave you and John to your own devices. There are many things I need to do and lots of places to go; and besides, I noticed last time the two of you can carry on exceedingly well by yourselves."

"I thought you were asleep."

"Strictly outward appearances, my dear."

"Why can't you stay? You told me you could be in different places at once."

"Right you are, child, but I'll put it this way—there are moments to be seen and moments not to be. This is simply one of the latter. I wish you luck and look forward to seeing you both again soon. By the way, I've left you some more refreshment—if you'll just look over here."

Basil points to a tiny table where a large teapot sits. It has the same handsome and ornate nature motifs as the cups and saucers we're holding.

"God keep you." he says, motioning goodbye.

"Hey, thanks!"

"Right'o . . ." John sticks his middle and index fingers up in the air. "'Til next time, and thanks again for the great rap."

"You are more than welcome, my friends."

He rises and begins to stroll toward the grove of oak trees, then vanishes into thin air.

"Just you and me, honey," John rasps in a low actor's voice.

I pretend to kick him in the shins. Then, trying—poorly—to imitate Greta Garbo, "The moment I've been waiting for . . ."

In my own voice I say, "John, you really look good. What have you been doing since I left?"

"There's so much to tell you. I hope I don't talk so much you can't keep up with me."

"Well, just don't talk too fast—that's when I can't keep up."

"I'll do me best. Now, there's so many things we didn't get to the last three times you visited," he says, standing up to pour himself another cup of tea and checking to see if mine is empty.

"Meanwhile, I see we're both gettin' so much outta this. It's a great setup, don't ya think?"

"Oh, it's a great setup, but—off and on—I feel I've got a lot more to learn."

John fills my cup to the brim.

"I'll admit I've been a bit too much in yer space recently, and I apologize for that! You've been so open to me . . . I took the chance to make the most out of it."

"Yeah, well, this is something I wanted to discuss with you. It's really not good for me, at certain moments, to have you come so close. For instance, when I'm in bed with my husband—couldn't you be a little more discreet?"

"Aye," John says, trying not to laugh, "but you've gotta put me further out of your space before you go and *do* something like that. I mean, of course, I find it interesting! Don't you think I've got beautiful memories of those luv'ly earth games myself?"

"Don't you miss it?" I ask, again inspecting the designs on my cup.

"Of course I miss it. There's nothing like it anywhere, on earth or in heaven! But remember when I asked you if earth was separate from its creators? Our lower levels of heaven certainly practice sex and procreation, it's just not my trip right now. An' those old Greeks weren't crazy when they observed mythical characters being involved in all sorts of celestial lovemaking, nor were the other primitive cultures whose religions had the same idea."

"But most of the world has forgotten about them."

"Because western religion tried ta hush this up, makin' folks think only heaven's upper levels were worth a damn—the place where our angels hang out. Not to put 'em down—some of me best friends are angels—but they weren't foremost in constructing the earth and never wanted to Express there. Don't ask me why. Angels are perfect, so they don't hafta learn the way we do."

"Why not?"

"It's part of the hierarchy, and too complicated fer now. Look, I'm sorry if I intruded, but you need to be more aware of making better divisions when you don't want me hangin' around—as you recently came to realize yerself. Otherwise this kinda thing is undoubtedly gonna happen."

"No, you're right . . . it's my fault. I'd been listening to you singing one of your love songs to Yoko that evening and forgot to put you out of my system."

"Love and learn! You've been keeping me near and I reacted to it, ya know. I've been busy in your space because you chose to invite me in . . . and I found it lotsa fun!" He's got a big, naive grin on his face.

"I've been learning by watchin' you," he continues, "and bein' part of the process you're going through, part of your human scene."

John studies a bright green beetle crawling up the leg of his chair.

"And do you keep in regular contact with your family?"

His eyes remaining focused on the beetle, he appears more reserved. "There's a lotta dream communication, and I'm actively *around*, even though they forget it at times. But that's normal. Julian is often hardest to reach, but it's no wonder." John looks up at me, pained. "He's got the most anguish to bear concerning how his life went as a youngster—a repeat of me and my mum."

"It often works that way."

"Right," he says weakly.

I decide not to ask more about his family now; it doesn't feel right. "But it must be remarkably absorbing seeing people pass through worldly trials and tribulations."

"Oh, yeah! For instance, I noticed recently that when you taught yer classes you were more out of balance than I've ever seen you, mainly because of the influence of my presence in your space. 'Cause you allowed me into this space—something you wouldn't normally do with just any entity."

I laugh out loud. "You're damn right."

"You lost your own balance . . . sorry about that. But I recommend—and this is one critical groundrule of your apprenticeship—when you bring me so near, you should keep in mind the normal methods of psychic protection. You need ta have a filtering system in order to keep in harmony with your own essence and not get it mixed up with mine."

"I recently caught on to that, concerning this entire undertaking with you . . ." I pause. "But the way you describe it, I have to learn to function like a metaphysical coffee machine. Do you prefer yours strong or weak?"

"Oh, strong as all shit," John answers, his powerful eyes gleaming once again. "I realize you know a lot about this subject, dear, but you'd better take Basil up on his proposal to help out."

"You're perfectly right. I was being an ass, I'll admit. But I've begun to mend my ways, haven't you noticed the difference?" I look at him, disappointed.

"Ah, yes—you've been doing just fine! I don't mean ta criticize. I love it when you trust me so much; but at the same time, you shouldn't forget the experience you've had communicating with yer guardians—and what it means to keep bein' yerself, as you're starting to do. It's been a good lesson."

"Well, I'm glad you guys are concerned about my psychic welfare, because staying myself in the midst of what other people want and think is one of my weak spots, as you already know."

"I'm aware of that. But don't you see how much you and I are the same? This is one of the subjects I talked about with

Basil while you were gone. He's gonna help you with this, if you ask him—like he's gonna help me."

John looks youthful. His cheeks have taken on a rosiness and it's plain that Basil's fatherly influence has been healing.

"I often forget to ask for help," I add. "It's dumb, I'll admit. But I'm grateful for your concern . . . I don't want to burn out before my time."

"Like I did. Hah! I can tell you about *that*, of course—not only from my last Expression on earth but quite a few before."

"All in a row?" I look troubled.

"No, not quite. There were easygoin' ones, too, where I got to rest a bit and pull meself together." John folds his arms, crosses his legs and looks me straight in the eyes as if preparing for my next question.

I look at him, blushing slightly. "I feel myself becoming you in certain ways. And it's tempting to have another entity so near—comparable to being pregnant. It definitely goes against the things I teach at my psychic school about protection and all of that. At times I think I'm brave and adventurous. And at other times I think I'm going crazy and should be committed to a mental institution."

"Join the club, dear."

"And I have an inkling you really *are* an old friend of mine, as Basil says. I feel different things for you, actually," I falter, my cheeks becoming redder.

"Sometimes I become obsessed with you. Our kidding about being alone together is sprinkled with grains of truth . . . although I can't separate my motherly inclinations for you from my sisterly or romantic ones. I'm not sure what's going on. I'm confused."

"My God, maybe you *should* be committed!" John chortles. "I understand—I'm not as daft as I look. But you've gotta see that my nonphysical reality helps me keep the picture much clearer than you can keep it for yerself. These sentiments arise naturally when people like you and me communicate so intensely. And bein' able to trust enables the communication to begin. Once two beings have this kind of contact, love can only become deeper."

"Uh-huh," I answer, finding it difficult to look at him.

"But this love we're talkin' about is very distinct from the love most earthlings are able to share. This love that you and me are sharing is called agape."

"A-what?"

"Agape . . . A-G-A-P-E. That's an old-fashioned Greek term for a kind of love akin to brothers and sisters loving each other unconditionally. This is some of the great stuff I've been learning here at my school. Ya see, you can share this kind of love on earth, and you can also share it out-of-the-body. It's a love of no limitation—of total freedom."

"We could use more of that kind."

"The love of Eros is a whole other ball game, though! There's a lot I could tell you about this, too. It was one of me favorite subjects when I was in a body and able to enjoy it. Eros love is as important as agape love, it just gets you into more bloody trouble, that's all." John chuckles sarcastically.

"You don't have to tell me!" I look down at the surprisingly green grass. I'm having a flashback and realizing one of the reasons I'm able to empathize so easily with John is that we both share a backdrop of colorful—if not dubious—earthly encounters. Specifically, I'm aware we both experimented with sex and drugs. Not that I boast of these endeavors in my present life, but I know they played a major role in my last Expression on earth, until my death in the car accident which I had related to John. Not only had I led a turbulent life, but I'd been a musician and singer as well.

John is slurping tea, fiddling mindlessly with a piece of loose tarp on his chair.

"Now," he continues spiritedly, "I think this whole subject of love, sex and partnerships is bloody important in how the earth is gonna develop. As I said in a song, "The center of the circle will always be the home." I'm noticing a lotta themes you and yer man are working on are similar to the ones I came to believe in."

"For instance?"

"Fer instance—the prospect of being a *friend* to yer lover. Or, how does a person love a partner both erotically and in the spirit of agape? This seems naive to folks on earth; there is a stigma attached to simple love, because modern human beings are easily bored. Free love, free sex and free AIDS . . . this is the world's modern heritage, right?"

"Sadly, yes—for many people. But, John, it was your relationship with Yoko which set you on this new path, wasn't it? Since I've been reading about you and accumulating impressions about your relationship, I feel an increasing link with Yoko."

"Yer right. Maybe I'll tell you more about my relationship with Yoko later. There are many aspects to our tale, Linda. It's very complex. Like me, she's done reckless things in her life, which, with hindsight, she might have done quite differently. And, Yoko has had her share of the self-inflicted pain and sorrow crazy artists attract. That's why we needed each other so much when we started out—we were a helluva lot alike."

"And—a lot different?"

"Yeah, you could say that too," John utters with an odd look on his face.

"You must have learned tremendously from each other."

"I'm sure she won't disagree with you! Yoko was learning— and still is—what it means to face the dark side of her nature, to make friends with it and love it . . . and be able to love herself better."

"Have you told her this?"

"Yeah, I've told her." John's expression turns into a fragile smile. "But I'm not sure she wants ta hear it."

He's reclining now with his feet resting comfortably on the arm supports of Basil's unoccupied chair, and I stare inadvertently at his freckled legs.

"And in those songs on your last albums, I understood you and Yoko were singing about finding that foundation of faith in one another."

"It was an *ideal* . . . but I'm afraid we were, in those last days, painfully far from our goal. But I'd rather go into the details some other time. It's a whole subject in itself and . . . I don't know if I'm ready for it."

"Okay. Sure."

"We believed—when we were strong enough—in this other kinda love. Because, ideally, friendship can make it possible for yer own kinda freedom and originality to flower—not only with other humans but in yer relationship with guardians, God, and the whole universe."

"If you give each other the space for it, that is."

"That's why I say 'ideally,' because within a relationship, we're all trying to get to know each other better and to understand our role as a spiritual being which outshines our personalities. We're trying to combine this searching and growing with having a stable relationship with a partner. And that's askin' a lot, don't you think?"

"Sometimes I think it's too much to ask of any mortal."

"So do I . . . but you just hafta carry on."

"Anyway, you're still quite busy with this."

"Heaven is a place of learning, just as earth is—only a bit different."

"A bit?"

"Well, quite a bit. But there's hard work to be done Here—and that's the god-awful truth." John sets his teacup carefully on the ground.

"It strikes me, too, from listening to the emotional development in the lyrics of your music, how you seemed to acquire a need for simplicity—the need for one true partner, one simple home."

"Linda, I discovered this is the most fulfilling place to *be*, although it wasn't always easy! Home and family became my temple on earth. But ya know, even temples can have their leaking roofs."

"Home is where the heart is."

"That's what I mean."

He peers at me with sharp eyes, puts his feet on the ground, stands up and begins to do stretching exercises while continuing to talk. It amuses me to see him do this; it seems so incongruous.

"This concept of simple love between partners is something people on earth need to look at with new insight. Moral codes or religious dogma don't teach people anymore, so you've gotta figure it out on yer own. Learning to love can't come from authority figures and can't be imposed on anybody from the outside. It can only come from the depths of yer own soul."

"But don't we basically teach each other?"

"Right. You get a great resonating effect once you allow yerself to be more loving . . . it bounces off the other and straight back to you, like a good game of tennis."

John pants a little bit and his face becomes red as he keeps on stretching.

"How funny to hear you referring to sports, when you couldn't stand them in your last Expression."

"Don't forget the limitations of the ego-personality, luv. I'm not only speaking from Johnny's point of view," he adds, putting his hands on his hips and making rotating movements with his pelvis.

"Oh," I say, feeling my own stiffness as I watch him. I spring impulsively from my reclined position, so suddenly I frighten him.

"Jesus, you scared the shit out of me!"

"You mean, you still do that too?"

"I tell you, kid, we do anything here we damn well please," he answers, bending over again.

I imitate him and it's a luxury after so much sitting. The wholesome air fills my lungs, wonderfully rejuvenating me. Hanging my head back to stretch my neck, I open my eyes and become lost viewing an eagle soaring high in the sky.

"Hey, don't break your neck!" John says, sitting down again. "I hope you folks on earth realize too much freedom can be as harmful as too much of anything else. From my perspective, it appears that AIDS is a cosmic message—a way of teachin' people in a tough way about their limitations and how ta find new forms of lovin' each other. Total freedom has become as damaging for many as very little freedom. Human beings need ta learn to be free in new ways."

I'm sitting again. "And that's difficult to learn. Personally, I find monogamy easy—that's not the point—but I'm concerned about those subtle areas which relate to being committed to the relationship, while also being open to individual needs and imaginative whims. Where are the limits of freedom, and at what point does it start to make either partner unhappy?"

"It always made *me* unhappy when I didn't find a good balance between my needs and hers. Human beings need to feel safe, loved and appreciated. And everybody's got those needs—you can't get around 'em."

"We're all babies at heart."

"Aye! And I dare say moral codes and religious teachings have worked against themselves—made matters worse by forbidding things people need to figure out on their own. What makes you happy? What makes you unhappy? You can't learn this from an authority figure—you only learn it by yerself, from firsthand experience."

"That makes me think of the statement you made about the Beatles being bigger than Jesus Christ."

"Oh my God, spare me . . ." John says, throwing up his hands. "I got into more trouble from that one fuckin' statement. It was entirely misunderstood."

He has a disturbed look on his face, as if he had tasted something bitter.

"I wasn't meaning to put down Jesus! God knows I'd be the *last* one ta do that. Young people were looking for answers and inspiration which they weren't getting from the church. The Beatles were more interesting to this generation because they could speak directly to them about things that really mattered in their lives. Young folks could see themselves reflected in the Beatles songs more than in church hymns."

"It's a good defense, although it sounds as if you still haven't totally recovered from that misunderstanding."

"Another reason ta put it down on paper and get it straightened out once and fer all! I guess this misinterpretation of a sudden, frivolous reflection of mine symbolized my earliest heavy-duty realization of the power I was wielding in the world. To be taken so seriously by so many people! It was far from any kind of ultimate statement."

"It was taken out of context . . ."

"Exactly. And, it represented the beginning of the end of my *modest* existence on earth. I discovered for the first time what a burden and responsibility it was to be so *bloody famous*. It came as a painful shock, actually. From then on, I felt I had to mind every word, as if the whole world was listening."

"Is this a good example of how too much freedom can end up making you unfree?"

"Right on . . . that's it."

"Considering this," I say, "I suppose it's marvelous for you to be totally anonymous in ye olde Infinite Dwelling."

John is looking more relaxed again. "Right, 'cause yer talkin' to a small part of *me* now, and you can dig that. No one knows about these other parts and no one needs to know—at least for now."

"And you're no longer vulnerable—I guess you can afford to be more open again."

"I'm not bein' watched and manipulated like I was on earth," he says, resting his legs on Basil's chair again.

"So how is it to be back on stage again, now that I'm going to be writing about you?"

"Bloody good! I've got me own space here and I've got me rest. It's entirely unlike the life of being a superstar on earth—an immense relief, actually. I don't recommend being famous to anybody, unless they thrive on vanity, stress and paranoia. Can you imagine how stupid I felt becoming world-famous and discovering what a self-made prison it was?"

I don't answer him, but only nod.

"It sobered me into maturity—made me grow up in certain ways, although in other ways I never did—didn't want to! Hey, let's walk over there to that little creek, d'ya want to? We've been sitting here long enough."

"I'd love to. I was just about to go home, but there are a few more things I want to ask before I leave."

John stands up happily, like a boy who has the notion to go fishing, and we walk quietly toward the stream which has been gushing and gurgling since the first moment I came Here. We've taken off our shoes and the soft grass is caressing our bare feet. Dandelions, meadow buttercups and daisies are everywhere— suddenly I'm wearing a delicate, light-yellow summer dress.

"I don't mean to bug you about the subject," I say, walking next to John, "but do you believe that after so many years of separation, you, Paul, Ringo and George would have gotten together again as musicians?"

"I think we probably would have tried," he answers in his somewhat nasal tone, "eventually—as a joke. Maybe when we got older and wanted ta have a good laugh. But, you've gotta see the reason the Beatles were great is that they could get off on bein' a group. Later, this changed! And just because some folks come together for a period of time doesn't mean it's meant to be *forever*. This is what most people hafta learn about loss . . . and it's the same with an intimate partner. Amazing things might happen, but once yer time together is up, it's up! You can try to force it and hold on . . . but you'll only make yerself sorry. This is one of the most painful things to learn."

"No, it's not easy."

As I look at the mysterious grove of oak trees nearby, again they seem to be enticing me to venture near. I force myself to focus on John, who keeps moving in that special waltzing gait of his. As we approach the brook, he saunters over to a spot where there are big rocks surrounded by thick foliage and searches for a place to sit. Seating himself on a large, smooth boulder next to the creek, he begins to chomp on a long stalk of grass.

"We were talking about relationships . . ." I remind him.

He stops to chew on the green stalk. "Right. I definitely put myself through hell because of 'em. It had ta do with pride and fear and the pain of my childhood. Because of my unstable emotions, I had fear to contend with, especially in relating to a partner."

"That's what I gather," I say, still searching for the right place to sit.

"This is where I found Yoko to be such a help to me initially; we provided each other with a quality of communication—of sharing and giving—which was new for both of us. And, of course, we had many other Expressions together on earth."

I have settled on a flat rock next to John's and shield my eyes from the sun as I look at him.

"And does everybody on earth know their lovers more than once?"

"Yeah, almost always. That's what Life's all about! It's normal to spend many lifetimes with the same partner-soul. It takes more than one Expression to learn essential things from one another. Thank God we have the chance."

"You make it sound so romantic."

"It is . . . if you allow it."

He throws the broken stalk into the water and follows its course downstream.

"Do you intend to return to earth in the near future?"

"No, oh no. I need a rest! But you can never be sure. I haven't decided yet. First, I need to go through with my school—gotta figure out things from *this* perspective."

"Are you going to tell me about this school?"

"Of course, but it has to be in the right order."

I observe John gazing peacefully into the streaming water and I think that Life out-of-the-body definitely seems to have its positive features.

"I suppose," I say, "you wouldn't exactly be chomping at the bit to come back."

Appearing to be lost in thought, he doesn't answer.

"But, is it true you and Yoko were the English poets Robert and Elizabeth Browning? Both of you had seen, or maybe I should say 'received' information about this right before you died. You bought Yoko a portrait and signature of Elizabeth Barrett Browning and were going to give it to her for Christmas."

"Yeah, that was luv'ly."

There is an elated stillness in the air as John stares into the water. I wait for him to continue.

"You believe in our story," he says, directing his glance toward me. "We felt it was true . . . and now I'm sure of it."

There is another long silence.

"Would you sing the song you wrote as a take-off on Robert Browning's poem?"

His face is kind and responsive. "Ya mean, 'Grow Old Along With Me'?"

"That's the one."

He stares into the distance for awhile, takes off his glasses and puts them into his breast pocket. Then, as he closes his eyes, I hear that famous, transparent, falsetto tone blending itself with the sound of flowing water.

"Grow old along with me, the best is yet to be . . . when our time has come, we will be as one . . . God bless our love, God bless our love."

He waits, watching the stream, and then closes his eyes again.

"Grow old along with me, two branches of one tree . . . face the setting sun, when the day is done . . . God bless our love, God bless our love."

His voice has become raspy and he clears his throat.

". . . Spending lives together, man and wife together . . . world without end, world without end."

Then, his voice becomes stronger and brighter.

"Grow old along with me, whatever fate decrees . . . we will see it through, for our love is true . . . God bless our love . . . God bless our love."

I can't say anything as John looks at me. I can only nod—a painful lump in my throat. He looks at me compassionately, and I feel warmth trickling down my cheeks. For the first time, he doesn't know what to say, and this strikes me as so funny I burst out laughing. He looks relieved.

"I used to do that a lot, too," he says casually. "Had ta face it before I could move on, before I could get outta the clouds . . . and release all those emotions to the universe . . . and into the marvelous future I'm planning for myself. For better or for worse, Yoko and I will be together again someday—and she knows it too."

~5~
The Way of the Stream

I desperately wanted to do some research on the poet, Robert Browning. I was provoked by this subject of past lives, or "Past Mode Expressions," as John had described them. What was it about this subject that left me upset?

In my library I opened The Cambridge Guide to English Literature *to page 107 and was dumbfounded by the imposing portrait of Browning at the age of forty-six. I gasped— perhaps it was my imagination—I could see John Lennon's dark eyes peering out at me as if to say, "See—isn't this great?"*

Browning's countenance looked similar to John's. I felt waves of goosebumps raising on my arms. Turning another page, I began to read a summary of his life and work. Born in 1812 and died in 1889. Grew up in Camberwell—once amid green fields—now a suburb of London. Eagerly, I read further . . .

"The young Browning's appreciation of the arts also extended to music, which he learned at home, and his talent for drawing was admired by Rossetti. As a boy Browning was, he said himself, an almost compulsive rhymer, and by the time he was 12 or 13 he had written enough poems for a small volume . . ."

I read through the entire passage. These were facts which fit perfectly into John's life and I was becoming increasingly fascinated. Listed right before Robert Browning was Elizabeth Barrett Browning; again, I felt chills rising on my skin. As if superimposed upon the portrait, Yoko Ono's face seemed to be ogling me with knowing eyes and powerful demeanor.

I read further, seeing more parallels in the unfolding story with John and Yoko's life. For instance, Elizabeth Barrett Browning had been a devout spiritualist. She was six years Robert's senior and had already made a reputation for herself as a poet when they met and fell in love. She bore her first child when she was forty-three and died prematurely at the age of fifty-five, leaving Robert alone with their only son.

"Theirs is one of the great romances of literary history . . ." I finished reading and closed the book.

I was shaken, partially because I had not expected such a strong physical reaction to my investigations. This time it had been goosebumps . . . my body was telling me something my mind could not.

About a week later, I was again in trance, wondering if I would locate John still perched on his rock by the water. Now, I only needed the tape recorder for my voice—my resourceful inner ear was able to provide the birdsong, gentle breeze and babbling brook. It was tedious repeating aloud everything I was hearing inside, for it went faster than I could keep up with.

The entire affair was becoming increasingly one of learning to be patient and quietly receptive. My mind and imagination would race, fly, then nosedive back to earth, leaving me anxious and frustrated. Modern human beings are accustomed to flashy movies and television, while the inner movies of the mind are less noisy and imposing. Like putting a seashell to your ear and hearing the ocean surf—it's all there—you just need to listen with a different ear.

I see John sitting where I left him. He has another green stalk between his teeth and is looking at the moving water below.

"Catch anything yet?" I say from my position next to him.

"Hey, hoity toity! How's it going?" John turns to regard me.

"Just great! It's fun to be back. Have you been having a good time?"

"Oh, yes. It's a wonderful spot."

Looming clouds are casting intermittent cool shadows upon us and I see that both John and I are wearing something unusual this time. I'm in a full-length, heavy cotton gown with a string of light green emeralds around my neck. John has a full beard and is wearing a suit made of this same rough material. Hanging from his neck is a thick golden chain with a beautiful blue stone, mounted in gold, which appears to be lapis lazuli. Both of us are wearing soft, brown leather boots which lace up the ankle.

". . . this is certainly an interesting get-up!" I laugh, inspecting my garments.

"I hope you like it . . . we're gonna be taking a hike."

"And these are gorgeous!" I finger my new necklace and stroke the velvety boots. "A hike? I think I'm ready for that. Where are you taking us?"

"I beg your pardon, lady. Yer imagination has ta be as lively as mine, remember?"

"But I'm entering into *your* world—as a curious visitor from earth."

John throws the stalk out of his mouth and smirks at me.

"Yer right, but we're both responsible for what happens to us Here. You're an earthly visitor to my world. But once you possess the knowledge and ability to *come* here, you make yerself a co-creator along with me. The advantage you have is you can manifest this trip in the physical world—something I could be jealous of."

"Is that really true?" I look deeply into his eyes.

"Yes, that's really true, Linda."

"But I thought you were happier Here."

"That's not the point. I *am* happy. But there are things you can do on earth which can't be done anywhere else in the universe."

"What, for instance?"

"Fer instance, meetin' yer partner again in that unique, tangible place—in that special way—which only the two of you can remember together."

John's eyes reflect a distant sadness.

"Let's get off these fuckin' rocks—me arse is achin'!"

He jumps down onto the thick grass and I follow him.

"Anyway, there's this pathway I've discovered which I think we should be taking . . . wanna go?"

"Of course."

John has turned and is walking along a narrow pathway surrounded by high, thick foliage.

"I should tell you," I say, hurrying after him, "what an interesting time I had looking up the Brownings. It was fascinating."

He pivots. "Good old Bobby Browning and his wife Eliza B— now there's an attractive couple! Yeah, it's riveting, once you begin to examine this stuff. It happens to be what I'm busy with myself."

His voice trails off as he tromps ahead of me. We're surrounded by endless shades of green. In the silence, I hear the melancholy song of a willow-wren.

Suddenly, we're out of the dense foliage on a broader pathway. John is humming contentedly as we amble along. I look up at the clouds which appear to be performing a slow dance in the sky above. I've not witnessed this kind of weather Here before, and it's putting me into a totally different mood than our meadow. It makes me think of Ireland and certain parts of Northern California, and I wonder if I actually smell a salt breeze.

"I began by looking up Robert Browning in my English literature guide," I say. "I almost died when I saw a portrait of him. He looks so much like you, John! His eyes practically jumped out of the book at me. He's got that same depth of sensitivity . . . the humor . . . that touch of cynicism."

He looks at me and raises his eyebrows in jest.

"The portrait of Elizabeth Barrett Browning looks less like Yoko—maybe because of the Japanese features in her Present Expression. There were sparks flying from her, too."

"We had the same reaction to the portraits!" John says. "It was so much fun for Yoko and me to trip on the whole idea. That was right before I died, actually. Since coming Here, I've been exploring the similarities and contrasts of our key relationships. You know Elizabeth tried to open Robert to new spiritual concepts—which he stubbornly rejected. He was a mystic in his own way, but too arrogant. He refused to accept that a person could talk to spirit."

John fondles the brilliant blue stone hanging at his chest.

"And then, Elizabeth died at a young age, just as John did."

"Is this a game you enjoy playing with each other?" I ask pessimistically.

"Undeniably, we've been folks who chose to experience contrasts! It's a tough way to learn. With the death of Elizabeth, Robert was forced to live alone with his son—who was part of the soul Yoko and I brought into the world again as Sean. In both Expressions we formed a triangle which created a Repeating Interchange among three strong souls."

"Repeating Interchange?"

"Ya know—when souls keep meeting in numerous Expressions in order to learn fundamental lessons."

"To work out karma?"

"Aye."

"And what was this triangle teaching you then?"

"It forced us to learn from our limitations."

"With each other?"

"Yeah, and ta see what happened when we tried to fight against those limitations."

"What did happen?"

John places his hands on his chest. "We isolated ourselves, not only from the world, but from each other. We'd forget our hearts. In retrospect, those particular moments were a plain waste of a good time."

Our pathway is following a meandering stream. The landscape is becoming filled with larger rocks and shrubbery.

"I've been reading some of Robert and Elizabeth's poetry, and obviously both of them were extraordinarily strong individuals."

"That they were! And yet, there was this powerful element of love between them, for they clearly recognized they were twin souls."

"What does that actually mean?" I ask, captivated by the swirling water nearby.

"To be twin souls, ya mean?"

"Right. I've heard that term so many times, but I can't completely relate to it."

John stares mischievously at the ground, then, looking up with raised eyebrows he says, "When the universe was created, Mr. God and Mrs. Goddess got lonesome together and wanted to have more fun—so they decided ta have children! They begot all of these minuscule little pieces of themselves, called them 'souls,' and sent them off on their merry way—out into the universe—to be just as inventive as they were. Very soon it became apparent that each of these souls was actually comprised of *two parts*—called 'polarities'—which made them prone to argue! At a certain moment, Life became quite unbearable for them, and these two parts said to each other, 'fuck you, I'm goin' me own way!' Then each one stormed outta the house for what seemed to be for good."

I look at John, trying not to laugh.

"Now, each original soul had split into two opposite parts and had become a *new* soul in its own right. The real *ironic* part of the story is these polar opposites—these two parts of the whole—thought they could do without each other, so vain they were! But oh no. Not a chance. When these two parts of the whole decided to Express on the material plane, they kept running into each other. From the far corners of the earth, one part would say to the other, 'Hey—you again!' "

"Sometimes this meeting was extraordinarily fun—the most fun they could ever remember having! And this was when the concept of 'heaven' was born. Yet, at other times, their meeting went sour—and when it was bad, it was awful!"

"These unfortunate two parts of the whole had forgotten their inception as one. They couldn't possibly imagine why they were so irresistibly attracted to one another. In their Expressions on the physical plane, they continued swimming deeper into the seas of love and hatred. If things didn't work out as they expected, they would become agitated. It was during this period of the souls' evolution that the concept of 'hell' came to be."

"Reflecting each other like perfect mirrors, both pointed the finger at the other in blame, forgetting their noble origins in the cradle of their celestial parents. But sometimes, when lying blissfully entwined in each other's arms, these two parts of the whole *could* remember. They would wonder how they could have made Life so difficult for one another. And this, my dear, is the story of twin souls—fer better or fer worse."

"Thanks. I think I understand now," I say, grinning at him.

"Of course this is just a thumbnail sketch . . ." John begins to whistle softly.

Following the way of the stream, which is gradually becoming wider, we are now surrounded by a thick mist. Putting my hand to my head, I touch a dampness that has caused my hair to curl. Together with the salty air, I am beginning to smell, unmistakably, a familiar coastal fragrance—fennel and other wild vegetation—which blends deliciously into the increasingly wet atmosphere.

"Is there anything more to tell me about the Brownings?" I ask.

"Oh sure." John moves his hips playfully to right and left, holding his hands and arms aloft, as if he is going to dance like Zorba the Greek. He stops to catch his breath.

"Bobby and Eliza were very possessive of each other, yet at the same time they sought love which was not imprisoning. They adhered to the belief that when you can trust, you can also be free."

"They were a very romantic couple."

"Yes. They believed in the closed circle."

"What was that?"

"It's yer basic monogamy. In those days it wasn't unusual, of course. The closed circle establishes a nice, warm nest and a safe base—it's nothin' ta be ashamed of."

"You don't have to convince me," I proclaim, giving John a forceful glance.

"So often partners think of their jealousy or possessiveness as a *negative* thing. More often it's just telling 'em, very plainly, that their relationship needs more attention or more privacy. John Lennon was such a jealous guy, ya know."

"That was a great song."

"Well, it was terribly true. There was a lot behind it."

Again, his eyes follow the ground moving under his feet. He strokes his beard thoughtfully.

"This circle I'm talkin' about is the traditional symbol of the wedding ring. All those conventional trappings didn't interest John Lennon the slightest in his youth. But later, he came to see their real symbolism, especially in regard to his parents. Within the closed circle is openness. And this extends to the sexual practices of a couple. It ties in with the idea of tantric yoga—the yoga of sex."

"Now that's an interesting subject."

"I know! And tantra cultivates those pure energies which a couple can generate together—through sex—energy which can move mountains."

"But so many people are ashamed or afraid of sex. They think it's dirty."

"Right, because they don't understand how ta use it. In traditional tantra, sex energy is considered *holy* and can serve as a gateway to heaven."

"Is this where your story of the twin souls ties in?"

"Sometimes—if yer lover happens to be yer twin soul—you've really hit the jackpot," he answers casually. "But in any case, this tantric type of physical union can become a doorway which each partner is capable of opening for the other. To pass through it means to merge with the harmony of the universe. The beauty of the concept is this: as partners of flesh we can be Adam and Eve creating Paradise. That's why the circle needs to be closed—to reach this degree of consciousness as a couple—to reach the center together."

"But don't you think this is too lofty and abstract for most people to grasp?"

"Not if they realize it's *time* for them ta grasp it, especially if sex hasn't worked out for them."

"You know, you're referring to a hell of a lot of people right now."

"Sex can serve either creatively or destructively. As everyone knows, there's a lot of misdirected sex energy in the world today. Yet, if harnessed—watch out! It's one of earth's most up-and-coming spiritual energy sources, just wait 'n see."

"Will we be able to run our washing machines and light our houses with it? I doubt I'll be around that long."

"Oh yes you will—only who knows in what form?"

We look at each other and grin.

"Now, if you check it out from another perspective," John goes on, "a couple can be part of a much larger circle of relationships with children, family and friends—right? Each circle has its importance. There's always the need to keep things clear, because Life is filled with too many emotional contradictions."

"You sound as if you speak from experience."

"Whadaya think? It kept me preoccupied most of the time."

"I guess you're saying to people, 'keep it simple.' "

"The simple shall inherit the earth," he says.

Our conversation has been so engrossing, I hadn't noticed our trail diverging from the river, nor the fog partially lifting. We are climbing sand dunes now and I can smell the pungent, spicy odor of the sage growing in low, pale-grey bushes. A cool breeze is blowing and both John and I are now wearing exquisite, golden-colored, linen capes for warmth. With his beard and brown cap covering his long hair, John looks like a refugee pirate.

"Aye-aye, mate, we're returnin' ta the sea," he quips, picking up immediately on my thoughts. Then, climbing a dune, he tries to catch a glimpse of the coastline.

"Nothin' yet, but we only need to walk a bit further—if you'll accompany me, dear."

John motions me onward, but it's difficult walking in the sand, and I trip clumsily over a clump of grass as I try to keep up.

"Hey, wait for me! Do you see anything?"

"Just a bit further this way and we'll be there."

I can barely hear John's voice as he trudges ahead, talking into the wind. It sounds as if he is speaking a strange language.

"His personality has changed," I think, "since we left the river and began to climb these dunes."

Suddenly I feel insecure; and at this moment, John spins around and screams loudly, scaring the daylights out of me.

"Dammit! What are you trying to do?" I yell, exasperated.

"I thought ya might need a little more excitement!"

"It's been exciting enough as it is! But what language were you speaking just then? What are you doing, for God's sake?"

"Be ye a billigen—or a bodsmire?" he cackles, then rushes toward me like a lunatic.

Shrieking, I run away and we both fall into hysterics. Tears are streaming from my eyes and my sides are aching.

"What have I gotten myself into? You're totally insane!"

"The pot callin' the kettle black! Come on! Let's find the fuckin' ocean!"

He darts away in the direction of some larger sand dunes, but I can't keep up because of my long skirt. I wish I had something else on and, instantly, I'm wearing a pair of pants. John continues to dash ahead and nearly trips over his cloak as he runs in the direction of an even higher dune. Following him with my heart thumping, I run slightly downhill, then upward with great difficulty, to the top of a huge mound. I hear John yelling and my chest pounds as if it is going to explode.

~6~
Mystical Ocean

"There she is!" John screams in the brilliant sunshine. "Come on! Hurry up—take a look!"

He is standing at the top of the dune. Seagulls cry shrilly overhead. I climb the last stretch to reach him. Gasping for breath, I near the top, and my ears become assailed by the thunderous pounding of a mighty ocean surf. Finally standing next to him, I behold a stunning, blue coastline with enormous, rolling, white-capped waves.

"Well, glory be! There she is!" John pants in satisfaction.

"Wow, this is fantastic!" I exclaim, still gasping. "It's so *big* and *blue*! Did you know it would be like this?"

"Well, yeah . . . I've been here a couple of times before meself, but it never looked quite like *this* before!"

Removing our cloaks, we spread them out and sit cross-legged upon our sandy knoll. Gazing at the immense body of water, I try to comprehend it. I get the message that this is an ancient place, as well as a familiar one. It reminds me of my youthful days on the Pacific Coast—yet it is more than this. There is an odd power and mystery surrounding us now which I can't define. It is like a *presence*. Or is the sky coming closer to the land?

"Where are we?" I ask, stupefied.

"It's the Mystical Ocean."

We listen to the surf crashing on the gleaming shore. A delicate salt mist rises into the air.

"I enjoyed your story about the twin souls," I say, breaking the spell.

"It's a subject I have pondered for many Expressions," John answers quietly. "The study of relationships has always kept me deeply occupied."

"But isn't this what every soul is busy with on earth?"

"Of course. But there are those who choose to specialize." He gives me a piercing look, then stares again at the waves.

"Few folks could understand the difficulties I put myself through in my relationships."

"Many people saw you as a victim."

"I realize that. It needs to be rectified." He clears his throat. "My difficult periods with Yoko were part of a larger soul strategy than folks were capable of realizing."

I have an uneasy feeling in my stomach. "People were angry with her . . . perhaps because she seemed to take you away from the Beatles and from your music."

John snickers. "As our great friend Basil would say, 'Strictly outward appearances, my dear!' "

"Could you explain it?"

"As twin souls, Yoko and I were paying off old debts. In our adversity, balance was bein' restored."

We observe the colossal, foaming tide. It effortlessly sweeps in upon a glossy shore and becomes sucked out again by a powerful undercurrent.

"Each person has their own shadow side," John continues, "and, at times, a person can become blind and ignorant of who and what their partner truly is. Each of us has an ugly side which can produce evil—yet ends up generatin' *good*—because it forces us ta search more deeply and demand more truth in our relationships."

"You're saying this ugly side forces us to learn from our errors?"

"Correct."

Closing my eyes and absorbing the abundant sunlight, I inhale damp, salty air.

"To be honest, John, it's a pity you and Yoko were such an isolated couple."

He doesn't answer immediately, as if he needs to think.

"Isolation has both good and bad points. The good part is Yoko and I were on an inward pilgrimage to reach our own soul connection and achieve a new balance. The bad part is too much isolation can make you crazy."

I open my eyes and look at him carefully. "Were you able to attain the soul connection you were searching for?"

"Yes and no. I ended up Here anyway."

I shift my position and lean forward to hug my knees.

"If you look at John Lennon's life," I say, "you see he started off being about as extroverted as one could possibly get—and ended up nearly a recluse."

"That happens when you let fear take over," he says, stroking his beard. "The lessons were big ones."

"What were you afraid of?"

"I had abstract fears, as well as tangible ones, and they revolved around the fear of *loss*—which generated more loss! I was lacking confidence, which made me consistently weak. I was beginning to break through when we came out with our new album in 1980 . . . but by then it was too late. My life had become irrevocably complicated."

"What do you mean?"

"I had lost control of it by then. And there was no way of retrieving it."

I look at him without answering. A flock of shrieking seagulls pass above, then land awkwardly on the shore.

"How can a person go from one Expression to the next and be so totally different?"

"There's lotsa reasons. For one thing, we're usually not able to see how everything is perfectly connected . . . just like those beads around yer neck. We can only see one bead at a time and don't understand how they can all hold together."

"It's difficult to accept how a person can be like a saint in one Expression and a criminal in the next. Isn't there any evolution?"

"You don't totally understand, dear. There is only evolution in terms of *learning*, not what it *looks* like from the outside! Now take your saint and your criminal, fer instance. The saint may be wise and lovin' and all of that, but he has to learn to come down-to-earth, to appreciate the value of material things—to learn to respect the laws of nature without trying to escape them. So, he chooses an Expression in which he hurts people and steals from them in order to become *involved* in the classic earth game of ego-manifestation. This is something which the soul—in spite of its goodness—didn't know enough about. And he sets it up so the saint in him isn't going to be gettin' in the way to interfere with his chance to learn something important. See? The saint is there—keeping track on the sidelines—but he wants ta learn more about the earth plane. Not just in his intellectual discerning, but in his gut, in real experience. In another Expression, he can have more insight into other people's problems—because he's been through it all himself. Get it?"

I nod.

"Ya see, there's no Great Chap sitting on a throne Here, it's all *inside* us. We're makin' up the script of our own drama, whether it be farce or tragedy, in order ta learn about physical and nonphysical manifestation. And that's it."

"But you make it sound so empty and nihilistic."

"Not at all! Did you forget Mr. God and Mrs. Goddess? And besides, there is this wonderful thing called universal truth, which works the same for all of us and which is joining individual soul consciousness into one mind-boggling whole. These universal truths end up teachin' us that Love and Light are supreme—there's not one case I've ever heard of, *anywhere*, where this ain't true."

"As you tell me this, I believe you're right—because the hair rising on my arms is telling me so."

We pause. John stretches his legs and gives me a sidelong look.

"I guess you've been wondering about some of the other Past Time-Mode Expressions I've shared with Yoko on earth."

"Of course! You realize I have little understanding."

"Right. Well, once upon a time there was a little fishing village in southern Italy . . ."

He raises his eyebrows, and I listen in suspense.

"Somewhere around 749 A.D., a fisherman lived in this village with his wife and five kids in their modest hovel. It wasn't much of a life because everyone had ta work hard—no time for fun and games, mind you. The fisherman worked his ass off every day and came home at night loaded, smelling of fish and ready ta give the ol' wife another good thrashing! Year in and year out, she had ta tolerate this crap, and managed to pretend as if it was the normal state of affairs—which, in those days it was! Obviously, this dame had a deplorable life, not only caring for the household chores and the kids all by herself, but also havin' to deal with the fact that when her husband drank too much, he would beat her up and squander all their dough."

I stare at John in puzzlement.

"One fine day, this little woman had a flash of inspiration chargin' through her. She was gonna dye the wool she was spinnin', weave it into beautiful cloth like the family down the road and try ta trade it for food and household goods. She even got a couple of her older daughters to help. And fer a moment in time, her existence was lookin' up."

He hesitates, giving me a calculating look.

"But what d'ya suppose this bastard of a husband had ta go an' do? He saw he'd lost his grip, you see, and of course that could *not* be tolerated. So the filthy bloke not only beat up his wife and two daughters, but proceeded ta throw all the fuckin' spindles and looms outta the house—over a bluff and into the sea, to be exact—together with all the beautiful wool. From this moment on, the wife became grey-haired and empty-headed and didn't complain to him again. And this, my friend, is the end of my dismal tale."

I smile warily at John.

"Was that you and Yoko?"

He nods.

"And you were the fisherman?"

He nods again.

"At least you have the guts to admit it."

There is a lapse in our conversation.

"And what about your happy moments together?"

"Ah, those were certainly many!" he says brightly, pulling up his knees, leaning forward and staring out again toward the sea. The repeated sound of the breakers has begun to lull me into a colorful, dream-like state of suspended animation.

"Egypt . . . 1252 B.C. A beautiful, teenage girl was living in her father's court. From her earliest days, she had been trained to play a lute-like instrument and to sing as beautifully as an exotic bird. Since her childhood, she had been in love with the handsome son of a nobleman, who was a talented artisan in the royal temples."

"Eventually, these two paradigms of loveliness and prosperity were married, inherited land and wealth and bore children. Not only did they have a deep bond of trust as lovers, but they recognized themselves to be twins of fate, sheltered and guided by Ra, the great Sun God. In this Expression, the couple promised themselves to each other, not only in the transience of the flesh, but in the world beyond. Of course, they lived happily ever after." John smiles at me smugly.

"So that time you were definitely another kind of guy."

"You mean *gal* . . . Yoko was the man and I was the woman that time around."

"Hey! You're kidding."

"Nope. Why would I kid you? You see how different and contradictory each Expression can be—all for the sake of wisdom."

"Do we have to learn the same lessons over and over again?"

"Not necessarily—only if we need to learn them *better*. The crucial question is, 'how easily can a person put their wisdom into practical use?' "

"That's a good question. Do twin souls always meet as lovers, then?"

"Often, but not necessarily! Would you care to hear another wee tale?"

"I'm all ears."

"Once long ago . . . in 803 A.D. to be exact, there lived in Japan a rich woman and her adult son whom she dearly loved.

Many years earlier, the husband of this woman had passed away, leaving her with two sons. Unfortunately, one of these boys died in his teens, leaving the woman doubly bereaved.

"One year in late spring, the dowager began ta make plans—as was the custom in those days—for her son to marry into a family of wealth and high standing. Her hopes for the future were focused on this event, and she set herself to the task with utter resolve.

"Yet, unbeknownst to the unlucky dowager, for several years this cherished progeny had fostered an illicit love affair with one of the humble maid-servants in his mother's house! When it became plain that a wedding was in the making, he was torn by anguish and bewilderment. The young man was forced to admit to himself he had fallen hopelessly in love with the girl-servant. Be she rich or poor, he could not abandon her for another bride! I suppose you've guessed the outcome already."

John focuses dramatically on me.

"No . . . I mean, go on!"

"With great pluck and candor, the cherished son revealed to his mother his love for—and desire to marry—this blameless girl. It's hard ta describe the emotional scene that followed. The dowager was beside herself with distress, bordering on madness. A dreadful jealousy had possessed her—to the depths of her being."

"A frightful argument followed wherein the son refused to obey the wishes of his mother. She was forced to disown him. In her deepest core, it was as though he had *died* like her other son. She spent the remainder of her life in spiritual desolation. Meanwhile, the young man married his true love and managed with great difficulty to build a new life based on his own merit."

I have been so engrossed, I don't notice the sun slipping down toward the sea.

"What a tale!" I exclaim.

"Ocean Child had some awful lessons to learn about detachment," John nearly whispers.

"Ocean Child?"

"That's what 'Yoko' means in Japanese."

"And you were her son?"

"Yes. It was a life in which I did not know fear."

He looks at me wistfully.

"Believe me, dear. I'll venture again to the other side of this ocean—and pick up where I left off. Because Life is like that! We're all blind fools . . . looking forward ta the love, forgetting about the pain."

A fiery, copper blaze of sun is making its plunge into a violet-colored sea.

"I have to go home now," I sigh wearily.

He pats my shoulder. "Sure, I'll be here waitin' for you! But you'll be going on a long vacation before you return. It's not what you think—but you'll see."

"I can't imagine why."

"Life is filled with surprises, kid."

"And where will you be staying?"

He switches to his deep actor's voice. "I'll sleep with the stars . . . in a bed full of chortling virgins."

In his normal voice he says, "I'm not alone, Linda—you don't have to worry about me."

The last thing I remember is the tinge of bronze and violet reflecting on John's face.

PART II

Forces of Change

~1~
Behind the Scenes

John warned me I wouldn't be coming back soon to his place and I hadn't considered it possible. Funny enough, he was right, for after our last visit at the Mystical Ocean, I had no inclination to return. I trusted this was okay, yet frequently wondered if I still had the honor of being John's apprentice or if the spell had somehow been broken. In any case, it felt like I had come to a natural stopping point in the development of the project.

Nevertheless, I often met John in my dreams. When I awoke, I would feel exceptionally open and for the rest of the day his presence would be obvious. This was always the earliest signal that I had made contact with one of my spiritual guardians—whether through night- or daytime musing: I could clearly feel their presence in my heart. It was fervent and exciting, as if I was in love—not eros love, but that nice agape kind which John had told me about.

Besides Mr. Lennon, there were other spiritual guardians I dreamed about and was specifically aware of, such as beloved Basil, a motherly individual named Lydia and a comedian called Rags. The importance of these relationships did not seem to lessen because of the current one developing with John, but rather, only seemed to intensify.

Having an active relationship with a spiritual being often made me think of how a child communicates with a teddy bear or an imaginary friend. It was tempting to believe I was lost in a world of projection—that I was odd or didn't want to grow up somehow. At the same time, I was convinced of the validity of my adult perceptions and the genuine existence of my guardians.

As John and Basil reported, "soul" is composed of so many abstract layers of being that it would be impossible to show all of it to an earthling. I could grasp that the entity I was calling "John" must have been busy on many other levels unknown to me, yet I always recognized his presence by the dry humor, the distinctive voice and by the way I got to look at things through his hip, yet pragmatic perspectives.

Behind the scenes, I was learning spiritual entities often choose to express themselves by means of the personality they had left most recently on earth or which had been a favorite of theirs in terms of imaginative expression. I was discovering that in order to communicate effectively, a spiritual being needs to pick a character and a form to use as a means of improving or enhancing the dialogue. I knew John chose the personality he had lived in his last Expression because I needed him to be that way—and I figured, so did lots of other people if they were going to be following along in the adventure.

On the other side of the looking glass, I began to see myself and my personality from many new angles. My ties with John were influencing the way I acted and felt. My self-confidence was soaring. I cared less about trying to please the status quo and found it easier to voice the humor and individuality of my younger years. After a long stretch of hard work in my adult life—having married, borne offspring, divorced and then re-married—I positively valued this new carefree attitude.

I thrived on listening to John Lennon's music, starting with all of the original Beatles stuff and continuing through every record he'd recorded until his death. Listening to John and Yoko singing to each other on their last two albums gave me a notion of where their sentiments had been—with each other and with themselves—up until the very last days. Many people had written books about John after his death and I made it a hobby to read this material in my spare time.

I felt John's attention on me, too. It seemed he was gathering information about how I lived my daily life and how I resolved various emotional problems. John appeared to be a highly sophisticated, yet very needy, soul. This contradictory combination of qualities was at least partially responsible for his power and charm over me, for it told of the duality of my own existence.

As deeply as I was immersed, I would often step aside and take a more rational look at my interest in John. Countless times I asked myself if I truly wanted to get so deeply involved. And, if I was going to take the project seriously, was I ready to deal with the consequences in terms of a big, commercial world? Would I end up sorry I'd ever begun? It seemed to be the story of my life: in spite of my fear of heights, I was always eager to jump off the next cliff.

Nineteen eighty-seven had come and gone. In January of 1988 I began to rework the material I had written. The tapes needed editing and this proved to be more work than I had expected. It hadn't always been pure inspiration coming through; there was plenty of gobbledygook which needed to be refined and boiled down to its most essential ingredients.

There came a phase in my life in which I didn't have the energy or focus to write. This was probably due to our recent move into a new house and my need to work harder on my relationship with my husband. The natural flow of existence seemed to be thwarted by a bottleneck of stress. I had many inspired plans concerning work and family, yet carrying them out could be so physically and mentally tiring.

Perhaps a deeper underlying factor in my anxiety was the fact that my husband and I wanted to have a child together. When I awoke one morning—knowing I must be pregnant—I could hear John's voice remarking,

"Bein' a mother is like bein' number one on the universal hit parade . . . if yer good at it, there's nothin' that can make you happier."

"I am good at it and I'm terribly happy! But what is to become of *you* and the rest of my career?"

"Pshaw . . . you didn't come off the banana boat yesterday! Use yer head. Don't forget—Life is what happens to you when yer busy making other plans."

In spite of the changes taking place, I could always be sure of John's happy and carefree proximity. I could often sense him hanging around, both at home and at work. He seemed to be eagerly absorbing information and I surmised that this process was as important to him as the process of getting a story written. As he'd told me more than once, it all needed time. His presence made me want to smile and jest—it was never dull with John around.

Meanwhile, the infant growing and moving spiritedly inside of me felt bright and cheerful and symbolized the hope of the world to come. Our daughter was born in August 1989 and cast her beautiful, magic spell upon us. Life flowed on like a river, carrying us wherever it wanted to go.

~2~
In the Throes

Next to all the joy and fulfillment a baby had brought into our lives, it felt as if a miniature bomb had exploded somewhere inside of our psyches. It forced us to pick up the pieces and learn how to build entirely new structures within the family alliance. During this time, I decided to stop teaching; clearly I had more important things to do.

Reworking the written material I'd collected so far, I could easily hear John's voice in my thoughts. He seemed as much a part of the editing as the original story-telling and was literally sitting on my shoulder, helping in the writing process. He gave me friendly hints about how to describe something more effectively or bring out the true flavor of the story which he and I had initially constructed.

This heralded an entirely new phase in my apprenticeship. I was beginning to understand how I could visit his world simply by having him present with me at the word processor. Our relationship had become so advanced—I didn't have to go through elaborate procedures—I could simply hear, see, smell and touch the world we were inventing together.

Besides the "instant conveyance" I was experiencing while in a light trance at the word processor, I discovered I still needed the frequent consolation of deep meditation—without the typing. This was necessary to broaden my understanding

and clarify impressions I was receiving. Afterwards, some-
times I made notes about what had happened; more often I
would allow the impressions to flow freely.

This particular aspect of writing could be likened to prepar-
ing the ingredients for an elaborate soup—washing, cutting
and cooking, adding the necessary salt and spices—then
letting the entire concoction simmer gently on the back burner
of my mind. I enjoyed accumulating ideas throughout the day
and liked the freedom to savor this fanciful soup as well as
the fast food which "conveyed" writing was feeding me.

My work was going on whether I was conscious of it or not.
I couldn't stop the process anymore—not because I didn't
value my free will—but because it had become too vital to my
existence, like watching an additional child growing up.

It had been a long time since I had worked on the story line
with John. On a bright morning in February 1990 this
moment finally arrived.

I am walking along the beach as clouds sail through the sky
like large ships. Sand is sinking under my feet and I swing my
arms freely with every step. I need this walk—alone—to empty
my head and attune myself to my surroundings. Looming far off
on the horizon are craggy rocks which seem to dwarf the beach.
Looking to my right, I see sand dunes scattered with patches of
tough, grey-green turf. Beyond the dunes lofty, enchanted mountains appear blue and green, crowned with a silver mist.

Enjoying the rhythmic movement of my arms and legs, I think
how peculiar it is that a physical body and its reality can be
appreciated even in its nonphysical form. I wonder when I'll see
John or if he might play a practical joke on me. Then I see him,
waving from atop a nearby sand dune.

Running toward him, I hear him chuckle.

"Ya managed to find me again, funny lady! I thought you
needed ta walk alone fer awhile."

"Well, I did . . . but I became curious about where you'd be
and what you'd be like this time."

"Oh! You do remind me of myself—lovin' me freedom but,
at the same time, longing for companionship."

Moved to see him again, I become shy. He looks strong and refreshed—and very different. I get the impression he has accomplished many things since I last saw him Here.

"Linda, congratulations! You've become a mother again . . . and it's part of the greater plan. You've changed, I see; and it becomes you!"

"Well, thanks. I was going to tell you the same thing," I say, sitting down next to him on thick clumps of grass.

"It's good to be back—better than I had hoped! I've appreciated the camaraderie, John. You've helped me a great deal, even though I didn't actually come *Here*."

"That's natural. Give yerself a break, will you? This isn't a marathon we're runnin', ya know!"

"Yeah, I tend to forget that and allow myself to get anxious."

John looks at me solemnly.

"Hey, tell me something," he says. "Are you doin' this for yerself or for other people?"

"That's just the point. I've pondered that question for a long time. The only way this experiment will work is if I stop thinking about other people. I have to do this for myself."

"You've passed the test, dearie. That's the mark of any artist—he *needs* ta create, not just for the results, but for his incurable compulsion. He knows if he doesn't do it, he'll end up goin' mad or dyin' of frustration! A true artist is perpetually obsessed and will create at all costs."

"But why do so many artists create and destroy themselves at the same time?"

"Because they need to learn to respect themselves as much as what they're creating—and to realize they're conveying a power comin' to them from higher realms—it's divine. This realization might cause artists to take better care of themselves."

"Do you think the concept of the 'the starving artist' is passé?"

"It will be when the artists' overall love-of-self improves—when their connection with earth improves."

John squints at the blue water and continues, "As our old friend Basil once told you, artists and other imaginative folks need to realize *they* are the modern healers of planet earth. They are supplying the world with pictures of what reality is all about! Imagination is what makes the world go 'round, no matter what level yer working on. And in order to be imaginative, you need ta be able to *feel*."

He fixes his intense gaze on me. "It's not the old trip of 'losing yerself to yer emotions' and all of the negative crap humans have associated with bein' in a body. It's learning to dig what a miracle it is to have a body, emotions and feelings in the first place! How many folks don't know this? I mean, they need ta learn how pathetic it is that they haven't learned to feel! Feelings are each person's measure of truth."

"But the trouble is," I say, "many people don't welcome or know how to get in touch with their feelings. They fear those feelings will be painful or destructive."

"They only get painful or destructive for folks because they haven't learned that all emotions are okay."

"Do you attest, then, to the innate goodness in us all?"

"I believe all humans have the capacity to be loving if they're given the chance to express their negative side in a genuine way and still be loved for it."

"That's called unconditional love."

"Aye. We're all lovin' beings if we can love ourselves. And we learn to do this from those who bring us back into the world—and know how ta make peace in themselves with Darkness."

"And how do you propose they do this?"

"They learn to recognize that all good things have a difficult twin. If you make friends with this difficult part and accept it as necessary, you have the power to transform it."

"That makes me think of your story about the twin souls."

"It stems from the same principle. One of the reasons there's so much darkness on earth today is because people aren't trained to confront and deal with it. This comes out of fear. Usually the darkness gets swept under the rug and just sits there until somebody comes along and stumbles over it! By avoiding darkness, you become it."

"Is this another one of those universal laws you were talking about?"

"As my teachers are always tellin' us, a problem is like a little seed—dark, hard and bitter. Accept it, sow it, water it and love it . . . and you've got yerself an exquisite flower."

Hearing a faint rustling beside me, I glance to my left and am startled to see Basil there.

"My good people!" he says. "As soon as I gathered the nature of your discussion, I knew I had to join you."

"Why, hello!" I exclaim.

"When you start talkin' about the forces of change," John says, "you can expect this guy's around—lurkin' behind a rock or tree! Greetings, Bas. How's it goin'?"

"Greetings to both of you! I'm pleased to see you at this remarkable place, but it doesn't surprise me. You are hopelessly addicted to the search for understanding of soul force, and you couldn't have found a better place."

He looks at us with gentle eyes.

"I wasn't sure I could get back here, Basil, it's been so long. You've seen the trials I've put myself through."

"Quite a few of them, yes."

"Lately I've been thinking family life is as complex and challenging as any strict yogic discipline."

"Something like learning to lay oneself comfortably upon a bed of nails?" John retorts.

"Something like that," I laugh. My expression becomes more serious. "But at the same time, I realize how lucky I am."

"Life is strange," John speaks with emotion. "The theme of a genuinely difficult family life on earth has kept repeatin' itself for me, in one way or another, for many Expressions. As John Lennon, I suffered pain because my parents weren't with me when I was young—and my mother was killed at the time I thought I had her back! Me Dad was always 'off at sea' in my mind—whether he actually was or not. Near the end of my life, something *new* happened."

He looks at us with an odd grin.

"I discovered, in goin' out ta sea, that I could survive there—on my own. While sailing to the Bahamas with Sean, there was this big storm . . . and much to my amazement, the boat didn't capsize. I actually made it through—alive—with my son. I felt reborn! I had been able to take charge in a novel way."

John's countenance is open and vulnerable.

"Immediately afterwards, I could write music again—after a stagnant period of nearly five years."

"Because you had redirected the course of your life," Basil declares. "It is appropriate the two of you are here together . . . drawn by the primordial sea of creation—which embodies the elements of sound, sight, smell and touch; male and female; mother and father; light and dark; and the supreme love which ties every atom of the universe together. Here you can accept, heal and transform the pain you have endured in Life—the agony of separation from the things you hold most dear! By loving and accepting the act of creation, one can accept the pain which has tormented us for thousands of years. How many times has a mother screamed in pain while giving birth? How many times has a child screamed for its parents?"

"Basil, you must stop . . ." John whispers, bending his head and covering his face. Clutching his shoulder, I feel him collapse with choking sobs.

Basil regards John with kindness. I realize how much of a teacher he has been for John since we began to meet in the meadow.

"The supreme beauty and love of Mother Earth and Father Sky," Basil continues, "the ultimate pain of separation and the attempt to describe it in our artistic quests . . . this is the never-ending epic of beloved planet earth."

As John's weeping subsides, he uncovers his face and blows his nose loudly into a handkerchief.

"I'll say this much," he sniffs, "I'm tired of makin' the same fuckin' mistakes." He stares at us with deep, flashing eyes.

"But you've entered a new era, son. Anyone connected with the earth's evolution at this point in its history is being given the opportunity of healing thousands, even millions of years worth of mistakes."

John claps his hands together. "Hot diggedy dog! I'll be a god-damned monkey's psychotherapist!"

His white face is hard and cold.

"No, really, John! Basil is right," I protest. Wanting him to take these words more seriously, I give him an authoritative look. He becomes pensive and stares for a moment. I know he's going through some fervent soul-searching.

"I was told that stuff when I first got here," he answers in a hushed tone.

"And . . . ?"

"And, it didn't interest me," he says, looking away, "I was too pissed off."

"And now?" Basil asks.

"Well, ta be honest, it was different *then* from the way I feel *now*." John looks at him and rubs his eyes. ". . . as if I can finally dig what that actually means."

"It's always that way with learning," I venture mildly, "you'll only hear something when you're ready to hear it. But, practically speaking, Basil, how are we going to transform a million years worth of mistakes?"

"For one thing, mistakes aren't really mistakes, as both of you already know. When people start disliking themselves, they think in terms of mistakes—right and wrong, black and white, good and bad. As you know, mistakes are part of the mechanisms of change. It means braving both sides of the coin of Life—in order to learn. And planet earth is in the throes of an extraordinary metamorphosis—it's in the stars and has been since the dawn of time. Your world is preparing for revolutionary transitions."

"It better be, or there ain't gonna be no folks left," John sings in a little ditty.

"That's correct," adds Basil, "and many beings on earth are finally getting this message, thank goodness! The celebrated day of reckoning is at hand and is literally forcing every conscious person to examine his or her deepest wishes and motives. The future of your world is waiting for their answer."

"But hasn't this always been the case?" I hazard.

"True," Basil says. "But timing is the issue here. Human beings have had a period of grace in which to confront the power of their own imagination and destruction. This period of grace has ended. And just as adolescents grow into adulthood, mankind is entering a new era of maturity. He either becomes a co-creator with God or looks forward to a planet which is uninhabitable. Yet all difficulties have their precious counterpart; by gaining lifetimes of learning about Darkness, humans have more incentive to choose the Light. This is the irony of their existence."

"Are you saying it's not gonna be easy fer folks ta straddle the fence?" asks John.

"Precisely. This period on earth is one of learning to make conscious choices."

I furrow my brows at Basil. "You say that by gaining wisdom about the Darkness, people will have more power to choose the Light. Do you believe they actually will?"

"I do. Human beings have gained knowledge and experience about the effects of free will and how it can bring them into Darkness. They are remembering *they* possess the divine power to manifest the Light. Through trial and error, this special power— which all humans possess—has become apparent to them . . . and they are beginning to acknowledge it."

"And what about John's idea that you have to love Darkness as a necessary companion to Light?"

"I agree. The brighter the light, the darker the shadow. It's all in how you perceive and relate to it. In order to transform it, darkness must be respected—just as anything else."

My mind is assailed with questions.

"You say people are realizing they are divine. But what about the millions who don't know it yet, and won't for a long time?"

"Indeed. The majority of people need countless lives on earth to learn these lessons."

"Won't it be too late, then?"

"Not necessarily. Because of the increased potency of love manifesting itself upon your planet through a minority of spiritu- ally-conscious beings, there will be enough to counterbalance the effects of those who have not yet become conscious. This awakened minority is steadily increasing and growing more powerful every day because it realizes how to direct its spiritual wisdom for a purpose. It is capable of loving, healing and teaching itself in the ranks of humanity and will be capable of initiating improvements for the good of all."

"So," I add, "it's important for conscious people—especially those straddling the spiritual fence—to make big decisions in the coming years."

"Truly, this is the time to live out one's convictions and not just contemplate them anymore."

John stretches his legs on the white sand, staring past Basil and me.

"It's one helluva challenge for any mortal," he says soberly.

~3~
Back on Stage

I didn't want to complain. Life was good. But letting go of teaching—concentrating on mothering, night feedings and the daily grind—had been more painful than I anticipated. It was less glamorous and I was confronted by myself. Wallowing about in the laundry basket of life, I was searching for new elements of meaning which could tie all the parts together. Why was I jealous of my husband when he came home with interesting stories about students and other teachers? Why, at times, did I feel we were growing apart? It wasn't serious, I reasoned. My writing seemed to be separating us more, bearing me along on a solitary journey away from our comfortable connections.

He wasn't jealous. But there were divisions between us, daring us to let go of our fears and trust in Life; daring us to trust we were being guided to do what we needed to and our relationship would grow stronger, not weaker.

The forces of change persisted in provoking me. Perhaps because of John, I had a yearning to return to my music. There seemed to be profound meaning in the fact that John Lennon had been a brilliant musician as well as a spiritually-gifted being. Sometimes I wondered if Consciousness Conveyance would develop itself into a musical one, even though I wasn't sure one could successfully combine violin with rock-and-roll.

Several times I dreamed I was playing in a band with him and woke up exhilarated.

One day while meditating, I made a shocking discovery; it went like this:

"Hi, John . . . are you ready for the next wave of adventure?" I sense his proximity.

"I most certainly am," he says. "What've you got yer eyes closed for?"

"I want to *be* there. I want to be at our Mystical Ocean."

"Okay, you close yer eyes—and I'll meet ya there."

"Gotcha . . . roger and out."

My attention is retreating to the sound and smell of the sea, giving me a rush of longing and nostalgia. Immediately I feel cold, wet sand sinking under my feet. I am wearing that bronze-colored cape again, the muslin gown and emerald stones. The skies are grey and overcast, and I'm cold. I can't find John and wonder where he is.

I am upset to see a totally new person, someone other than John or Basil. A short man wearing a wig is hurrying toward me! He is wearing a red brocaded frock coat with gold emboss-ing, breeches with white stockings and big-buckled shoes. This guy has to be from the eighteenth century or thereabouts. Who is he? I haven't time to think.

"Good morning, my dear lady!" he says enthusiastically, nod-ding with a bow.

"Uh, hello!"

I'm taken aback and look around for a sign of John; but the beach is empty except for myself, this funny guy and a couple of seagulls.

"Are you enjoying this magnificent place? I am astonished how the sounds and smells of the ocean shore can produce such deep responses in a human heart."

This little fellow is quite something. He doesn't seem like a stranger and has a thick European accent—not French, not Dutch. German, maybe? I take to him immediately, but he is not what I had expected to meet on this beach. Amused, I search my mind for an intelligent response.

"Have you been here long?" I smile politely.

"Oh, no. I was taking a walk in the countryside, and then, boom! Here I am!" he giggles.

He has the face of a child and it sparkles with a bit of madness.

"Well," I say, "doesn't that scare you?"

"Oh, no—of course not. This happens to me all the time."

"Really. Well, where do you come from . . . if I may ask?"

His eyes twinkle at me playfully.

"By all means, my dear madam. I am Austrian, if you can't hear it on my tongue. Austria has glorious mountains, which I could never abandon! Yet, when I am in this miraculous place, I wonder how I could live without it."

"Do you come here often?"

"Oh, yes—almost always in my dreams! This place inspires me greatly. It is the source of all my joy."

He makes large, sweeping movements with his arms in the direction of the crashing waves.

"It's funny," I say, "but I thought I would meet someone else here . . . and you show up."

As we walk along the wet sand, the sky remains cold and grey. A chilly wind causes our garments to flutter.

"Who is this someone?" the short, funny gentleman queries.

"Oh, a friend of mine. He's, uh . . . his name is John . . . John Lennon. Have you heard of him?"

This squat man with the powdered wig and puckish eyes begins to laugh uproariously.

"God! Hah-hah-hah! God, yes! Hah-hah-hah!"

It's all I can do to keep from becoming consumed myself; I howl right along with him. "What's so funny, though? Do you really know John?"

"My beautiful red-haired madam," the fellow says, taking my hand in his, "John Lennon is someone I know most intimately."

Then he proceeds to kiss my hand, and I'm thinking to myself, "Help! What's with this guy anyway?"

I attempt to hide my embarrassment. The situation is becoming awkward, yet this character has me intrigued. He has an aura of greatness about him, yet I'm confused. In one way, he appears pure, mystical and childlike. In another, I speculate he would like nothing better than to end up groveling with me in the nearby sand dunes.

"I've seen guys like this before," I ponder uneasily. Yet there is more going on. His face seems so funny and familiar. If I could just rise above the awkwardness by asking him more questions. And make sure we remain at arm's length from each other . . . I jest silently to myself.

"What is milady smiling about?" the Austrian inquires.

"Oh, nothing! I was thinking how curious it is that you know John Lennon and what he might say to you if he were here."

"Oh, I presume he *is* here, milady, but you can't *see* him."

"I'm used to that. But, in this place, I'm usually able to see and talk to him."

Secretly, I am irritated John hasn't appeared, because then I might have more of an idea what to do. I'm accustomed to him and Basil, but this person has me perplexed. I'm not grasping the meaning yet and consider leaving. As these ideas play randomly through my mind, the expansive sandy beach becomes drenched in sunshine. The clouds are drifting away and I see large patches of comforting blue sky. Next, my lively friend cries out in delight and runs ahead like a youngster, holding his wig with one hand.

He has now run quite a ways ahead of me. The colors of our surroundings have altered drastically and the ocean waves are emitting an overpowering blue-green resplendence. His bright-red frock coat suddenly contrasts brilliantly with the water. From a distance, I see my companion stop abruptly to face the thundering, white-capped breakers.

Suddenly I hear the exquisite tones of classical music. They seem to be coming from everywhere: from the sky, the water and the ground under my feet. Not only are my ears perceiving this music, but my entire physical body. It starts softly and gently and gradually builds in strength. An indescribable emotion is welling in me, and I am becoming lost to it.

Because of this intensity, I'm not sure what happens next. The little man in the red jacket is suddenly juxtaposed on the beach with a large group of people materializing out of nowhere. They are taking on the form of a great, powerful orchestra as my new friend goes to stand on the podium and conduct them. He is moving violently, passionately, gracefully—then, tenderly with the music—as someone possessed. I stand in awe of this miracle, baffled by the intensity of perception which engulfs me. I am overwhelmed by pure joy—my heart is going to burst.

My stupefaction has prevented me from realizing I am listening to the music of Wolfgang Amadeus Mozart. It has become apparent the funny little fellow moving on the podium in the frock coat is this man himself.

I doubt I am capable of going further, yet the daredevil in me screams "yes!"—and fortunately so, for there is something of great importance to be witnessed in this display. As I near this orchestra and inspect its players, I see with great shock that one of the male violinists is myself . . . in another Expression! He is performing one of Mozart's violin concertos. As I watch, I begin to weep. My body convulses in great sobs as I view him transmitting this heavenly sound through body and instrument, giving him an amazing, joyous strength and vitality.

The tears puddling in my eyes cause my vision to transform this eighteenth-century violinist into a young woman. She is about fifteen years old, dressed in modern clothing and I see her playing the concerto with her high school orchestra. I see myself in my present life as a teenage violinist playing first chair. The vision grows into one of attainment, showing mastery of the instrument. Had I been meant to walk the musical path? In a flash, I fathom why my life has unfolded as it has. My path had to be different this time around.

The music continues; and I stand on the shore, witnessing the revelation of a lifetime. There are so many things happening, I doubt I am comprehending everything . . . I feel almost insane.

"What a pity John hasn't been here to see this with me," I whisper.

Looking again at the orchestra, I see it has reshaped itself. I no longer hear Mozart's music, but another kind of orchestral music. It sets off bright, cherished memories. They're playing "Sergeant Pepper's Lonely Hearts Club Band," and new instruments and people have begun to materialize. John Lennon is standing on the podium—dressed in a red coat, white breeches and stockings—playing the guitar and leaning into a microphone to sing.

"Oh, no!" I bellow, putting my hands to my face. "That's why he looked like someone I know!"

Collapsing to my knees in the blinding sunshine, I look like somebody praying. As the music plays on, I want to curl into a ball and go to sleep. I lie on the sand, in a stupor, for what seems to be a very long time.

Suddenly, silence surrounds me. I look up to see the orchestra and its players have disappeared. The surf continues to pound and the seagulls call. Sitting up, I see John walking toward me on a long expanse of dry sand.

"Well, did ya like it?" he asks with a roguish grin.

He's still wearing the red coat and I reach out to touch it as if it were the holy shroud.

"It's quite a trip, isn't it?" John beams.

"Why didn't you tell me before?" I say, practically ruined.

He sits down beside me, now in granny glasses and with long sideburns and short, curly brown hair.

"I didn't tell you because I knew it would be too much for you in the beginning."

"And now?"

His hands are playing with the warm sand. "And now, you can handle it . . . especially if we talk about it . . . and you have time to work it through."

He looks at me virtuously, and I still feel insane.

"You know what this means, don't you?"

"Yeah, it means yer going to be sticking yer neck out even more," he continues in a deep actor's voice, "about this spiritual, New Age foolishness."

"Do you really think people are going to buy the idea you were Mozart?"

"It's irrelevant whether they buy it or not," he answers flippantly. "The important thing is what you experienced for yourself—and the truth you and I are sharing Here. It's a pity anyone else has to know about it."

I look at him in disbelief.

"Just between you and me, there's a lot to relate, kid. This Time-Mode Expression stuff is mind-blowing if you get into it."

"You can say that again! Is it true I played violin in one of your orchestras?"

"Why do you think it was so easy for you to learn as a child? Why do you think you always played first chair?"

"It was totally familiar to me, yes! And when I played, I felt an unusual exuberance which seemed to come out of nowhere."

"And now you know."

"But hell, John, this is going too far!"

"Linda, that's bullshit, ya know! As we told you in that luv'ly meadow—there *ain't no* famous souls in the Infinite Dwelling. Once you've left yer body, you're joining with the true or false God within yerself, whatever that may be! No one here *cares* what you were on earth. They only care whether yer bein' honest."

"So, from your perspective, Wolfgang Amadeus Mozart is just one of the gang—no big deal."

"Of course it was a big deal—he produced miraculous music, and that required a special kind of human genius which millions of people have appreciated. But take a look at the rest of his wretched life! Don't you think he had a helluva lot of home-work to do once he left his miserable, neglected body and got Here? I want you ta understand that Mozart may have conveyed a new level of musical genius on earth, previously known only by angels, but he was one helluva wreck by the time he got Here!"

John looks heated and indignant.

"What do you mean?" I ask carefully.

"What do I mean? Take a look at his lower life-wheels! Be-cause he was such an astonishing medium, he was open to one bloody lot of negative—and positive—energies. He allowed his earthly *base* to become unsafe! And *that's* why he lived in fear, attracted so many problems and died at a young age in spite of his amazing gifts."

"Sounds like someone else I know—if you don't mind me saying so . . ."

I look at him cautiously; I've never seen him quite so annoyed. He gazes sullenly into the blue ocean waves, his hands kneading a million grains of sand.

"Don't worry, I won't clobber you!" he says, cracking a smile. "I learned me lesson about that, I think."

I had read that John Lennon, as a human being, had been very aggressive at times; and this was something I never witnessed. I wonder if this part of his character has improved since journeying to the Infinite Dwelling.

"You've gotta realize that even Lennon's Expression on earth wasn't half as tumultuous as Mozart's. I had a wonderful rest as Mr. Browning, in spite of the emotional pain I suffered losing Elizabeth. I had a long, full life which connected me with the world of nature and the earth principle, and I had a chance to grow old! Browning died in 1889 and John Lennon wasn't born until 1940. That was a chance to rest, which I did, in a way— but I managed to slip one Expression in between."

"Oh, yeah? Well, don't tell me it's somebody famous again, or I might start disbelieving all of this." I look at him harshly.

"I know I've been addicted to genius sometimes, but don't forget the appalling difficulties that went with it! Okay, in the Expression after Robert and before John, I skipped genius and settled for wisdom, strength and sincerity. I was a black woman living in the rural southern United States. And this person *really* got me in touch with the earth principle! But it's hard to achieve true balance, which is why I almost hated physical labor by the time I ended up as John."

"What a change!"

"I was born in 1901 and died during childbirth at the age of twenty-six."

I look at him, astounded.

"There's a lot more fer you to discover about this particular Expression, but you need time to deal with the impact of our wayward little Austrian first! You shouldn't go too fast with this discovery business, otherwise you might end up blowin' yer own mind."

"What if this has already happened?" I look at him with crossed eyes.

"Go on . . ." John gives me a playful push and I struggle to keep from falling over.

"No, you're right," I say. "We shouldn't go too fast. My mind can't cope with it. My curiosity says 'yes,' but my mind starts to protest. It can't deal with it now."

"It can eventually. But it's not good to push things."

"I've been busy with the concept of past—what you call alternate—Expressions for more than twenty years now. But I think it is one of the most difficult things to accept. It's easy to assume in an intellectual way, but when it comes to actually feeling and knowing, in my body and soul—it comes as a tremendous jolt."

"This is because western human minds aren't taught to deal with it. They stumble upon the many pieces of this mysterious, multi-dimensional puzzle—lying scattered about in their conscious and unconscious minds—whether they want to or not. They find it shocking, even though they may think they're prepared."

"And my mind is bushed!" I sigh. "It's the perfect moment to go vacuum my dirty house. Thank you, John, for sharing this with me. And thanks for being so honest. You're very good at that."

He nods contentedly, fondling the bronze buttons on his jacket. Then, a blink of my eyes, a shift of focus and I'm gone.

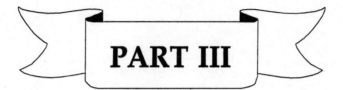

PART III

Discoveries
on Earth

~1~
A Tarot Card

Winter turned to spring 1990 and the river of life was gushing swiftly along. Writing and family were demanding, yet fulfilling. Aart was becoming increasingly interested in the John Lennon project, and we talked about it often.

After my last visit to the Mystical Ocean, I had been impressed with how the evolving themes could fit so perfectly with my own existence. A certain resistance had dropped away. I was remembering to ask myself why I had particular problems and what I could learn from them.

Since the launching of the project, I'd graduated from typewriter to word processor. I hadn't felt ready to deal with a real computer and it had been my opinion I couldn't learn to use one.

One afternoon I asked Aart to help me "re-format" the material I had on a diskette. It contained all that I had written about John Lennon. Checking it out, he discovered the diskette had been filled and was determining his next move. From downstairs, I heard a terrifying cry emanating from the upstairs study. Every bit of color drained from me as I heard his tortured exclamation, "It's gone!"

He appeared in front of me holding that piece of plastic, looking like a madman. He had pressed a key on the word processor which had erased the Lennon diskette. After several futile attempts to retrieve it, we were soon convinced that all of the information—the work of about three years—was gone!

Fortunately, most of what I had written had been printed out, but a great deal of the editing and some of the new story had been lost. We were stunned beyond words. What did it mean? Was it a message from John, or some other guardian, that I wasn't supposed to continue? Was it a warning? Were my worst fears being confirmed—that I was not up to the task of completing such a book, that I had dared to do something I should never have begun?

We couldn't eat. Staring at each other blankly, I said, "Let's pick a tarot card."

I shuffled through the "Mythic Tarot" deck—a modern deck based on Greek mythology. The card I picked was "The Wheel of Fortune," and the interpretation read as follows:

"On a divinatory level, this card augurs a sudden change of fortune. This may be 'good' or 'bad,' but whichever way the Wheel turns it brings growth and a new phase of life. We cannot predict what will come to meet us—or rather, what we will turn to meet. But behind these changes stand the three goddesses of Fate, an image of the centre within. Thus the Seeker is thrown from his complacency and begins the descent to his own source."

I went immediately to my room, pondering this message.

"Why . . . oh why?" I moaned.

"Poor thing!" John snorts in reply. "But losing the characters on that funny plastic thing is telling you you're working on a project which is getting too big to have on your machine— it can't even make copies, for Christ's sakes! Yer bein' warned—just in time, mind you—before you have even more to lose."

"What are you getting at?"

"Dearie, this is one of those rites of passage. You should start using a computer—a real one, not that half-assed thing you're using now."

"That's impossible."

"Oh no it's not. You just think you can't! It's idle fear."

I don't believe him, but try to stay positive.

"Okay. I'll consider the idea . . . just for you."

"That's a good girl. Nice idea, the tarot cards . . . a great way ta get a proper message across."

"I suppose Basil was involved in this too?"

"More or less. We couldn't allow you to keep on basking in ignorance. You're working with tools which can't serve you, kid. It could fuck up the whole project! It's not worth the risk."

John seems annoyed, but so am I.

"You must be right . . . but it's easy for you to say! I'm the one who has to learn to use the damned computer and rewrite all that stuff!"

"You've got a good point, but at this moment yer fear is naked illusion, believe me."

"So, you think I'll be able to learn to use one of those things, do you?"

"I'm sure of it. In fact, it'll improve yer creative powers—just wait 'n see."

"Well, if it brings growth and a new phase of life, as the tarot card promised . . . what's so funny?"

"I was thinking about how often Yoko and I consulted the tarot. Now I see how it looks from This Side."

"Yeah, you guys can sit and laugh yourselves silly. It must be wonderful," I say sullenly.

"In those days, we were convinced we could get help from our spiritual benefactors by using oracles. Now that I see how it works from this angle, it's obvious we sometimes went a bit overboard."

"How do you mean?"

"We were lookin' *outside* ourselves for answers. Since I've been here, I've seen how important it is to consult yer own soul as often as yer guardians. A good balance is important."

"I believe you."

"It's easy to set yerself up and become too gullible! If yer not clear, you'll attract entities that aren't clear. If you use oracles to get help from cosmic sources, you need to trust *yerself* and yer capacity to solve the problem."

"That's easy to forget."

"I know. When I look back at my last Expression on earth, I laugh! We would get so serious about 'messages from the other side,' thinkin' our spiritual guardians were *so much smarter*! They do their best to help. But there are limits to everything—especially in taking responsibility for somebody else's decisions."

"Sure," I say. "But guardians have a broader perspective. We know you can help us because you can see more of the total picture, right?"

"If yer lucky! It depends on the dude yer workin' with. I know a lotta guys who get their kicks in screwin' people up!—like they've made a hobby out of it."

"Great. So what's the solution?"

"I told you already. Make sure you trust *yerself* before you start lookin' outside. 'Cause there's something called fate—and that's different from predestination."

"What's the difference?"

"Fate is 'cause and effect' in its purest form. You know, *karma*—reaping what you sow. Predestination is a word I don't like, 'cause it implies everything is permanently ordained by some big bastard in the sky, before you know it yerself! But it ain't true. Our futures are *not* set. We've got an assortment of possible futures when we're born. It's up to us to choose the one we want."

"How can you defend tarot cards, then—or any other oracle?"

"They give folks *ideas* about the possible paths available at any given moment. It's not meant to tell them, 'you gotta do this,' or 'you gotta do that.' Take responsibility for yer own actions! Don't try to leave that up to some joker in heaven."

"So, if I understand you, it means I still have a choice about this computer business."

"Of course you've got a choice. Apple or IBM?"

I knew John's bantering by now and waited a couple of days for events to sink in. But while making phone calls about the price of computers, I still felt depressed. I was afraid it would take me years—now revised from a million to at least several—to learn how to use one. What would happen to Consciousness Conveyance in the meantime?

I was soon to discover, however, that this sudden revision of fortune was forcing me to acknowledge, again, the positive side of modern technology. As usual, it was a matter of faith. My experience with the word processor was enough to get me launched; in less than two weeks, I was sitting pertly behind a personal computer, thanking heaven I was living in modern times. I soon wondered how I had functioned without one. The arduous task of re-typing the story had begun, yet a new and better version was evolving steadily with help from John.

"Everything has a light and a dark side," I could hear him whispering into my ear.

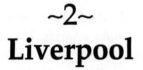

~2~
Liverpool

*Reaching down to plug in my computer one morning, I was amused to see a tiny picture of John Lennon's youthful face on the **Life** magazine lying next to my desk. Lately, I was constantly bumping into things relating to Beatle John and his home town. Every time I entered a store, I would hear him crooning away. A student at our school had been born and raised in Liverpool. A man camping nearby during Easter vacation had been from this fabled city. While buying canned salmon at the local grocery store, I inspected the label to find it had been canned in Liverpuddle, of course.*

While perusing the paper one evening, I saw there was going to be a concert in Liverpool in May, sponsored by Yoko Ono, in memory of John Lennon's fiftieth birthday! This was the last straw.

"Well . . . it's totally obvious now," I said out-of-the-blue at the dinner table.

"Obvious about what?" asked Aart, "What are you talking about?"

"About going to Liverpool."

"Don't spoil my appetite," complained one of the older girls. "I don't like liver."

We appreciated her joke, but when I told Aart how often the subject had come up recently, he snorted.

"It does seem clear," he said.

"But, I'd be uncomfortable going by myself—I haven't done anything like that since 1977 when I came to Europe as a hippie."

"Well, be a hippie again! I'd love to go with you, but there's no way with the kids."

I was perplexed, but when I awoke the next morning, I knew I had to be in Liverpool for the concert. After breakfast I decided to pull another "Mythic Tarot" card.

As I was shuffling the deck, I was shocked to see that my hands had turned into John's hands. They were the ones I had seen on certain video tapes as he played music or held headphones against his ears. They were large and round. Those hands had drawn "The Wheel of Fortune" card—the same card I drew after losing the diskette!

". . . but whichever way the Wheel turns it brings growth and a new phase of life . . . thus the Seeker is thrown from his complacency and begins the descent to his own source . . ."

★   ★   ★

*Gaping at the clouds from the airplane window, I was feeling absurd. My innate passion for adventure seemed to soar with every passing hour. The further I flew from home, the more I could hear internal laughter. The fact that I had settled in the Netherlands was due, after all, to this brand of courageous enterprise. I'd been idiotic for not realizing what a fabulous free weekend I was going to have **sans enfants**. I chuckled aloud, causing the gentleman next to me to look away uneasily.*

The evening's bus ride from Manchester Airport to Liverpool was pleasant. From my front-row seat, I watched as it became dark. The moon was becoming full, shining down upon gently rolling fields. A black woman whom I had admired at the terminal was sitting next to me, never once turning her eyes away from their fixed gaze out the side window.

She only looked in my direction as the bus was coming to a stop in downtown Liverpool about an hour later, and it occurred to me to ask if she had heard of the Adelphi Hotel. Her demeanor switched entirely. Not only could she tell me where the hotel was, but she would be happy to take me there. Stepping off the bus and looking around in the twilight, I had a sense of déjà vu—it could have been San Francisco. I told her about the John Lennon concert, and she also had a ticket. As we approached a big white building to our right, the female stranger wished me a fine weekend.

The Adelphi Hotel was old and had once been the grandest hotel in Liverpool. I was to discover a few months later that not only had John Lennon's sea merchant father, Freddie, worked in the Adelphi as a bellboy; but this was also where he and his wife, Julia, had celebrated their honeymoon in 1938—two years before John was born. Unaware of these facts on the weekend of May 5, 1990, I was merely impressed by the ambience of the place—in spite of my uncomfortable bed.

Out of habit, the first thing I did when entering the hotel room was sit down and clean it out. I don't mean vacuuming or dusting—I mean closing my eyes and visualizing any disagreeable energies which might be present in the room draining—like water from a bathtub—into the ground. Next, I made it clear in my mind that the room belonged to me at this particular moment in time, and not to the thousands of people who had come before me. In my thoughts, I painted the walls, floor and ceiling beautiful colors. It was cozy now, like a room in my own home.

Dropping exhausted to the swaying mattress, I wondered if I could sleep on it. I switched off the light and reached for the miniature tape recorder I had brought with me, assuming it would come in handy.

Picking up the tiny device, I described recent events. I still felt odd here, alone in a foreign city, and was gripped with stage fright. Lying frozen for a moment, I stared at the ceiling, waiting for my muse to join me.

*"It's basically whether or not one's situation can be seen as **amusing** . . ." my voice faltered into the recorder. Now, a tiny bit of magic began to divulge itself. I withstood the temptation to call my husband on the telephone and began to penetrate this enchanted world. I knew I had to stay here alone until my mission was accomplished.*

Well, not completely alone. I could feel John's presence distinctly—perhaps more than ever before. Was it because I had come to Liverpool? Excitedly, I looked out the window at the moon.

"So ya think yer gonna be able to sleep on that lousy bed, do you?" John grumbles.

"Hey—hi! Fat chance I have of getting another room at this hour. The hotel is filled with people wanting to go to *your* memorial concert. Besides, I'm rather attached to these quaint quarters."

"*My* concert . . . yeah," He hesitates. "I guess Yoko has been busy organizin' this thing . . . it means a lot to her, *me* turning *fifty* and all! I tell her to relax a bit . . . she's workin' too hard. But she won't listen to me. You women! Why do you have to get worked up about everything?"

"Hey, I beg your pardon! What would you be doing in this situation?"

"Okay, yer right! To be honest, I'm a nervous wreck."

"You mean spooks get nervous?"

"Yer damned right! There's some things you gotta do for me, Linda. You don't realize it, but they're important. I was delighted when you bought the plane ticket to come here this weekend. Yer gonna help me by being here. Yoko and Sean are here, too! Did you know that?"

"I wasn't sure. I had hoped."

"Do you know how happy I am? It's *terrific* what's gonna happen here. But I'm gonna need help."

"How, then?"

"Sorry, kid . . . I better tell you the rest tomorrow mornin'. You've gotta get yer beauty rest and all that."

"Jesus, John! I probably won't get any sleep! You know I can't sleep when I'm preoccupied . . . especially in this ridiculous bed."

"Don't worry. I'll sing you a lullaby."

"Okay . . . that's great . . . thanks. Goodnight."

I put the tape recorder on the desk next to me and began to do a breathing exercise. I centered my attention on my toes and made them golden-green. In the background I heard John softly singing "Julia" as I fell asleep.

~3~
Get Back

The next morning I was awake at 5:30, feeling remarkably fit and ready for my escapades to begin. Opening the window and peering out, I saw a fair sky with a touch of fog. Breakfast wasn't served until 8:00, so I decided to use this time for meditation.

Having dressed and made myself a cup of tea, I settled down in a big, red, over-stuffed chair next to the open window and started to free my mind by focusing on my body—and the energy in and around it. I felt myself becoming more open and better connected with the earth. As I did this, I was noticing an unusual heaviness in my system and couldn't reach the free-and-easy mood I was used to. I had done my best the night before and again this morning to tidy up the atmosphere of the room. It felt fine, but as I tried to tune into John there was something getting in the way. I soon discovered it was because he was surrounded by total pandemonium.

"John, what *are* you doing?"

"Yeah, hallo! Say, this is the stuff I *knew* I was gonna need help with! But I didn't wanna hafta bother you with it right away. It's kinda like a *disease*, don't you think?"

I feel him sitting, facing me, at the foot of the bed about a meter away.

"For God's sake, John, what *is* it?"

It's as if the room is filled with an infinite number of colorful, noisy, confusing images which are surrounding John like a swarm of fanatical bees. It makes me feel crazy.

"It's gotta do with all those *pictures*—those *thought-forms*! Do they get me down! It's gotta do with the earth sphere, ya know . . . it's what I get fer bein' so fuckin' famous. I warn anybody who'll listen—avoid it at all costs!"

"But . . . this never happened to us before!"

"Right, I know. But, occasionally it *does*! If I enter the earth sphere in a particularly stupid way—getting involved with things which touch me personally or connect me to my past—it can happen. I hadn't told you about it before, you'll hafta forgive me! But sometimes I get so stuck. Jesus, this is bad!"

He swats at the vast, impervious cloud. "Most of it has ta do with Liverpool and the Lennon Memorial Concert. There are so many people thinkin' about me right now, it's not even funny."

"Do you mean it bothers you when so many people think about you all at once?"

"That's part of it. But the real problem is people enjoy projecting their hopes, wishes and emotions on a mythical figure. People need heros! And if I just happen to be in the wrong mood . . ."

He sighs in frustration. "I didn't learn what this could do to somebody until it was too late. Remember how I looked right after I died?"

"Yes."

"Well, it's the same idea. I've got to get me energy and consciousness strong enough ta deal with those projections when I cross into the earth sphere. Get it? Sure ya do."

"You mean it's like learning to protect yourself psychically, only out-of-the-body?"

"Yeah. Only it doesn't work quite the same. To begin with—body or no body—when somebody thinks about somebody else, part of their awareness often makes a connection with the awareness of the other. Few people know this, and most folks can't think about someone else without going outside of themselves."

"Uh-huh . . ."

"So it's a drag when people do this with me! They need to learn to stay in their *own* center—regardless of what they want to share or communicate."

"Is that why that weird stuff is surrounding you?"

"You've got it! When you don't have a body, it can be difficult to escape these crazy things."

He makes a comical motion by flapping his arms like a bird.

"I believe you," I say, "but meanwhile, you need healing! Just stay right here."

With my eyes closed, I focus on John's essence sitting in front of me. He looks pathetic now—fragile, thin and depressed. Funny enough, he's dressed in a suit and tie.

"Try to relax, John . . . you'll be okay, I promise."

I start to hum—from deep inside my belly—a low, hushed tone. It's a sacred Sanskrit word, AUM, meaning roughly "all that is." This gentle sound is filling the tiny room and helping me feel safe and strong.

"This'll get us going," I mutter.

A special quality of light has entered the room. I lift my hands and direct this power of Light toward John's ethereal form. After a few minutes he opens his eyes and looks at me with a sheepish grin.

"Wouldn't it be funny to see the maids walkin' in right now? And they wouldn't be able ta see *me*."

From the depths of my trance I think, "Hah! You're reading my paranoid thoughts! You'd enjoy that, wouldn't you? Now shut up—I was just starting to get somewhere."

As I work with this new power of Light, I am coming into contact with my own fears. I'm getting closer to John than ever before. It brings an abrupt lack of sensitivity to my heart and feels like dead weight. I have traveled to Liverpool to do what I am doing now—to communicate with a soul more real to me than ever before—and I want to get up and leave. I realize it's easier to deal with someone when they keep their distance.

It makes me cry, not only in my thoughts but with actual tears running down my cheeks. This is my strongest test—in general, concerning my apprenticeship with John; specifically, concerning my entire quest in Liverpool. I wonder if I am up to it.

The tears are washing away my fear . . . gradually bringing a sense of homecoming. Blowing my nose, I check my points of trance and ground again.

John looks meek. A phrase pops into my mind: "You've got to get back to where you once belonged."

Paul McCartney had sung that once. John needs to regain his sense of wholeness, which will connect him with his earlier life, particularly to those moments when he had been vital, happy and open to the world. Many of those moments had taken place in this town.

As I reconnect with the Light, John's form begins to modify. His hair has become shorter, and he becomes younger and fatter, exuding impudence, defiance and wit. I cringe thinking of the pain and suffering he will endure over the years; but now he has the gift of openness and optimism—showing naiveté and sophistication at the same time.

"You're obviously much stronger now," I say to him.

"I don't doubt that, luv, but how do I rid meself of these fuckin' pictures?" He tilts his mopped head to one side and looks at me helplessly.

"To be honest, I'm not sure myself. But don't despair!" Sitting as I am, I wait for the right solutions to reveal themselves.

"You look so much younger now . . ." I whisper.

I had always been amazed by the contradictory moods and personalities John Lennon had displayed to the world, as if he had been a multitude of individuals.

"If you can manage to let go of the stuff surrounding you," I continue, "you'll get further with the changes you want, especially learning to be stronger—both in-and-out of a body."

I have been sensing the presence of Basil and other high guardians for some time. Now they seem to be officially greeting John and me, and the work resumes. I see hundreds of red roses surrounding us, so real and vivid I pick one and press it to my chest. I know the roses can help me—and John—heal the pandemonium. I offer one to him. He accepts it and holds it under his nose, looking again as I'd envisioned him right before he died—gaunt and vulnerable.

"John—listen! It's *clean-up* time."

My attention is focused on that special luminescence permeating the room. Again, I place my palms facing John and hear the deep droning inside me—the sound of universal healing and restoration, the sound of many voices singing AUM. Then I hear a chorus of angels, joining to blend with the other earthy tone. Speaking aloud, I utter a powerful Sanskrit prayer of protection. As I pray, the atmosphere in the room becomes increasingly calm and steady.

At the end I say, "In the name of the Father and Mother, the Son and Daughter and of the Holy Spirit. For the highest good of all concerned."

"Jesus, Linda, it sounds like a bloody exorcism . . ."

"It is. Sshhh!"

John sits straight and I continue using my hands to disperse the images engulfing him, repeating these words over and again, "This is not yours anymore . . . this is not yours."

The cloud surrounding him is resembling a haze of light rather than a swarm of bees and is not as dense as it was before.

While working, my point of focus becomes concentrated. Steadily, the energy cloud surrounding John has begun to get smaller—and smaller—and more concentrated. It has gradually begun to convert into a small golden cube which fits easily into the palm of my hand and radiates an intensity of life-force.

"John?" I say, breaking the silence, "You need to give this back to God."

I lean over and give him the cube. He holds his open palms together to receive it. I see the image of Michelangelo's God—an old man with a long, flowing beard—appearing as John presents the treasure to him. He takes it with a smile, kisses John and glides away. Superimposed on these images is the slow-motion picture of a long elephant's trunk appearing to take the golden cube as if it were a piece of candy, all the while making loud, slurping noises as the cube disappears into infinity.

John whistles and starts to clown and sing. The energy field surrounding him is now a powerful combination of gold, light-green and marine-blue.

"You look beautiful!" I exclaim. "We can certainly thank those guardians for helping—it was fantastic."

"Don't forget to thank yerself too, dearie. I'm . . ."

We are interrupted by the sound of Paul McCartney's voice singing, "Get back, Jojo . . . get back to where you once belonged."

"Did you hear that?" I ask.

"Good ol' Paul . . . the dirty ol' bastard."

"Is that any way to talk about him?"

"Oh sure, he knows I still love him . . . no problem. Hi Paul!"

"I think you should visit this town more often," I say.

"Hey, you haven't had breakfast yet, poor thing," he answers, his voice fading. "Get yerself downstairs, eat and we'll be off to the suburbs."

~4~
Gravestones

Having eaten breakfast, I returned to the hotel room and switched on the radio. A local station was playing "A Hard Day's Night."

A DJ's bright voice piped, "The fifth of May—Lennon Day! How's everybody doin' this gorgeous Saturday morning?"

It felt like a national holiday. In the morning I was planning to go to the suburbs of Allerton and Woolton—the neighborhood of John's youth—and to the Cavern Walks and Albert Dock in the afternoon. The outdoor concert was scheduled for the evening. Guided tours were available through the Beatles old neighborhoods or most taxi drivers would have shown me the house where John Lennon had grown up with his Aunt Mimi, but I couldn't take these routes. The subject felt too personal for me to see these places in the presence of strangers. John had told me we would go to the suburbs together, and I was hoping he would lead me to the places I needed to go.

Soon I was sitting in an old relic of a train, looking forward to my quest. The large, worn seats faced each other on two sides. As we began clickety-clacking out of the station, I could feel John sitting across from me, gazing quietly out of a dirty window.

"Say, Lin . . . this is great! The station is just a few blocks away from me mum's old home."

"Are you going to show me where that is?"

"Oh, just wait. We'll see."

I was happy the rest of the car was empty except for an old man sitting behind me in one corner, facing in the opposite direction. The train was moving through an open tunnel heavily decorated with graffiti. All at once we were traveling high above the ground, where the houses appeared tiny and depressing.

Looking to the opposite seat, I suddenly have a vision of Aunt Mimi sitting with a boy of about five. It is so real and moving—I am almost grieved. The boy is holding his Auntie's hand as they return from a shopping trip in downtown Liverpool. They are going to visit John's mother, Julia. Suddenly, it's as if they are flesh-and-blood and I am invisible. Taking no notice of me, they chat and argue in their distinctive Liverpuddlian voices. John is bright, beautiful and brazen. Obviously Aunt Mimi has her hands full. She loves him very much, but often finds custody of this child-wonder difficult.

I snapped out of my daydream. The houses outside were becoming larger and more attractive, and there were more trees lining the streets. Stepping out on the platform in Allerton, I felt ill at ease and unsure of myself, almost despondent. John seemed very far away, as if he hadn't gotten off the train with me. I began to look apprehensively in all directions and noticed the weather had become hazy and a bit colder. It felt again as if my entire belief system was being severely tested. I had no idea where to go and was doubting my mental health. What could have possessed me to come here with no plans except to walk around, hoping to discover John's old house?

*"Okay . . . don't forget to be **amused**," I muttered between my teeth. I began to stroll with renewed optimism through this hilly neighborhood. The atmosphere reminded me of my own*

*girlhood suburbia. On these tranquil streets a man was whis-
tling as he washed his car, and further up the hill a woman
was unloading groceries. I saw a large, open space which
looked like a park. As I walked further uphill, I soon found
myself at the entrance to a large cemetery. I tried to listen to
my inner voice or hear a message from John, but there was
only dull silence. What kind of joke was this? I entered the
cemetery.*

*Rows of gravestones lined both sides of the wide avenue. As
I continued, I saw it was devoid of any living beings except
for myself. Eventually, on a pathway veering to the right, I
glimpsed a young man with his dog in the distance. I felt
tense and self-conscious. What deceased personage was I
visiting here? Did it matter? I began to hum quietly to myself
and tried to locate my sense of humor, which seemed now,
like John, to have disappeared. Birds twittered about and a
trace of sunlight tried to fight its way through the mist.*

*As I continued walking, I came to an old section which had
more interesting and attractive gravestones than those I had
viewed from a distance. My question when entering this place
had been: "Am I searching for John's mother's gravestone?"
Now, close enough to read the engravings, I began to
decipher names and dates of the deceased. I was disappointed,
however, to see they were much too old to include the name
of John's mother. I searched further. The man with the dog
was getting into a van and driving away. The birds began to
sing louder and more sunrays were forcing their way through
the atmosphere.*

*Then I saw an intriguing old gravestone in the shape of a
celtic cross which read "George Stanley—1910," and
sprouting in front of it was one single dark-pink rose—the
only flower in sight. At this moment, the full sun broke
through to enhance the vividness of its color. The name
Stanley seemed to ring a bell, and I recalled this had been the
maiden name of John's mother and his Aunt Mimi.*

"Is this family, John?" I asked eagerly.

No answer.

"Okay, if that's the way you're going to be . . ."

Suddenly, I knew I had to leave. I became filled with an increasing sense of uneasiness and foreboding. I was wandering alone in a city of the dead, in a foreign city and country.

"Let's get out of here!" I cried, practically running through the gates of the cemetery. Continuing uphill, I reached a small park filled with stately trees. There was a group of people talking and laughing together in the bright sun. Encouraged, I entered the park gates and discovered beautiful, rolling green hills beyond. Here the suburbs stopped and the countryside began. Leaving the park, I was walking on Woolton Road and wondered if I would find a familiar name like Menlove Avenue or Strawberry Field. Trying not to get lost, I wandered through streets lined with neat little houses, then decided to go downhill to the train station. I knew I wasn't going to locate John's old house this time—I hadn't even brought a map!

Perhaps I was meant to explore this territory simply for what it was—devoid of any commercialized hype. I felt this was another test of faith, but it seemed pretty dumb. I didn't understand my trip to the graveyard, although it had definitely made an impression on me.

Taking the train back to downtown Liverpool, I decided my next stop would be the John Lennon Art Exhibition inside the Cavern Walks on Matthew Street. It was a newly-renovated shopping complex adjacent to the infamous Cavern Club—the spot where the Beatles had first shaken the musical world.

Entering the shopping center, I saw a gigantic bronze statue, on wheels, of a guitar-playing John Lennon in parody. A mediocre street-singer was standing under it with an open guitar case, crooning old Beatles songs. He was surrounded by hundreds of milling tourists and shoppers.

I was fascinated with John's lithographs, yet the commercial atmosphere in the gallery detracted from the gravity of the artwork. John seemed far away, as if he resented the Lennon tee-shirts, calendars and mugs as much as I did. I had no desire to remain here. When John was treated as a public, commercial institution, it was impossible for me to understand my involvement with him. My mood nosedived into confusion as I felt the inner and outer worlds of my reality clashing. Nevertheless, I continued to the Cavern Club next door.

Standing at the entrance guarded by a doorman, I lost my nerve to enter. This timidity perplexed me; I was too shy to enter the Cavern Club alone! Frozen and embarrassed, I stared stupidly at the large front door, preparing to walk away.

"Do you want to go inside?" a friendly female voice inquired from behind me.

It was a young woman with whom I had chatted during lunch inside the Cavern Walks.

"Well, actually . . . yes. It's just that . . ."

"Never you mind! I'll go down there with you! It would be a pity fer you ta miss goin' in, wouldn't it?"

"Sure . . . thanks."

My affable friend led the way down winding stairs and there it was—the celebrated spot where John Lennon and company had fashioned their incredible happenings. I recognized the stage from Beatle documentaries. In my mind I could hear and see those performances as if they were still taking place. I stood and gawked for a few minutes, then looked around at photographs of the Beatles, as well as other performers I didn't recognize.

Suddenly, I had the urge to leave this place as fast as possible. I'd expected to be more cheerful after my visit to Matthew Street, but instead, I left feeling muddled and melancholic.

Once outside, gravity was pulling me downhill toward the fresh air and the sea. I was going in the direction of the Albert Dock and Pier Head—where the concert was to be held—and became happier and lighter with every step.

Approaching the docks, I could feel John starting to grin, too.

"John! You creep! Why did you abandon me out there?"

"I didn't abandon you—you did it to *yourself*. You were too anxious to communicate with—you were such a different person! And downtown—well, you know those were just yer basic mercenary establishments."

"Is that why I felt so uninspired?"

"Yer not as green as you are cabbage lookin' . . . but it turned out great, anyway." Then, as an afterthought in a deep actor's voice, "I was proud of you."

"Is that true? I can't imagine why! What about the Stanley gravestone?"

"You're gonna hafta figure out that kinda crap when you get home. Besides, I'm not *supposed* to tell you about it. It's one of those great mysteries of Life."

"Let's not get too philosophical. I had the idea you didn't want to prove anything to me when I was there. Is that part of the mystery?"

"It's part of the reason, but not all of it. You'll just hafta be patient! The pieces are gonna fall into place eventually."

Now I was standing on the piers where John's grandfather, Jack, had arrived from Dublin long ago and where John's father, Freddie, had once sailed as a passenger-ship steward. The blue, rippling water being lashed about by the wind was the broad river Mersey making its connection with the Irish Sea. On the other side were the broad shores of the Wirral Peninsula.

I could hear John let out a sigh of relief. It seemed he was as happy as I'd ever felt him to be, for all of Life's cares could be cast away here. His essence was free to drift in a blissful sea of peace, contentment and safety—like a baby floating in the womb.

I sat on a bench and watched sightseers pass and stare. Now and then I could hear the strains of loud electric music—a rehearsal of "Give Peace a Chance" blowing with the wind from the concert area.

~5~
Lucy in the Sky

Several hours later, under a nearly full moon and nebulous sky, I entered the concert grounds. It was heartening to see how many children were there and how many American voices were blending in with the hubbub. I didn't know who to expect on stage other than Yoko, Sean and the Royal Liverpool Philharmonic Orchestra—which was to accompany some of the performers. I enjoyed the suspense and waited to buy a program.

Since my visit to the docks, I hadn't felt John's presence. I was dazed by the magnitude of this event and by the people coming here to celebrate his fiftieth birthday. The two realities—of my inner and outer worlds—were again engaged in fierce battle. I chose to tune out those subtle planes of psychic perception in favor of an oblivious enjoyment of the music beginning to issue forth from the stage.

Gigantic video screens were illuminating images of the performers as well as flashes and movies of John. Musicians had gathered from all over the world. The show was opened by a black Baptist minister-turned-singer who walked spiritedly across the stage, microphone in hand, his fantastically-alive voice singing "All You Need is Love."

Sean and Yoko were helping to host the show—I was getting my long-awaited glimpse of John's illustrious woman and their fourteen-year-old son. She was strong and attractive with very short hair. He bore a haunting resemblance to his father—down to the round wire-rimmed glasses—and was living proof of the "Beautiful Boy" John had once described in song. Both mother and son were obviously apprehensive as they peered through blinding lights at the crowd.

Prerecorded video clips of the performers told about John's influence in the development of their music. Other artists who weren't appearing personally were shown on the screens— including Paul and Ringo. They wished John a happy birthday, and Ringo ended his piece by saying John had the biggest heart of any person he'd ever known. Enormous spotlights were shooting their powerful beams into a darkening sky while helicopters circled overhead.

A commanding black woman moved onto the stage and began to sing "Lucy in the Sky with Diamonds," sending a tidal wave of goose bumps rolling across my skin. As my body swayed with the rhythm, I dropped my head back and gazed trance-like into the heavens. The moon was hot-white and surrounded by a magical circle of colored light.

"The music's all there, all the time," John had once stated in an interview. This message was now reaching its pinnacle, as was another indisputable message coming from the performers—no one can replace John Lennon; his music is unique.

What he had done for the development of music on earth became evident to me. My thoughts turned to Wolfgang Amadeus Mozart. I looked around and wondered how many of these concert-goers could fathom Past Time-Mode Expressions and spiritual phenomenon in general. What would they say about John's astonishing past?

The concert was over and Yoko and Sean were still being projected on the television screens. They were noticeably affected as throngs of performers moved onto the stage— giving handshakes, kissing and hugging as the crowds milled enthusiastically.

Elated, I began my mystical moonlit ascent toward the Adelphi. My mind was blank. My body, docile from the demands I had placed on it this day, seemed oblivious to the fact there were no taxis or buses in sight. I was swept along with the crowd of people who were acting as if it were midday—I barely remembered getting into bed.

The rest of the night was filled with lucid dreams. I kept seeing the face of fourteen-year-old Sean as I had seen him magnified by those video screens. His handsome, boyish face radiated the features of Yoko and John—in perfect harmony.

Images of Yoko were interwoven with this. I was talking to her about relationships. She looked pale and tired, yet was extremely happy. She was telling me about the two aspects of her life: the public and the private. In one respect, she still wanted to be John Lennon's partner. In another, she needed to allow her life to continue to grow and take on new forms.

The alarm woke me early Sunday morning, for I needed to be at the airport by 7:15. After packing, I intended to sit one last time in the overstuffed chair and talk into my tape recorder. The events of this weekend had evoked in me a multitude of emotions. Which ones belonged to John, Yoko or Sean? Which ones belonged to me? It was difficult to distinguish.

"John Lennon made a new myth on earth," I said sleepily into the recorder, ". . . a new legend for the modern world. Maybe it can be compared to the old legend of King Arthur. The new myth emerged at a time when human beings needed a new kind of hero—an idol who could show not just the strong and brave side of life, but the weak and the vulnerable side, too."

I pushed the pause button to think.

"Today, John Lennon's Knights of the Round Table are the freethinkers, musicians, poets and artists who want to reshape the world. Their Holy Grail is the realization that planet earth is a conscious entity seeking a new equilibrium through peace. The Round Table has grown to encompass the entire

globe—its knights are the colors of humanity. John's son
embodies East and West coming together in love . . .

"It's important, though, not to confuse the myth with the
man. The myth can serve countless numbers—the man cannot!
He can only answer to his own small part within the whole."

I hesitated. Speaking these last words, I could sense John
zeroing in.

"So there you are!" I say. "Help me finish—I've only got a
few more minutes!"

"Yer up bright and early, dear—what stamina you've got!"
His suit is wrinkled, his tie loosened. He looks older again.

"I've got to catch my plane to Amsterdam."

"Yesterday . . ." John begins to sing and dance.

"John, really! I only have ten minutes before my taxi comes.
Is there anything you want to add to this concept of the myth
and the man?"

He sits on the edge of the bed, growing more serious.

"Folks need ta realize I was just a human being like
them—with the same problems, plus more. I've gotta get free
of that myth. It can live on its *own* now 'cause the man needs
ta keep movin' and growin' in his own private sphere—just like
Yoko—just like anybody."

"Thank you."

"Yer welcome."

~6~
Dragon at Work

I returned home without incident. The taxi driver had talked about the Beatles and how he'd once met Ringo Starr. Pulling into the airport terminal, I asked him about the meaning of "scouse," a word I had heard repeatedly associated with Liverpool and John.

"A scouse is an Irish gypsy without meat," he explained, turning to me and grinning. He was referring to the impoverished Irish immigrants who had once sailed over from Dublin to find a new life—John's grandfather, Jack, among them. As I climbed out of the taxi, his last words about John Lennon were, "He never should have left Liverpool."

Now it was summertime, and I was constantly lost in reverie about my pilgrimage to that city and more emotionally involved with both the myth and the man than ever. I supposed it was part of the apprenticeship and couldn't discern any negative effects from this involvement—other than during those early days when I first started.

One night I dreamed I was visiting a home for handicapped children and wanted to give a donation in John Lennon's name. I gave several people money and received a receipt from a computerized cash register which had the word "prevention" written on it. I made note of the dream, wondering what it meant.

I had read that John chose to give donations to charities all over the world, including some in Liverpool. As a youngster John had enjoyed making cruel jokes about handicapped people. Was he now feeling guilty about it? He wasn't available for comment.

There were other ways I could interpret the dream. Perhaps John was being healed of his emotional handicaps and I was playing a role in helping him. The word "prevention" made me think about preventive medicine; if John's healing was successful, he would avoid suffering in the future.

I wanted to learn more about this dream. I also wanted John to become real again to me as he had been in Liverpool, but he remained aloof. Eventually I perceived images which seemed either too silly or too cynical to take seriously: John showed me a white handkerchief, shook it out, laid it on the ground and defecated on it. "What the hell," I thought. "What is this supposed to mean?" I became irritated.

Later that morning, I became ill. As the day progressed, I felt increasingly strange, as if coming down with a bad flu. Also, I was becoming fearful about various subjects. I decided to lie down and practice a healing exercise: I struck up a conversation with my belly and allowed it to take on the form of an animal for easier communication.

My belly began to change into an enormous, oriental, fire-breathing dragon, who told me he was "burning out the fear." With his fiery breath, he told me some of this fear belonged to John (which I was helping to transform) and some belonged to me. The dragon declared I had many of the same fears as John, and that's why we were able to help each other.

This didn't surprise me. I had more in common with John than I'd been willing to admit. This was the first fever I'd experienced in twenty years. I was burning hot and cold—our dragon was at work! Growing totally obsessed—half-delirious—I saw myself wandering endlessly around the suburbs and the cemetery of Liverpool. The mood in these places was old and awful. In the background I heard tracks *from the Beatles' **White Album**, and recalled a bad mushroom trip from my university days.*

Cold and shivering, I decided to take a hot bath. Lying in the water, my inner voice kept telling me: "You're cleaning out!" I sang and tried to heal myself.

*I was shocked to see gruesome images of John at the time of his death. I could see his face and the clothes he was wearing. Then I **became** him and felt myself being carried by a police car to the hospital.*

I am slowly leaving my body. I'm in pain, yet I feel nothing. Letting go of the earth sphere, I am swimming in a sea of blood, sorrow, fear, pain, loss and shock. I miss my family. Then I'm dead in a morgue and someone sneaks in to take a photograph of my naked body! Bony, white, cold death. I see pictures of Yoko—she's hysterical and has to use sedatives.

I become Linda again. I want desperately to turn the images off and climb out of the bathtub! But more images are coming to haunt me. Next I see myself getting killed in my last Expression. A blond woman is crashing down the mountainside in a black sedan. The old nightmare moves in and engulfs me.

I know I must convert these images before getting out of the bath, but it's going to take intense concentration. I need to put these "death pictures" into a gigantic white rose—it's my way of getting free. But first I chant, "Hello Death, hello Death! I love you, Death. I love you, Cold. I love you, Fear. Hello, hello, hello!"

I say "hello" until the death pictures move into the big white rose, which is eventually devoured by an even larger, red rose. Then it explodes, releasing a brilliant, transforming light. With John, I chant every name I know of for God: "Dios, Jaweh, Allah, Gaia, Shiva, Vishnu, Indra, Brahma, Bagawan, Deus!" These names become mantras while I receive the brightness of the exploding images—a golden-white glow which surrounds me.

John has been resurrected. I see images of him just before he was killed. The young blond woman is alive again. She and John linger in this golden resplendence, growing younger, changing into small children and finally into babies. I repeatedly tell the babies, "I love you."

With difficulty, I climbed out of the bathtub and into bed, thinking how lucky I was my husband was home to care for the girls. Under the covers, I heard a new song from within. It was "Miss You Like Crazy" from a record I'd recently purchased by Natalie Cole. She'd performed "Lucy in the Sky With Diamonds" at the concert in Liverpool. I had been captivated by her but didn't understand why "Miss You Like Crazy" made me sob every time I heard it.

I got a good night's sleep and felt better the next day, although not entirely recovered. Lying in bed, I was obsessed with reflections about death and John Lennon. I couldn't think of a way to disentangle my thoughts from his. In fact, I felt powerless to do anything.

"How's it going?" Aart asked, entering the room.

"Much better . . . but it's so hard to stop thinking about John! It's as if I'm slowly losing my mind."

"Perhaps that would be an interesting subject to write about," he answered ironically.

"Right! My mind has probably been gone for quite some time already! I think I need a healing."

Sitting on the edge of the bed, he prepared to look at my energy body with his inner eyes. As this was happening, I concentrated on how I might separate myself psychically from John. Not that he had been bothering me—it was my broken record this time which needed fixing.

I thought of the challenge John had received while sailing to the Bahamas with Sean. I pictured him taking another successful trip there, leaving me alone in The Netherlands for a good rest. This worked immediately, as I seemed to retrieve more of my own energy and reality every minute. Meanwhile, Aart had been working on me and began to tell me some of the things he had seen.

"You have similar karmic problems as John, and that's why this has been happening. You've been using his problems to help clean out your own."

"How funny! That's exactly what the dragon said."

"One theme you and John have in common has to do with being abandoned: for you, in other lives—and for John, in his last life on earth. There is a theme of loneliness—and neediness—which brings you into another theme shared by most humans—learning to accept the painful side of Life. To love yourself even though you aren't perfect."

***"That** theme again."*

"In your last life, not only were you abandoned, but you abandoned yourself and were killed at a young age. These are the things which link you with John's last life."

Listening from my sickbed, I did my best to stay positive.

"John has been helped by your conscious—and subconscious—efforts to heal yourself because you know that spirit can learn from the physical world. You know that spirit is eager to guide humans to work out their unsolved themes—this is one strong factor which binds you and John together! Besides, the two of you have been close in other lives . . . but I don't think we should deal with that subject today, do you?"

"It's something I've wanted to know more about."

"I think you should wait, Linda. Meanwhile, this aura of yours . . ."

He stood up and began to direct energy to numerous parts of my physical body—and energy body—with his hands.

"I think I'm getting sick again . . ."

"Focus on yourself! John's entity isn't near you now; he's fine—(jokingly) he's off to the Bahamas! Think about helping and loving yourself more, not always someone else! It's a wonderful avoidance game, you know. Feel your own sun and grounding now, okay?"

There was silence as Aart proceeded, carefully, to move his open palms around me for about five minutes. Then he sat down on the bed again with his eyes closed.

*"Your connection with the earth looks better now . . . that's
the positive side. There are many good things happening
through this. Look how much stronger you've become."*

"When will I learn?" I whimper.

*He answered me in Dutch. "When will you stop trying to
be perfect?"*

*Then I thought about my dragon. I had to admit the terrible
fear seemed to have vanished, and my faith in the process
with John had been renewed.*

*Aart opened his eyes and looked at me. "It all needs
forgiveness . . . self-love and forgiveness. Let yourself have
that, okay?"*

"I'll do my best. Thanks."

*It was as though I had received a successful house-call from
the local doctor. The prescription for health was forgiveness
and self-love. I knew this was as true for John's soul-aware-
ness as for mine. Subconscious layers had been reached and
penetrated, and this was important to the pursuit of health
and happiness. The dark side of Life had been revealed and
accepted. This had been John's cryptic message with the
handkerchief! I chose not to think about him, but in the back
of my mind, I continued to see a small, graceful sailboat
navigating over smooth waters toward sultry lands.*

*"Heaven sustains earth, and earth sustains heaven, and
always the twain shall meet . . ." I said aloud. But it was not
my voice.*

"Basil! How are you?"

"Keep it up, my girl! You're progressing splendidly. I'm
pleased for you."

"Thanks. It hasn't been easy."

"That's why you have needed so much help; and I must say,
you've been graciously receptive."

"It often seems," I say, "that I'm just plain crazy."

"Nothing of the kind—it's your typical growing pains."

"Spiritual, you mean."

"Indeed. And they are especially felt when pioneering areas unrecognized by people around you. You are fortunate to have a helpful husband."

"I know. I'm getting luckier each day. And I do want to thank you, too."

"Heaven sustains earth, and earth sustains heaven . . ."

". . . and always the two shall meet," I hear my inner voice drowsily finishing Basil's phrase as I fall into a deep sleep.

In a dream I'm back at the pier in Liverpool. It is nighttime, very dark and people are milling about. John is standing at the edge of the pier, looking at the bright stars shining above the horizon. I'm looking down, as if I am invisible and suspended in air. Sometimes it's like I am John, and this reality becomes synonymous with the other. The stars are emanating clear beams of light and we wish to see them better. John/I are alone in the crowd—in a mood of confidence and tranquillity.

~7~
Hypnotherapy

After my illness, I was determined to look into my past with John. There were many ways I could do this, and, until now, I'd preferred the cautious approach of asking my subconscious for information while meditating. I had often explored Past Mode Expressions this way, just as I had explored them in my dreams. Yet, there was another more direct approach used to discover information about the past—hypnotherapy.

I'd been regressed by a professional hypnotherapist before. The experience left me feeling like I'd been having a vivid daydream. It was amazing how complex stories could surface merely because someone systematically relaxed all the parts of my body and counted from ten to one a few times. Occasionally, Aart and I helped each other reach a deep trance this way in search of information otherwise difficult to obtain.

I decided it was time to look at my Past Mode connections with John Lennon while under hypnosis. It would be interesting to work with someone other than Aart because he was so familiar with the subject. We agreed another therapist would be impartial. Also, I wouldn't mention the name of Lennon, only John.

On a cold, grey, rainy fifth of June, I made the long train ride to work with our healer-hypnotherapist friend, Hans. It seemed odd to keep my secret from him, but felt I should. I

described my objective: I wanted to communicate with a
guardian named John to discover what significant connections
I'd had with him in other lifetimes. After meditating together
for a short while, Hans asked me to recline in a special chair
and fitted me with wires that would indicate the depth of my
hypnotic trance. As I stared at a fixed point on the ceiling, the
tape recorder was switched on and Hans began to speak in
a slow, soothing voice. I was accustomed to this method and
knew it was bringing me swiftly into contact with deep
subliminal levels of awareness.

". . . and what do you see, Linda?"

"Beautiful, colored flowers," I reply in a soft voice, "light-violet, pink and magenta—they are hanging from trellises. It's real warm outside . . . It seems sort of Mediterranean."

"Where is it?" Hans asks gently.

"I think it's Greece."

"Can you see what year it is?"

I chuckle. "It doesn't fit. It's 1900 . . . it doesn't fit."

"Why doesn't it fit?"

"Because I didn't think I had a body at that time."

"Perhaps you are spirit, then?"

"Yes . . . perhaps."

"Are there other people around?"

"I'm with John . . . but I'm not sure if he's with me in body or in spirit."

"What are you doing here?"

"It's a terrace, a patio . . . we're looking at the water, a bay."

"Is the water the sea?"

"Yes."

"Are you speaking about something special?"

"I'm talking about politics. It's difficult there—many conflicting ideas . . . but . . . yeah . . . as we're talking about politics, it's as if we're seeing into the past. There's a big arch from the present to early times. . . it's not—it doesn't feel so much in present-time. It's as if we need to go into the past. It's like looking at a movie . . . hard to describe."

"Are you a man or a woman?"

"I'm trying to see . . . I think I see two men."

"And what age are these two men?"

"One is thirty-two and the other is fifty-six."

"And you are speaking about politics . . . and people—concerning your government?"

"We're looking at the whole situation—how it has gone and wondering how it will turn out . . . our thoughts keep returning to ancient Greece. We were there once, and now we're in modern Greece. We're looking at its entire development."

"Do you work for the government?"

"Hmmm . . . I think so. Yeah—I think we have uniforms."

"Military?"

"Yes."

"And what's your political attitude?" Hans searches for the proper words in English.

"I want more freedom."

"Freedom for what—for the military?"

"No, for the individual . . . but it's going in the wrong direction. It's . . . to get . . . well, I want more of the old spiritual values."

"What is old?"

"The heritage of Greece . . . very free . . . human life is valuable."

"And what is the political attitude of the other man?"

"He's less convinced that it's possible. He thinks the world has to be more disciplined, that you have to be stronger and more . . . authoritative."

"Are they friends?"

"They're members of the same family—they trust each other . . . but you have to be careful of what you say."

"What do you mean?"

"It's dangerous to talk of freedom in these times. You'll end up dead . . . or in prison."

"Oh? And what other things are important in your life here?"

"I don't seem to be attached to anything . . . I can't seem to get anywhere. I'm stuck in this place."

In my hypnotic trance, I have the sensation that I'm not in a body in this little movie, nor is John. It seems we are viewing the actions and conversations of two human beings because it keys us into a world which is important to our journey. It is abstract and difficult to relate to Hans.

"Okay," he resumes. "Now concentrate on yourself and relax . . . relax again. Close the book you were looking into and relax. Let everything go . . . close the book about Greece . . . rest—relax deeply. Imagine you are continuing to wander through a library, and your hand is attracted to another shelf—go ahead and choose something else to look through. What is it this time? Is it a book or a movie? Photographs?"

"I see a movie . . . with a little boy running around in swimming trunks—in the garden—a little boy."

"Do you recognize this little boy?"

"Um . . . no. Wait. I think it's John."

"What is he doing?"

"He's running in the garden . . . now he's going inside his house with his aunt. He's running—looking around the house and running up the stairs. It seems as if he's alone for the moment."

I am clearly seeing Aunt Mimi's house which I wasn't able to find while in Liverpool.

"And where are you?"

"Huh! I don't think I'm . . . I'm not in a body," I sigh. "It looks like I'm . . . I'm a *guardian*!"

"A spiritual guide."

"Yeah, of his."

"Are you John's guardian?"

"Yeah!"

"Nice, huh?"

"Yeah," I smile.

"And what are you doing?"

"I'm helping—it's a difficult time for him because his parents are separated and he's often alone. Although people love him . . . he needs love and care . . . help . . . with his emotions."

"Yes . . . and what do you help him with specifically?"

"Hmm . . . I help him with the Light—to get in touch with the Light."

"Is this an old film you're looking at?"

"No . . . It's about 1944.

"And can you see where it is?"

"Yes, it's in England."

"And look at what happens to John as he gets older."

"Yeah, I know what happens . . . I know all about that life—he had to die. He suffered. He had an important life and . . . I know all about it. He had to die—tragically."

"How old was he then, when he died?"

"He was forty . . . he's been dead about ten years."

"And is there something more that John wants to show you?"

"Yes . . . I keep being pulled back to Greece, so I think we have to go there."

Comfortably reclined, it's as if I am wide awake, yet dreaming.

"And what has happened with you in Greece?"

"It's difficult to . . . I get war pictures, and then I get healing-temple pictures . . . and . . ."

"The war—where was it? Was Greece fighting a war with another people?"

"It was neighboring. I think they were fighting each other. It was on the mainland . . . and I also see Delphi . . . but it's—in another time."

"Take a look at the war," Hans says carefully. "Were you involved in the military?"

"Oh, I see Peloponnesia—the word Peloponnesia. It's the Peloponnesian War. I'm in the army. I'm young . . . eighteen—a soldier. John is here too."

"Oh, you've met John again. Is he also in the army?"

"I think he's doing something else . . . He was . . . my *mother*! And I had to leave her! Wait a second. There are people coming from other places. I'm not sure if they are other tribes—or bands—of people. It's hard to see what I'm doing."

"Do you have to kill people at this time?"

"Yeah," I respond heavily.

"How do you do this?"

"I have to wrestle . . . and use knives and stones. It isn't fun . . . it's not fun at all!" I begin to laugh nervously.

"Did you get wounded in this fighting?"

"I think I died."

"And how old are you now?"

"I'm nineteen. I never see my mother again . . ."

I become emotional and have to stop talking.

"Let go of this image now," Hans says soothingly, "and go to that other life you saw at Delphi . . . was it at the temple?"

"Yes . . . In Delphi."

"What do you see in this temple?"

"It's serene and safe—where I was living before the soldier lived. It's a place where I can go back in spirit to heal myself . . . after the soldier's death, too. I yearn for this place . . . because it's so peaceful and harmonious."

"What are you doing in the temple?"

"I'm a woman—healing people."

"How old are you?"

"I'm a teenager when I go into the temple . . . about fifteen."

"You are young to be healing."

"Uh-huh . . ."

"Do you heal only young people—or also older people?"

"Everybody . . . animals too . . . and birds."

"Are you healing on the physical level, or also on a spiritual level?"

"On all levels—body and spirit are one."

As I say this, my personality alters distinctly; it is exceedingly strong and certain, particularly for a young girl.

"And is John here, too?"

"Yeah, I feel his presence. He's in the temple, too. He's a man, I think."

"What is he doing in the temple?"

"He's also a healer. I think we're cousins. We work well together—balancing male and female energies . . . bringing harmony into the body."

"It's harmonious . . . tranquil."

Although I don't mention it to Hans, I get the impression John and I are fond of each other.

"When do you finish your healing work here?"

"It seems I'm here my whole life."

"How old are you when you die?"

"Sixty-seven."

"And why do you leave your body at this time?"

"Well, I'm ready!" I reply, giggling. "I'm light-filled . . . I become radiant . . . and I'm called to the Infinite Dwelling. I'm not needed at the temple anymore. There are new people and I've taught them—I've done my work."

"Can you tell me what period of time this is? Suppose there is a calendar, and you look at it and see . . . ."

"It's 1604—B.C."

"Now let those images go," Hans says, "and see if you can go to a life you've never seen before—perhaps not on this earth. Let yourself float—totally free."

"Yeah . . . I go immediately . . . there's a place I yearn to return to."

I'm becoming emotional again.

". . . and that's Atlantis."

"Tell me about it."

I sigh deeply.

"There's a tremendous amount of sun and light. It's golden and so rich with green . . . so mild. Spirit is so near the earth—intertwined with earth. Spirit is so *near*. The longer earth has been spinning . . . the further spirit has retreated from it. In those times, you could breathe spirit and *touch* it. Everything you wanted to manifest was nearer. Spirit was closer to human beings in those days. It's wonderful!"

"Yes."

"And the nature . . . the spirit of all living creatures was integrated into human life. There was *no separation*. It seemed . . . the mind of nature was the mind of humans. They were telepathically connected . . . *it was the same mind*. This was in the earlier phase—the beginning here—before the trouble. This was the golden age of Atlantis, before it was destroyed . . . before the tension and devastation."

"What are you doing here?"

"I see myself as . . . I see land and . . . a land owner. I see orchards and fields . . . many animals—wild animals. I'm not sure."

"Do you have a job?"

I notice my voice becoming louder and stronger.

"Yes, I'm doing healing . . . but it's on another level. I communicate with . . . people come to me for information about nature. I explain things about the sun and moon . . . and nature spirits—messages they have for people. I'm clairvoyant. People come for counsel about what they should do in particular situations. I think I have a family. I'm a man . . . and there are children. I see lovely pools where we bathe—beautiful blue enamel bathing pools. I see my children—they're important."

"How many children do you have?"

"I had five, and now I have four. One of them died. There are blond ones . . . and dark-haired ones . . . two colors . . . there are different races here. I know both races of people."

"Yes . . ."

"There's a little boy who comes to me. He's wearing a white tunic and looks the same age as . . . the boy in England. He looks like the same little boy . . . *I'm his father*. He's coming to me . . . *it's John*. I'm teaching him what I know—everything I know."

"Yes?"

"My name is Chief Ra Na . . . and he will succeed me."

I am tense with excitement.

"Relax again, Linda. Take a deep breath, nice and easy. And now you can see yourself going to that library again . . . and maybe John is there with you now?"

"Yes . . . we're together and—there's one strange thing—it's a pink color . . . I'm supposed to look at . . . not so serious . . . but . . ."

"Take a look . . . and if you've seen enough for today, let the light in the library become dimmer."

After a pause, Hans adds, "Tell me if the light is becoming dimmer."

"Yes, it is now. There's a funny little pink bird. It has a message . . . and I'm supposed to see what it wants. I'm supposed to take it to the window. John and I go there together and . . . the bird was kind of dark . . . and we let him out the window . . . and he flies away. It's the symbol of *freedom—creative freedom*. The bird becomes luminescent and flies into the future. This represents letting go of everything . . . *to let the future find its own form*. We close the windows—that's enough for now."

Hans slowly brought me out of my trance with soothing music, asking me to thank all the information which had surfaced during this session. He told me I'd nearly been in the deepest state of hypnosis a person can be in. This must have been true, for when I stood up, I felt dizzy and unreal. Hans had brought me back properly into present time, but I couldn't make it substantial yet.

Having been led into the living room, I found it difficult to concentrate on normal conversation with Hans and his wife. I was overcome by the things I had experienced in the last hour-and-a-half. At the same time, I wondered if I hadn't made it all up.

"That's what most people think," Hans replied in Dutch, chuckling, "but you were in a very deep trance—as you were the last time I worked with you."

We were now chattering away in Dutch. It was frustrating to not be able to share my secret about John and the writing, but I still had the message to wait.

*On the train ride home, I attempted to deal with these new revelations. Were they all true? If so, it was no wonder I felt compelled to write about John! I had especially loved the revelation that I had once been **his** guardian. This must have been after my death in the car accident—around 1943.*

A few days after my session with Hans, I began to review the dreams I'd written down months before. With a jolt, I understood the meaning of the dream about John at the Liverpool pier: I had been looking at John, "as if invisible and suspended in air." In this dream I sometimes thought

John and I were the same entity—his reality and mine felt interchangeable. "Of course!" I realized, "that's how it feels to be guiding a human being!" I was stupefied.

My recollections of the healing temple of Delphi and the Atlantian paradise were equally astounding. Few Expressions could have been so well-balanced and fulfilling as these; they must have been peak episodes in my long, sometimes tragic journey upon earth. My session with Hans helped reawaken in me a haunting curiosity about my own past. I would persist in investigating this subject as my writing progressed— through hypnosis, dreams, meditation or the helpful voices of my guardians.

~8~
Gracie

Autumn had arrived and there were vital pieces of informa-
tion still buried in my subconscious which were relevant to
my story. Trying to expose them would have been premature
up to now, for it had taken me the entire summer vacation to
integrate the last hypnosis session into my waking life. I had
decided to work with my husband this time, and we soon
discovered why he should be helping me instead of anyone
else.

"Feel what you feel," Aart says, after having led me down an
imaginary staircase. "Make contact with John. What comes to
your mind when you do this?"

My voice is slurred and barely audible, as if I'm mumbling
in my sleep.

"You said I would meet him at the bottom of the staircase, so
it feels like I'm going into a basement. He's down here waiting
for me. Now we're in a room without windows, sitting at a
table. He's wearing a cap as in a picture I have of him from his
L.A. phase. . . he removes his glasses so I can see his eyes."

"Is it light or dark here?"

"It's light . . . all white. And we need to leave this room . . .
there's nothing happening in this place."

"Okay . . . find a door leading out of the room."

"I want to ask him to show me the Expression he had before he was . . . John Lennon . . ." My voice trails off, then ". . . We're at the door . . . it's all black. We're floating in the cosmos. It's scary."

"Stay with John and make yourselves safe . . . your Friends of Light are with you, too."

"Right. Okay . . . we step out and . . . we're falling.

"We land on the ground and look around."

"Is it daylight?"

"Yeah. It's a *desert* here. It's pretty and expansive—southern California! I've been here before."

"John is taking you somewhere?"

"Yeah . . . he was and now we're just standing around. He's in white again and looks bizarre. When I look at his face . . . he looks like a straw scarecrow . . . he's wearing a weird African mask."

"Yes?"

"I almost didn't let that come in—it was frightening! Yes, it is *African*. He's wearing a hat and white suit. Everything looks curious and scary. He's surrounded by light, and we're going to Los Angeles . . . Yogananda is there . . . and the Self-Realization Fellowship."

"Yeah?"

"I'm there. The blond woman was there once, too . . . she met with Yogananda."

"What time-period are you in?"

"It's 1936. He came from India before that . . ."

"Yogananda?"

"Yes."

"Okay. Ask John now to take you to his last earthly body before he was John Lennon. Maybe you can be in a room again."

"I'm sitting on a train."

I blow out of my puckered lips in great agitation.

"I'm getting all shook up . . ."

"Don't worry about anything. You're totally safe."

"I'm traveling by train from California to the southern United States—where the blond woman was born."

"Relax . . . and stay neutral."

I take a few deep breaths.

"Look around and say hello, Linda," Aart advises me in a soothing voice.

"It smells like . . ."

My voice trails off to an inaudible mumble.

"Where are you?"

"I think I'm in Virginia. I see land . . . cotton fields . . . and other crops. It smells good here! It's hot and humid . . . peaceful. I don't see any cars."

"Are you still walking with John?"

"I'm not sure who I'm with. I'm . . ."

"Where's John?"

"He's in the kitchen."

"Hmm. How does he look?"

After a long pause, Aart continues, "Linda, what's happening?"

"He's black . . . a beautiful, black, teenaged girl. John is a black girl! She's wearing long skirts, and she's smiling and laughing. She's real funny!"

"What else can you tell about her?"

"She's open and pure . . . her hair is in braids tied on top of her head . . . she's radiant . . . innocent."

"Who are you?"

"I'm a little *white* kid," I say in a weak voice.

"What year is it?"

"It's 1916."

"And how old are you?"

"I'm five years old."

"How old is she?"

"She's fifteen or sixteen."

"Is she taking care of you?"

"Sometimes—she's my nanny."

"It takes so much . . . to allow myself to feel it . . . because I want to cry! I see her and smell the air—nice and warm. It's almost too painful to remember."

"Because it's so nice?"

"Yeah . . . everything is easy now, so simple!" I answer wistfully. "The world is . . . easy! I'm looking around the kitchen . . . it's big. I can't see myself yet . . . I can only sense myself. I want to know my name . . . I hear the name Grace."

"Hmm."

"Maybe *her* name is Grace. Yes . . . her name is Grace . . . *Gracie*."

"Gracie. That's nice."

"Gracie Powell."

"Powell. That's a nice name."

"Gracie." I whisper gently. And then I moan loudly, "Oh God!"

Tears rush to my eyes and I'm afraid I'm going to choke.

"What does this scene tell you, Linda?"

"I really like her," I say emotionally.

"Uh-huh . . . there's a lot of love between you? That's great," Aart says tenderly, "allow yourself to have that."

I begin to sob. "She was so nice!"

"Was she caring?"

"Yes," I squeak in a high voice, whimpering, "she could *see* me for who I was—nobody else *could*."

I sob.

"She *died*," I whisper, trying to catch my breath.

"How old were you when she died?"

"It was later . . . she left or something. It gets too painful."

"Are you on a farm?"

"Yeah. It's a farm. There's a big garden near the house. I didn't realize how much farmland there is."

"Did Grace leave the house because she got married?"

"I think so. I think she got married."

"How old were you when she left?"

"I'm about fifteen, and she . . . had to leave! Then, she dies . . . she dies having a *baby*."

"Did you know then that she died?"

"Yes."

"Had she gone far away?"

"No, she was nearby—I saw her sometimes. I missed her. But you're not supposed to be so attached to a black person . . ."

"Yeah. What else do you see?"

"I hear music! People are singing and dancing. That's why I like the fiddle . . . it connects me with this! And the black people are singing too . . . I love them so much . . . and all the great music here."

"Did Gracie play music?"

"Yeah! She sang and played the banjo. She taught me some of her songs when we were alone. We laughed until we cried! When I got older, I was a professional singer—because of Gracie. I thought of her when I sang, and she helped me get it *right*."

"Was she your guardian after she died?"

"God . . . I think so!"

"What kind of songs did you sing?"

"I sang the blues . . . wanted to sing like a black woman! My father disowned me, so I moved to California."

"How old were you, then?"

"I was sixteen."

"And what were your parents like?"

"I don't know. I can't see or feel my parents . . . as if they're unimportant to me! On an emotional level, they're not there. Gracie was more of a mother to me than my real mother."

"What year did Gracie die?"

"In 1927—she was twenty-six years old."

"Do you feel the theme of her life?"

"She could see me when no one else could. She was *wise* . . . and could see what was really important, while everyone else was so superficial! She could *see*—she was clairvoyant. She had a big heart and good values. She knew how to *love* me, care about me! And she was incredibly strong . . . with a great sense of humor."

"Yeah?"

"She didn't say much . . . she laughed a lot . . . behind people's backs, you know, at the absurdity of Life!"

"Could she see above everything?"

"Right . . . it's ridiculous she's only helping in the kitchen! She could run the whole farm—she could do anything she wanted."

"What lessons did she learn from this life?"

"The meaning of being connected with her own wisdom . . . in spite of what other people projected about her. She often talked about God . . . she relied on herself and on God . . . and didn't care what other people thought."

"But in a loving way?"

"Well, to people who didn't see her . . . for instance, people who weren't kind . . . she could be sharp and defiant. She knew how to stand up to them—unusual for a black woman at the time. Actually, she was like a saint who nobody recognized. Only a few people could comprehend her . . . she lived and she died. That was it."

"That made you sad . . ."

"It affected me for the rest of my life . . . I couldn't live up to it. I couldn't live up to Gracie . . . I was ashamed, somehow."

"Of what?"

"Maybe of the fact that I was white and she was black. I lived and she died—it wasn't fair. I couldn't keep the same truth alive that she could. I was weak and didn't like myself. That's why I ended up as I did . . . with drugs and bad relationships. I missed her too much."

"Don't you think you're being too hard on yourself?"

"Perhaps. But compared to her, my character was weak."

"What did you do after you left home?" Aart asks.

"I took the train to southern California, through that big desert. Years later, I tried to get help from Yogananda in Los Angeles, but he couldn't get through to me. I wasn't up to him, either, even though I wanted it so much! He said I had *promise*! He could see me, as Gracie had. But I had a deficiency . . . it couldn't be helped! I couldn't live with myself. Gracie was dead . . . and my brother was going to have to go to war—he was the only other friend I had."

"You had a brother?"

"Right. I see him helping Dad on the farm with the hired hands . . . Oh, that was *you*!"

"Was I your brother?" Aart asks.

"Yes!" I say happily, but my mood quickly fades.

"Jesus . . . you got killed in that war."

"World War Two?"

"Yes," I say, weeping.

Aart waits. I sense that he is moved.

"Linda, is there anything else you want to say before you come out of trance?"

"I was attracted to Europe . . . for John *and* for you."

"Were you my guardian then, too?"

"Yes," I say, heaving a great sigh. "How can the pieces fit so well together?"

"It's a miracle—they always do."

After a moment, Aart continues, "Is there anything else, Linda?"

"It's confusing. I loved you as my brother and now you're my husband. I thought I cared about John . . . but when I see Gracie, I cared about her even more."

"Well, same spirits, you know."

Aart guided me out of trance. I was exhausted from crying and talking and overwhelmed by my journey through time. These were the missing pieces of a puzzle I'd been putting together for years. I was shocked to discover how this other reality was bound so powerfully with my present existence.

Over the years I had uncovered various clues about my past Expression in the rural South, but now the picture had become complete. This knowledge would challenge me again, just as, in the last few months, the other Past Mode revelations had broadened my awareness. It imparted a new depth to my relationship with John's spirit and strengthened my commitment to writing about him.

~9~
Nothing Is Final

The more I reflected on the whole Gracie discovery, the more astounded I became. I remembered the black woman who'd sat next to me on the bus ride to Liverpool and then had shown me the way to my hotel. I thought about the memorial concert and how exhilarating, yet painful, it had been when Natalie Cole had performed "Lucy in the Sky" with such passion. I recalled how another song of hers called "Miss You Like Crazy" had made me weep for weeks afterwards. I hadn't understood any of it then—those emotions had left me confused—but now I was staggered by the implications.

My last hypnosis session had struck, anew, an extreme emotional chord in me about death. Again it was my fear of loss—this time, the loss of loved ones. I found myself growing unusually concerned about the lurking perils of existence, especially in relation to my family.

I had a hunch I was working, once more, on a problem concerning both John and me. Along with my recollections about Gracie and my brother, I repeatedly thought of John being raised by his aunt and of his mother's death when he was a teenager. I also thought of Julian—as a small child—losing contact with John, and losing him for good at age sixteen. And I remembered how Sean lost his father when he was five years old. I saw how my writing about John was constantly bringing up the subject of death and loss in search of healing and transformation. The act of writing had become, among other things, a prolonged therapy session.

The autumn days were growing darker. Walking in the woods with my family late in November, I continued to ponder this disturbing theme of loss. My fixations had grown out of proportion, I realized, yet I couldn't let them go. In an attempt to join their happy mood, I thought up a game to play with the children: each of us would hug a tree and wait for its message.

Hugging my tree, I harmonized with it and its benefactor, the silent earth.

"Hold onto Life," the tree says, "and embrace Life instead of people. If you embrace Life, people will always be there."

"Thank you," I say, feeling illuminated.

"My pleasure," my confidant replies.

With this message, the tree relieved me of an oppressive load. Its fresh insight was convincing. Suddenly, I no longer felt concerned with the fears of loss and death. Amidst the shedding of dead leaves, a new leaf of trust was living inside me.

Soon it would be ten years since John Lennon had been murdered. As December 8, 1990, approached, there were several articles about this in newspapers and magazines. It was a significant milestone for John and me to be able to celebrate Life's victory over the illusion of death and the triumph of love and understanding over fear.

On the night of December 8th, I had the following dream:

I am at the place where John Lennon was killed, but it is not the Dakota Apartments in New York City. It is in another city which resembles San Francisco, where I lived as a child. I am with a group of strangers and we enter a large courtyard which is shaded by an enormous linden tree. We are being shown the spot where John was murdered. Among several large stones, one is oblong and pointing up. Near the top is a small plaque showing where John hit his head when he fell. The stones are decorated with many flowers, including red roses. The monument makes me think of an ancient Irish gravestone.

Yoko Ono walks into the courtyard. She is wearing a flowing, white dress and her long black hair is beautiful. She has come to commemorate John and the group present is going to join in the ceremony. Like a Druid ritual, the cycles of nature are being celebrated, as well as the immortality of John's soul. I'm not sure who is leading the ritual because we're communicating telepathically.

After the ceremony is over, Yoko walks quietly out of the courtyard, remaining solitary. I attempt to follow her, but she has disappeared. Looking at the surroundings, I see the courtyard is situated on top of a hill. It's tranquil and reminds me of the district in San Francisco where I lived as a baby. The air is foggy and bracing. I've gone back to my babyhood state-of-mind and am sensing how safe this neighborhood is and how impossible it seems that someone would come here to kill John.

Then I find myself in a new setting which is more abstract and surreal. I am looking at John's tangible form and am responsible for helping him bathe. It's important for us to repeat this ritual in several houses. The act is more symbolic than physical, for John is being cleansed of his past.

The dream ends with an overpowering sense of compassion for the whole world, then for the whole universe. I hear the phrase "all you need is love," and it makes me ecstatic. This state of euphoria awakens me.

★　　★　　★

When war broke out in the Middle East a few months later, my euphoric phase endured an enormous setback. I tried to grasp the significance of the event in relation to my own belief system. What did the war mean to me personally? How could I stay positive when I felt so perplexed?

"War is over, if you want it . . ." John and Yoko had told us emphatically about twenty years earlier. The Cold War

*had, indeed, miraculously ended, the Berlin Wall had just
been torn down; why was this happening now?*

*There were too many contrasting themes playing nonstop
in my head. For instance, if I was creating my own reality,
including the war I saw on television, how could I stop it?
This war was demonstrating to the world how many disparate
kinds of reality can coexist on earth. I needed help to deal
with the confusion I was facing, I needed Basil for consolation.*

"This is getting me down," I sigh to him after switching off
the news and retreating into meditation. "This hideous war . . .
just when everything was looking so good."

His soothing presence drifts in to address me.

"My, I don't mean to be harsh, but you mustn't *worry* so!
Your dark thought-forms aren't helping anyone! They're making
things worse—had you forgotten?"

"No, I mean, yes! I can't help myself—it's too horrible and
frightening."

"But you must recognize this particular stage of earth's
development has been prophesized by many people throughout
the world and throughout time. It's difficult aspects are making
themselves more obvious . . ."

"You must be right, but my old-fashioned human instincts are
getting me down."

"That's normal for any sensitive person. But it's time to take
steps . . . to look further."

"I keep thinking of what I read once—according to the Mayan
calendar, the earth is experiencing the last 22 years of a growth
cycle some 26,000 years in length! According to it's prophesies,
there's going to be a painful destruction of many old structures—of what earth has built up during this period—to make
room for the *next* phase."

"Now you've said it. At this moment in history, even if the
world appears to reflect total chaos and disharmony on the
outside, its deeper nature is moving into the full splendour of
the Light. According to the time schedules of many old religious
prophesies, which have been confirmed by modern astrologers

and seers, planet earth is gearing up for a tremendous transfiguration of the established order. Slowly but surely, the connection between human and planetary realms are becoming strengthened. The Gulf War is living proof of this—and needs to be seen as such."

I know he's right, but still I hesitate.

"But what about nature? Why should oil-drenched birds and sea creatures have to suffer along with us?" I retort.

"Now you're thinking in restricted terms! Nature is part of us and we are part of nature—we're all in this together. Don't forget the never-ending cycle of death and rebirth, nothing is final in the world of spirit. Remember what you learned about letting go—about releasing the old forms to allow in the new! Take a good look at what you've already learned from John . . . and by your reunion with your old friend Gracie. Do you see my point?"

"You mean there's always more going on behind the scenes than we realize? If we comprehended it all, we would be perpetually amazed and would live in a constant state of grace. Hey . . . Gracie. That's nice, isn't it?"

"You've got my point. It's important to emphasize that humans are living in extraordinary times. It's crucial to view the chaos, darkness and pain now running rampant upon earth with an attitude of acceptance and hope. This isn't a naive hope based on ignorance, it's knowing you are traveling together in this procession toward the Light. And, furthermore, I suggest you use this war as a symbol and catalyst for your own inner warfare. It's giving every individual the chance to see their personal negative and destructive side! This is the underlying message of war."

"But, Basil, you know how hard I've been working on facing up to my dark side."

"True. But don't forget the most important work of all."

"What's that?"

"It's learning how to accept and forgive yourself. This is your key to change and perhaps the most important of all the discoveries to be made on earth. Because self-love is the food for all progress . . . and the warm refuge which humans will seek in the turbulent years to come."

PART IV

Arcadia

~1~
Return

Back at the Mystical Ocean with its roaring surf, mighty coastal winds and blowing sands—I shiver beneath my cape. Maybe I should have turned the heater up in my study before venturing here again; after all, it had been snowing outside when I left. Gazing around on this vast sweep of beach, I'm frightened.

Traversing the wet coastline, I gain comfort in my rhythmic gait. As usual, the colors of this place are remarkably alive. I take pleasure in the stretches of whitish sand surrounding me, the dunes and rolling hills and the distant blue-and-green mountains crowned with white haze.

"Not bad," I admit to myself.

The temperature is rising, and the more relaxed I become, the less the wind blows and the more sun and blue sky there is to greet me.

Soon it becomes so hot that I remove my cape, revealing what I'm wearing underneath. It is a delicate-pink, low-bodiced gown. On my feet are dainty, white, laced boots. My hair is swept up in the back and tied with a large satin bow.

"What's all *this*?" I murmur, wrinkling my nose.

By now it's hot and humid. I blink as I begin to observe how the surroundings have altered. The beach has become smaller, the surf is less pounding and the hills and mountains are gone!

I am carrying a parasol and quickly open it to protect myself from the intense glare. It has become sultry—every breeze is a welcome relief.

Strolling along this strange, new shoreline, I detect a tiny form in the distance moving in my direction! Adrenaline races through my body.

Soon I am able to distinguish woman's attire. There is something special about her—something dark. She sees me too! The closer we move toward one another, the more violently my heart beats.

She is a *black woman*, young and beautiful. Her plain, light-yellow dress stands out against her dark skin. Her hair is coiled neatly. I see her white teeth as she smiles at me with a mischievousness I instantly recognize.

"Gracie!" I wail, my voice choked with tears, as I drop my parasol and run frantically in her direction.

"Why didya hafta go'n *die*?" I sob, throwing my arms around her neck.

"Lord Almighty!" she replies, "Ain't this a homecomin'!"

"God, Gracie! Ah missed you so much ah thought ah was gonna die myself—and then ah went and did that *anyway*," I blurt through my tears.

"You shouldn't of done it, Miss Sandy . . . all them folks missed you and your poor brother somethin' terrible!"

"Well, that's how *ah* felt 'bout *you*, Gracie. Why did ya leave me?" I look searchingly into her deep brown eyes.

"Miss Sandy . . . you *know* why that happened . . . you know the Lord called my name . . . and ah had to *answer* Him."

"But yer *baby*, Gracie . . . yer poor little baby."

Sadly, she glances at the ground and responds softly, "Ah know Sandy . . . ah know . . . but my sister reared him as good as ah reared you! Ah made shore he got as much love as he could."

I stand and stare incredulously at this treasured soul; we giggle uncontrollably.

" 'Member this one?" Gracie bellows and starts to play a hand-clapping game with me. We shout funny, childish rhymes as we clap and then collapse into fits of laughter.

"C'mon! Let's go sit down ovah there."

Gracie points to a large, blue-checkered tablecloth spread on the sand, shaded by a large blue parasol. A wicker picnic basket sits on the tablecloth, and we race to it like frolicsome puppies.

"Miss Sandy, ah gotta tell you somethin'," Gracie says, acting like an adult again.

"What?" I worship the air she breathes.

"Miss Sandy, now you know why it went the way it did," she sighs, giving me a deep look.

"You mean . . . we both had ta die when we did?"

She nods wisely.

"Now you understand why. Now you can see why we had ta suffer, 'cause there was things we had ta *do* . . . and ta learn later on . . . alone an' tagetha! Ain't it just too perfect?"

"Oh, Gracie . . . you always amazed me! Ah think this must be one of the happiest days of my life."

"Honey, it does mah heart good ta be able ta sit here with you and realize our lives are eternal—that such love can abide without bounds of time, place or condition."

She looks at me with that old mystical gleam in her eyes.

"We're *free*, girl . . . totally *free*, we are!"

Gracie leans joyously to embrace me. Overcome with sentiment, I cannot look at her.

"Ah always knew that," she adds with determination, "but life can be hard on folks."

Inhaling deeply, I taste the sea.

"So this is mah beloved Virginia. Gracie . . . ah've missed it so! An' this is the beach where we used to play! You would come along to make shore we didn't drown ourselves."

"Them were the days!" she says, showing her luminous smile. The crash of the ocean breakers echoes in our ears.

"Heah." Gracie offers me a homemade, white roll stuffed with cold, fried chicken. We eat in silence, finishing off our meal with chocolate cake.

"My real mother, ah scarcely knew. You were always there, when she wasn't," I say dreamily.

"Why don't you lie down and take a nap, Miss Sandy? You been too busy with all them tears."

"Oh, ah will! Ah'm so tired! But, *please*, Gracie . . . would you sing me some of your old songs?"

"You shore could sing 'em good yourself, honey . . . I loved seein' you singin' 'em like me! We was real fine, Sandy . . . you was like mah own little sister."

Under the shade of the blue parasol, I lie down curled up on my side. She watches me with deep affection. I'm not going to let her out of my sight. First she hums softly, then her resonant voice begins to soar:

"Ah'm a long time travelin' heah below,
ah'm a long time a travelin' away from mah home . . .
ah'm a long time travelin' heah below,
gonna lay this body down!
Now when I kin read my title clear,
two mansions in the sky . . .
ah'll bid farewell to every fear,
ah'll wipe my weepin' eye . . ."

"God, Gracie, ah remember that one so well," I whimper when the song has finished. "Now sing the one about the angels, okay?"

She lets out a boisterous chuckle.

"You shore haven't changed one bit, Miss Sandy! Now ah gotta 'member how that one goes. Let me see . . ."

I watch with anticipation—then deep concentration—as she closes her eyes, tosses her head back and lets her voice sail out to blend with the sound of the Atlantic surf,

"Mah latest sun is sinking fast . . . the race is almost run,
mah strongest trials now are past, mah triumph is begun . . .
Oh come angel band! Come and around me stand,
bear me away on your snowy wings, to mah immortal home,
bear me away on your snowy wings, to mah immortal home . . ."

Her song is lulling me into a deep, untroubled sleep. Entering a dreamland of childhood memories, I recall the shimmering yellow heat . . . the abundant shades of green . . . the fresh, sweet, sweltering smells—always those smells . . .

~2~
Julia

I awake inhaling cool, moist air. Something heavy and musty is covering my body. My eyes focus on a brown cowboy boot and denim pants. Looking up with a start, I see John sitting next to me. His folded arms leaning against his knees, he stares pensively at a misty, white-capped sea.

"John!" I cry, sitting up and gawking.

"Well, hello there, dear! You've rested well—I thought you needed it." He grins at me sympathetically, pats my head and continues. "It's great to have you back. You've been through a lot! You have to take care of yerself."

I throw off the cape which has been covering me and inspect the rough, faded material we're sitting on. There is a large, white umbrella over our heads. I search for the picnic basket.

"Want somethin' to drink?" John asks casually.

He reaches into a weather-beaten wicker basket and . . . it's the same basket! Not only is it old and worn, but it looks like somebody sat on it.

"Sure, I'd love something to drink," I answer, entirely distracted.

Looking around, I see we are settled in a tiny cove at low tide. Slippery, green moss covers the wet stones on the shore-line, which is shadowed by huge, eroded boulders looming to the right.

"Have you been waiting a long time?" I ask.

"What's time to an immortal?" John says nonchalantly, handing me a cold can of beer.

"You know, John, I never counted on this being so real when I started off. I was afraid it was merely an artistic endeavor. But now . . ."

He blinks, looking worn. His long hair is ruffled and parted down the middle. He seems older and more weather-beaten— like a hardened sailor or sea captain—yet also feminine and refined.

"It's something I wanted to tell you from the onset," he says, "but it wouldn't have worked! It was somethin' you needed to come to on yer own—through yer own efforts. It wouldn't have been the same if I'd told you."

"I can appreciate that. It reminds me of being a parent—there are so many things I'd love to do for my offspring, to help them grow."

"That's what I mean. They've gotta do it themselves."

"I don't think I'll ever get over Gracie, though," I say sadly, sipping my beer.

"You don't have to," he replies, letting out a modest belch.

"But sometimes—she seems to outshine even you."

"She's *in me*, dear. Her Life is eternal. Remember?"

I lunge at John to hug him, spilling beer on the faded cloth.

"Help me to remember that, okay?"

"That shan't be difficult," he answers, joking in his deep voice. "Shall we go for a walk?"

He stands up and I follow, realizing my long, pink frock has turned into a kelly-green jumpsuit.

"If I had all these clothes on earth, I'd have to get a bigger closet," I think.

"Let's walk in that direction," John says, pointing to our left. "Actually, it was my idea to leave this place. That is, if you want to . . ."

"Of course!"

"I promised I'd show you my school, right? I'll let you in on a secret—in many ways, you've been attendin' parts of it with me. Yer part of my school this very moment! The principle of learning is at work everywhere."

"You mean we're always going to school?"

"Aye—starting with yer exclusive School of Life on earth, which specializes in instructing folks that within the physical world there are hidden universal laws which need to be complied with. And once a person leaves this material world, he enters another place of learnin'! Ultimately it's like goin' to the Quarry Bank High School for Boys, only a little nicer," John cackles.

"So, it's not something you can escape once you die, like most people think."

He laughs again. "Sorry. Everybody is *always* goin' to school, even if they know nothin' about it. Learning never stops, whether it be in the physical *or* spiritual world. You can't escape it, although one often wishes he could! You should understand more about the details—how it works for me. You could meet some of the gang I hang out with, some of me old friends."

"Like Basil, you mean."

"And you can't get a better friend than him. I don't know what I would've done without him in me latest Cycle a' Bloom."

"Cycle of Bloom?"

"That's what we call a period of growth which can be measured and reviewed," John says, motioning with his hands, "like a flowering plant tended by its keepers."

"What sort of keepers?"

"The teachers, and our higher self which illuminates our soul."

Breakers thundering to our right, we continue walking along this broad stretch of sand while I listen to John's explanation.

"Ya see, everything we do Here is bein' formulated by our awareness. Because there is no physical world Here, everything happens outside the realm of time."

"How can there be change outside the realm of time?"

"Change is awareness," he says. "Spirit is fluid, just like those waves."

"Oh."

"Your thought-forms are establishing yer reality on earth. It usually takes longer because it's a physical world you live in. Because of time and space on earth, a person can afford to make mistakes. You see, there's more of a gap between cause and effect."

I look at him with questioning eyes.

"There is more of an interlude between the projection of a thought-form and its eventual outcome in the physical world. If you recognize this, you can see why earth is like a kindergarten. It's good fer certain types of souls to develop a basic connection between what they *think* and what they *create*, without fuckin' up their physical existence the moment they have negative or destructive thoughts! In other words, it usually takes awhile on earth for people's thoughts to manifest. In the meantime, earthlings have time to learn what to do with negative thought-forms—to transform them into positive action. Get it?"

"I think so."

"That's the big trip on earth. No easy task!" John snorts. "As you can see, it's about a soul becoming aware of the fact that it's responsible for the reality it formulates—*every precious moment of it*."

He looks at me with enormous, animated eyes.

"And you mean to say," I ask, "on earth we're given the phenomenon of time to experiment with our inventiveness before we can actually screw things up?"

"Yeah. It's like giving a bunch of children leeway to indulge themselves as they learn. Time and space give them the chance to ponder their suffering. The problem is so many people screw it up, then get into a bigger mess. The souls inhabiting planet earth are primarily concerned with what it means to be responsible for their actions, both mental and physical, and to discover the deep-seated patterns, conscious or otherwise, which cause them to act as they do."

"And how does this differ from the learning Here?" I ask.

The sunshine is so bright that I wish I were wearing a hat, and instantly I feel cool shade covering my face. I'm wearing a white tennis visor now, but John doesn't seem to notice.

"Learning Here is instantaneous," he continues, "yet less consequential. In order to incorporate what's been learned Here into the system of the entity, the higher self needs to be grounded in physical existence on a planet which is willing to cooperate."

"Wow! That's what I've been waiting to hear about. Can you tell me about life on other planets?"

Skipping and jumping, I face John.

"Sho'nuff honey child," he says, giving me a playful push. "Many of 'em are just like earth! But you're gonna have to wait for the right time. First I'm gonna take you on one hell of a trip."

"But when you tell me a planet has to *cooperate* with somebody . . . ?"

"For a soul to ground its learning, ya mean?"

"Yes. What are you suggesting by that?"

He gets a mad gleam in his eyes.

"I mean 'the hip bone's connected to the, uh! tail bone, and the tail bone's connected to the, uh! leg bone, and the leg bone . . .' "

He starts to dance and gyrate his hips.

"John!" I pretend to hit him.

"No, I mean . . . every planet has rules and regulations which need to be respected," he continues, deadpan, "and a soul has to fit into a particular system that relates to its own awareness and perception. Otherwise it would be like tryin' to mix rock 'n roll with dixieland jazz."

He persists in dancing and playing, and then sings in a loud, nasal voice: "If you knew, Peggy Sue, then you'd know why I can't do, without Peggy . . . my Peggy Sue-ooh-ooh . . . well I love you gal . . ."

I stand still, giggling as John clowns.

"I consider myself very lucky, John," I shout. "I could have needed to write a story about my past lives with Nikita Kruschev . . . or Sigmund Freud."

". . . Pretty, pretty, pretty, pretty Peggy Sue . . . oh Peggy, my Peggy Sue-ooh-ooh . . ."

There is a frenzy of snickering as John races ahead of me with bowed legs, and arms spread wide open as if in pursuit of something.

"Mammy, mammy!" he cries in a mock-female voice.

I don't know what he is doing and am waiting for the next laugh. At this moment, I see a female figure in front of him who looks familiar.

"Why, hallo there, Julia!" I hear John saying brightly in a normal voice. The two of them embrace. I am stunned to realize this is John's mother. He spins around to look at me, his eyes sparkling.

"Linda, I'd like you to meet my mother, Julia."

I'm awe-struck as I stare at this slender, auburn-haired woman. She smiles impishly, and it's as if I'm looking at the female image of John.

"I'm thrilled to meet you!" I say, hurrying forward to greet her. With twinkling eyes she receives me graciously, holding my hands in hers.

"And I've heard so much about *you*, dear. It's not often we get visitors this far over! You enjoyin' yerself Here, are you?"

She lets go of my hands. I am charmed by her accent, which is identical to John's. I want to burst into laughter.

"Oh yes!" I answer. "I'm having the best time imaginable. I never realized it could be so much fun. Of course, I'm grateful to John for providing such lively entertainment."

She looks at her son with pride. "He's great at it . . . that's fer sure!"

"Ain't it grand ta see two lovely redheads standin' side-by-side," John boasts like a youth. "An' two old pals of mine ta boot!"

"Now, Johnny . . . have you shown her the Learnin' Tree yet?"

"No, not yet. But say no more, 'cause I'm savin' it fer a surprise."

"Oh m'gosh. I'm sorry if I spoilt it . . ."

"You haven't spoiled anything, Julia," I say. "I haven't the slightest idea what you're talking about. But I'm delighted to meet you this way."

"The pleasure is certainly mine, dear."

She grins at me again and runs a delicate hand through shiny, bobbed locks.

"Say, John, I just happened ta hear from a friend about the next Nine meetin'—you gonna be there?"

"Sure, Mum. I was planning to . . . 'twas great ta see you again so soon."

Mother and son embrace, then she is gone—vanished into the air.

"She's in my group, but not my sub-group," John informs me.

"Oh. What does that mean?"

"It means Mum and I are learning at the same school; we're in the same cycle group, but our theme and topic groups are different."

"Gee, that explains it . . . now I understand everything," I reply sarcastically. "Hey, I realize how tired I am. If I go home now, where will I find you next?"

"We'll be wending our way to the meadow! Then we'll go beyond—way beyond, in fact—but I miss the old pastures right now, don't you?"

"God, I'd love to go there. But, do you see your mother often?"

"Aye. Isn't she great? As I told you, she was one of the first ta meet me when I came over. We've been inseparable ever since."

A pelican with a flailing fish in its mouth lands on a rock offshore. We watch it rapidly gobble its ocean snack.

"See those dunes over there?" John points to the left. "Well, there's a trail that'll lead us back. But it's important fer us to take *that* trail. I mean, don't try ta go directly to the meadow."

"Whatever you say, Johnny."

"Way to go, Lin. I'm glad you're havin' so much fun."

"I wouldn't do it if it wasn't."

"Neither would I."

We hit our open palms together noisily and I'm gone.

~3~
Number Nine

The sky is a brilliant, cloudless blue. I am waiting to find
John on a hilly trail lined with dense vegetation: fennel, wild
mustard and radish, poppies and lupin. I walk slowly, experiencing every step, for in this world it's easy to merge with my
surroundings. I'm on a different path than the one we followed
on our journey toward the Mystical Ocean so long ago. I hadn't
expected it to end the way it did; I couldn't have guessed the
amazing things that would happen there.

As the path dips and bends, I see John sitting on a large
boulder to my left.

"Aye-aye, captain!" he shouts in a shrill voice. He's wearing
a funny, brown felt hat with a feather in it.

"No, you've got it wrong, Johnny—you're the captain!" I
retort.

Except for John's new hat, we look as we did before, down
to the white visor on my head.

"Oh, ye speak the god-awful truth . . ."

He hits his forehead with an open palm, knocks his hat off,
then puts it on again.

". . . why, what a madcap hath heaven lent us here!"

I wrinkle my nose. "Shakespeare?"

John nods in mock seriousness and jumps down from his
perch.

187

"Why do you lend such solemn brows on me? Think you I bear the shears of destiny? Have I commandment on the pulse of life?"

As he speaks, he stares at me with a crazy grin. He leans toward me and whispers, "King John."

"Oh really? You mean Shakespeare."

"How's it goin' kid?"

"Nervous."

"Whatcha nervous for?"

"Well, this morning as I lay half-asleep, you were telling me about your school, weren't you?"

"Yeah, I was. And you dreamed about me last night, but I don't think you remember it."

"After waking up, it felt as if I'd been busy. But I can't recall what it was about, only that you were telling me certain words."

"Such as?"

"Arcadia."

"Right! The name of my school here! Very good." He pats me on the shoulder. "Anything else?"

"Yeah. The Blue Ray," I answer cautiously, as if taking an examination.

"Excellent! The name of one of my sub-groups." John begins to bounce up and down. "Shall we mosey on? This path is gonna take us to where we started, with a little detour on the way—something extra you'll appreciate."

"I'm sure I will. Everything Here boggles my mind."

"Just wait 'til ya see where we're going!"

"Don't talk about that yet! I might get weird."

"The weirder the better, I say."

I glare at him. "Okay, spill the beans. Tell me about your school."

"Right. You know the name of it: Arcadia. Look up the meaning in your Oxford Illustrated the next chance you get. This school is large—one of the largest in our solar system. The place has assorted groups 'n sub-groups, beginning with the cycle group. Mine is called Number Nine."

"Huh. What are the other groups called?"

"They're numbered from one to nine, but each has its own theme and topic groups, so it isn't hierarchical."

"You mean, it doesn't indicate you're more evolved if you're a nine?"

"Correct. Everybody *is* evolved to a certain degree. To fit into the Arcadian School, you need ta be of a particular persuasion—we only get souls Here who understand and respect the laws of nature."

A magpie lands on a nearby rock and inspects us with dark, beady eyes.

"And how does a cycle group function?"

"Number Nine Cycle Group has all levels of development, just as every number has. A cycle provides the key elements needed by a developing soul for a series of Expressions—this varies from a few to several hundred Expressions, depending on what the soul is able to absorb and learn." John looks at me quizzically. "Get it?"

"I think so," I say. "Go ahead—this is *great*."

"Okay. The next major division separating the cycle groups into smaller, more homogeneous circles is the theme group. Mine is the Blue Ray."

"It sounds beautiful," I say, looking ahead speculatively.

"And the color of each theme or topic group has subdivisions, which is gonna get hopelessly complicated if I explain it in detail. That's why I put it off so long."

"That's okay. I get the basic idea, anyway . . . I think."

"Now, last but not least, me topic group is called the Green Wave. All of the Arcadian groups can join and overlap in the most peculiar ways. I'm eager to tell you about it, but I'm so awfully limited. It's known to be one of the most difficult tasks of all . . . to try to explain these realities to an earthling. Usually, they are only able to have vague dreams or recollections about it. Or they simply remember it all once they've returned—which might take awhile for some—depending on their circumstances."

"It makes me dizzy."

"I can imagine. That's the way I felt when I first came Here."

The broad path veers again, and we continue enjoying the scent of plants, flowers, balmy air and rich soil.

"John, can you tell me how many souls attend your school?"

"It runs into the billions, but don't forget, we cross over into other solar systems. There are other schools similar to Arcadia, but I didn't want to get into that right now."

"No, let's not! But tell me how many souls are taking part in your theme and topic groups?" I step over a large snail crossing our path.

"That's easy. There's about 500,000 in my Blue Ray theme, and 5,000 in my subdivision. My Green Wave topic has about 600, and my subdivision has seven."

"I hope I don't have to comprehend all this precisely."

John looks at me with his hat pulled down so it almost covers his eyes. He pretends to be stern and says, scowling, "Memorize all of this and turn in yer written report tomorrow morning!"

"Hey, you look like a high school teacher I used to have! Okay . . . I'm going to let this sink in a bit, if you don't mind."

"And, ta make it more interesting, yer gonna get ta meet the Group of Seven . . . once."

"You mean, the subdivision of the subdivision? How will I recognize them?"

" 'Cause I'm gonna introduce you, that's how."

"And Julia?"

"She's in my Number Nine Cycle, but not in the Blue Ray Large Circle."

"That means she has lessons similar to yours?"

"In many ways, yes. But there is a distinction between her methods and mine."

I heave a deep sigh. "I have so many questions, but I don't know how to ask them."

"It's a good thing, 'cause it's not healthy ta hear too much at once. It's not good for yer earthly brain."

"I suppose you're right."

At this moment, I'm startled by a man with short brown hair wearing a dark blue suit and tie walking toward us. He seems to be lost in thought and doesn't notice our presence.

"Hey Brian! You better watch where you're goin'!" John bellows.

"Oh my gosh . . . I'm sorry! I didn't see you. I'm in a hurry—I forgot an appointment!"

"Why don't you project yerself, then? Why do ya hafta *walk*?" John looks irritated.

"No, no! This is part of the designation. I must walk and enjoy the surroundings. Otherwise, the appointment will mean nothing—absolutely nothing!"

"Well, bloody hell Brian. Why the fuck don't you *enjoy* yerself then? Ya look like yer mother just reincarnated!"

"Oh cut it out, John! Do you always have to rub it in? You've caught me at an odd moment, that's all. I passed my theme evaluation with flying colors! That's better than you can say for yourself."

"Hey, Brian . . . I'm sorry. Yer right! I didn't get more than a six the last time. I promised the ol' teach I'd work harder in the future. Anyway, you'd better get going, or you'll miss yer meeting."

"Right'o! Godspeed!"

The man hurries away, doing his best to appear happy.

"John! Was that Brian Epstein?"

"It sure as hell was. Sometimes I wonder about that guy! He did seem improved, more self-confident or something."

"I wouldn't know. He certainly was introverted—he didn't even see me."

"One thing about ol' Brian, you shouldn't take his inadequacies personally. He has a lot to work out with women—but it's something he won't solve until he's in another body. Who can say? He might need to be a chick next time around."

"Yeah, why not? Might solve the whole thing."

"I wouldn't doubt it."

"But John . . ."

"Yes, my earthling?"

"Are all the entities we meet here part of the Arcadian school? Would it be possible for me to meet someone here from the outside? From another school?"

"That's a good question. Normally, the answer is 'no.' Under exceptional circumstances, we're allowed to break the rules and cross over into foreign domains. It would only be done under the supervision of a high teacher; and even then, it would be subject to constant scrutiny! A soul that becomes lost outside its own realm can become irretrievably misplaced!"

"Forever?"

"Sometimes . . . it depends. There *are* rescue missions. But a lost soul is a soul without guardianship or a system of reference, floating in a timeless sea of infinity! This rarely happens, so don't worry yer pretty little head about it."

"Well, thanks. So it wouldn't be normal for someone to switch schools mid-semester?"

"No, like I said, it would be rare. If a soul decides to attend another school, it might spend several Expressions taking the step . . . with help from the Sovereign Council. But, many of us Here have been coming since the beginning of our creation."

"And am *I* included in this Arcadian system?"

"Whadaya think? Of course!"

"I'm feeling dizzy again. Shall we sit down and rest?"

"Sure. I know just the spot. You'll have to walk a bit further ta get there. Can you handle it?"

"Oh sure . . . but I won't mind resting as soon as possible."

Hearing these abstract ideas has puzzled me. I decide to not ask more questions about Arcadia for awhile and sense John's understanding.

We emerge from the thick vegetation and approaching a wide, flat, open area which is covered with orange-brown grasses and sprinkled with grey boulders.

"There's yer resting place, lady. Why don't we sit on those luv'ly, smooth rocks. It'll be nice."

"Great. It's good to see open space again."

"There he is, the old beggar!" John says, slapping the side of his leg.

Directly in front of us, a disheveled man appears in a state of total confusion.

"Who *is* he?" I ask with alarm.

"It's Freddie, Freddie Lennon—me *dad*. But he can't see *us*."

"What's wrong with him?"

"Oh, it's part of his scene. Everybody Here is working on *some* aspect of their Past Mode Expressions, an' this role of beggar is one of 'em. But we've gotta be able ta leave each other alone! You need ta let folks be who they are. We're not allowed ta interfere with each other's process—unless it's ta give moral support. Too much sympathy can ruin it, ya know. It's not healthy ta take someone's problem away—they'll end up gettin' mad an' lookin' fer another one."

I stare horrified at the beggar.

"He'll be okay," John says. "I promise!"

We watch as he disappears clumsily into the bushes. Climbing onto a huge, flat rock and inspecting our surroundings, we look skyward to see an eagle flying toward the sea. John takes off his hat and sets it down next to him.

"Well," I sigh a few moments later, "a few weeks ago Aart felt compelled to go to a bookstore and look through the magazines, but didn't know why. He felt drawn into the store. What do you suppose he brought home?"

"Beats me."

"He brought home a Dutch magazine article about Mark Chapman! It told about what he's thinking and doing in prison. I was terribly affected by reading it, though it clarified things. He explains he didn't see you as a real person when he shot you, but as a personification of his own defeat. He projected his problems on you because he wasn't able to solve them himself. At the time, he was mad at you, and the act was an outburst of his fears and insecurities about personal mistakes. Murdering you was actually a kind of suicide . . ."

"Uh-huh," John nods calmly.

"What impressed me most is his remark, 'I am responsible for what I've done because I was refusing to accept my own problems at the time . . .' He's sorry he did it, yet has accepted his deed. In the last ten years, he's accepted responsibility for his actions, however sick they were at the time. Later in the article he says, 'John Lennon stepped out of the car and looked at me—he didn't smile—only looked at me very emphatically and then walked past. The devil was standing behind me at this moment, but after the shots were fired, he abandoned me.' What do you think about this—about the man who took your life?"

John looks at me with tranquillity. His brown eyes are wide and expressive, showing a strange kind of composure.

"I've got love and respect for the guy. He built his own hell and had the guts to admit it. He didn't blame anyone but himself. I suppose this is the biggest lesson a person can learn."

"But aren't you sorry he killed you?"

"It's a complicated story. On one level, of course I'm sorry. I would have preferred to stay with my family and end my life as a happy old fart living on a little island off the coast of Ireland. That was my idea of a good time. But like Mark Chapman, I'm accountable for the reality I made."

I look at him thoughtfully. "What do you mean?"

"I mean that killer and victim fit together like hand and glove."

"Yes . . ."

"And during my entire life, I had subconscious fears about getting shot. Sometimes, during periods of stress, they surfaced to consciousness. It was a morbid obsession. I didn't think about it every day, but when I got depressed or felt lost, I'd see myself getting shot and wonder what it would be like."

"Not very pleasant, I suppose."

"Yer right. It wasn't! I won't devise *that* particular incident for myself again. What I mean to say is I hold no grudges against, and even feel love for, Mark Chapman. I think it's important for him to know this."

"But isn't loving your murderer going a bit too far?"

"Not at all. I generated my own death. Not consciously, but I have ta take responsibility for the fact that my own fears attracted someone who had the power to kill me. If I had become free of that fear, I wouldn't have attracted a reaction to the fear. On another level, Chapman was *my* victim . . . don't you see the paradox?"

"I suppose I do."

"Chapman and I were made for each other, we satisfied the other's subconscious requirements. He talks about being driven against his will to kill me. And he talks about bein' tempted by the devil. These are his ways of describing his psychic bond with the dark side of Life and the greater cosmic plan. It took guts for him to do what he felt he had to!"

"But how can you actually love him?"

"I've been ta visit him in prison more than once. He wasn't aware of it, ya know—I'm sure it would be too much for him to bear. When I saw his face and eyes, I knew he was an empathetic and religious guy. He reminded me of myself! I wanted to tell him not to feel bad . . . it was painful . . . I'm still sorry for the bloke."

"Because he is still suffering and you're not?"

"Something along those lines. Because he's more alone than I am, even now I identify a lot with his state of mind."

I look at John and am shaken, for he resembles a guru or holy man at this moment.

"Is there anything you'd like to tell him right now?"

"I would like to tell him I forgive him. And that he can build a new life without guilt, fear or doubt—knowing,too, that he has been totally absolved by the high teachers."

My thoughts are being transported again to that Vast Ocean. With a strange taste of salt in my mouth, I am reminded of tears—not only my own, but those of an infinity of human beings as well. I know all sorrow and joy can be felt and cleansed at this place where water pounds on willing and receptive soil. I know Life can be forever turned anew.

"You okay, dear?"

"Oh, yeah . . . I'm okay. Sometimes it's just too much to take."

"That used to be one of my favorite aphorisms. I'm working on accepting that Life is as profound as you wanna make it. The sky is the limit—literally."

A tiny breeze has come up. I take a deep breath and observe billowy clouds in the sky. Two blackbirds land nearby and peck at the ground.

"John, there's something I want to ask you about this place."

"Shoot." He makes a silly face and I pretend to hit him.

"This abode which you call 'heaven,' or 'Infinite Dwelling,' or 'Arcadia'—is it always a paradise? I mean, it all seems so easy. What is 'hell,' then?"

John plays with his hat, then speaks. "You realize every soul is devising its own reality in any school you choose to participate in—physical or nonphysical—right? There are folks in Arcadia who are making their own hell at this very moment! We can't *see* it because, together, we have chosen to manifest something else. It's that basic. If a soul needs a particular lesson Here, it's gonna give itself an oil spill or two, or a toxic waste dump which is gonna kill off everything precious to it. There'll be no birds, nor beasts, nor verdant fields, 'cause it's all dead and gone."

"Then you're saying it's the same principle at work Here as on earth."

"As above, so below . . ."

"And do these souls get help to escape their own hell?"

"Thank God, they do! That's what teachers are for! No one is expected to solve their problems alone. There's always help and encouragement if you're capable of taking the responsibility for yer existence."

"I'm happy," I say, "you and I are sitting here instead of in a toxic waste dump."

"The feelin' is mutual, kid. But, to be honest with you, it hasn't always been this easy."

He looks up at the clouds with interest.

"How do you mean?" I ask.

"When I first got here, I was repeatedly caught in a relentless blizzard, gale, cyclone or hurricane. Or I'd find meself trapped in a fuckin' lion's den, runnin' away from a swarm of bees or drowning in a dark and creepy lake! Once—no matter what I did or said—I couldn't get the sun to rise! It refused ta listen. It was hopeless."

"What did you do?"

"In the beginning, I didn't care—I felt so humiliated. And then I prayed. I just fuckin' prayed! It was like givin' myself up to the teachers . . . to Mr. God and Mrs. Goddess, or whatever you want to call it. Initially it was hell because nothing happened.

Nothing! I thought I'd gone out of Arcadia—like one of those derelict souls, lost outside its domain! Irretrievably misplaced! I was scared shitless."

I look at him in suspense.

"Then it happened! As I repeated one of the prayers I'd learned from a high teacher when I first arrived—with every bit of faith and hope left in me—I perceived an exquisite sunrise on the horizon! It's impossible to describe my joy. It was something like—don't give up hope—there's always help somewhere you didn't know about, didn't remember how ta *see*. You just gotta be open to it in ways you don't expect. That's the key to it all, I think. I haven't been the same since."

~4~
Circle on the Stone

John puts on his hat and jumps to the ground.

"You up ta goin' further now?"

Adjusting my visor, I slide off the rock and join him on the soft soil.

"Naturally," I say. "Where to?"

"We're gonna meet people . . . souls. Well, you know what I mean."

"At the meadow?"

"Maybe. But fer starters, I'm gonna take you on that detour I was tellin' you about."

"Oh good! You certainly have a way of keeping things exciting."

He moves to our left through the tall grass, which soon leads us to a small, flat path. I see thick, green vegetation, sprinkled with greater stitchwort and its delicate white flowers. The path is becoming so narrow I have to walk behind John. As we walk, I hear him whistling softly.

After an interlude of peaceful traveling, I see a grove of trees in the distance and let out a deep sigh. John spins around.

"Too much for you?" he asks.

"No! Oh no. I'm excited and don't know why."

"You'll find out soon, sister!"

He faces ahead again, and we continue walking. I become pleasantly distracted—this time by the dazzling yellow and black plumage of a golden oriole.

Soon I realize the trees we're nearing are giant oaks.

"Do you remember those?" John asks, turning his head.

"I'm not sure. I don't recognize them."

"We're approaching them from the other side. Have you forgotten—on the way ta the stream—when we left the meadow so long ago?"

"Is that where we are? Right! I do recall them. I was intrigued—but didn't get the chance to visit. It's where Basil disappeared once."

John chuckles and points toward the groves.

"Shall we, milady?"

"We shall."

Walking the final stretch of path, we find two enormous megaliths forming a gateway into a lavish sanctuary of green foliage. Inspecting the gigantic, pointed stones more closely, I see many intricate, spiralled patterns chiseled artistically into them.

Passing through the gateway of stone, we are stepping into a new realm of cool tranquillity. Its imposing greenery imparts a strange awesomeness; these majestic giants are growing, unmistakably, in the configuration of a large circle.

They are obviously ancient. My mood has altered drastically since entering the stone portal. I am like a fairy queen who has unwittingly returned to her place of origin and suddenly realizes she is ready for her next enchanted calling. In the coolness of the surroundings, it seems alive with mysterious force—gentle, yet mighty.

I glance at John, who appears equally fascinated. We are subtly joined—yet totally separate—in our private worlds. There is no need to speak.

Shattering the silence, a terrifying squeal erupts from behind a nearby tree. It's a wild boar! Beside it is a fat sow with a litter of scruffy piglets. I see the image of them attacking us, and my blood runs cold. I see their sharp, protruding fangs! In the next instant, however, they move away from us—their short, stubby legs moving full speed.

Breathing deeply, we slowly begin to enter the circle of oaks—through thick, moist grass—trying to grasp the meaning of this place. The air is damp and earthy. Nearing the center of the tree-circle, we observe a small, standing stone. Inspecting it closely, we see a circle divided into quadrants deeply chiseled in its smooth, dark surface.

Again, I experience an odd cognizance of homecoming, as if I know instinctively why I'm here and what I'll do. I'm aware of John going through the same process. Silently, we remove our hats, shoes and socks, and roll up our pants. We walk in the direction of the line we saw chiseled on the stone in the right quadrant of the circle. With cold, wet grass sinking under our feet, we tread slowly and carefully toward one of the trees with our open hands facing the ground.

Approaching one of the aged, gnarled oaks, we place our open palms together in front of us, our fingers pointing upward in the posture of prayer.

"May there be peace in the East," we say in unison.

Beside these leafy giants, we continue walking slowly in a clockwise direction with arms at our sides, open palms facing the ground.

Coming to a specific spot along the circumference of the oak circle, John and I stop instinctively to face another large tree, repeating our stance of joined palms pointing upward.

"May there be peace in the South," we proclaim.

Captive in our world of remote recollections, a quality of understanding grows in me with every step I take. *Clearly, I am John's sister.* Together we are fulfilling appointed tasks as part of a well-known ritual. I look at him; he winks and turns to face another tree. The ceremony resumes as we walk around the circle until we come to another significant stopping point.

"May there be peace in the West," we say together in our special pose, near the stone gateway.

Then we embark on the last phase of our slow, clockwise transit which ends at another massive oak.

"May there be peace in the North."

More images flood my mind and I wonder, "Why didn't I remember this before?" I'm a different person—dark-haired and green-eyed—and my brother is reflecting my image like a shining mirror.

A primitive, abstract awareness in me intensifies. I quickly associate it with the scent of the surroundings. Continuing along the circle, we retrace our path toward the eastern tree, then back to the center.

"May there be peace in the Universe," my brother and I say stalwartly, standing again near the circle on the stone.

Stepping gently, we return to the eastern tree and travel around the circle, this time going counterclockwise. I slowly regain my own personality, and John is looking and acting like himself again.

As this is happening, a steadily-growing force is building in my mind and body. As our second circle is completed at the eastern tree, I have acquired a new level of perception.

"Go again to the center," John says calmly, yet firmly.

As we do this, it's as if I'm having a lucid dream or responding to a powerful psychedelic drug. When John looks at me, his eyes have a new depth that makes me shiver.

"The way you are now," he says softly, "is what it's *always* like to be in Arcadia."

I look fixedly at the colorful, shimmering energy field surrounding his head and face and try to focus on the significance of his words.

"You mean . . . you're always this spaced out?"

I try to highlight my visual attention on John's eyes.

"In a way, yeah. But ya get used to it. It's different for an earthling. This is as close as I'm gonna get in trying to describe it to you. I think you get the message."

"I think so! I hope I can function this way."

"It won't last, dear—don't worry. It'll help you understand things and become more a part of my world. So far you've always had one foot in yours and another in mine. I thought it might be a trip for you to experience this other state-of-being and try to translate it into words."

"That's difficult," I say, "I don't think I can!"

"Everything is possible, *Sis*. See what happens."

I stare at him, smiling, but bewildered. In this whirl and blur of light and color, there is something else going on. I begin to hear funny sounds like whispering. Yet the whispers don't always sound human—but rather like the rustling of the oak leaves surrounding us, sometimes turning into the soft murmuring of a brook or the song of a cricket. My four-dimensional perception seems to be growing steadily. I drop to the ground for comfort and safety.

"Listen! Listen to us!" the voices of the whispering leaves seem to be saying, slowly becoming more audible.

Resting on the grass now, I close my eyes and feel lucky that John is nearby.

"Listen! Listen to us!" the voices cry.

I must readjust my ears to be capable of hearing. I am used to the ways and words of the human whisper—not that of leaves! I am ill-prepared.

"I'm listening! Go ahead . . . speak!" I plead.

There is more rustling and swishing for a moment as I focus my concentration to receive the message, "Under the stone!"

"Which stone?" I whisper.

"Under the stone! The circle stone!"

As I open my eyes, I'm blinded by a bright light. I crawl toward the magic rock and touch it.

"How can I lift it?" I cry out. It puzzles me that John is not bothered by the brilliant light.

"Here . . . I'll help you!" he answers.

Together we push and shove, and I hear an unusual sound coming from underneath—the sound of stone grating on something hollow. As we manage to dislodge the stone and push aside the thick grass, we discover it is sitting on top of a small, weather-beaten, wooden trap door.

"Open the door! Enter the land!" the voices are calling.

"But I'm afraid!" I answer. My heart is pounding, and I have the urge to cry.

"Open the door! Enter the land!" the voices insist.

I look at John, who appears unruffled.

"Go ahead . . . let's do it. I'm sure we can manage."

Together we grasp a rusty iron ring connected to the trap door and start to pull. There is a creaking sound as the door budges with difficulty. My heart keeps on pounding, and I feel sick to my stomach.

"Enter the land! Enter the land!" the voices coax.

"I don't *want* to!" I yell, but it's too late.

~5~
Dreadful Things

I watch John slink down through the small trap door into a chamber of darkness. I feel myself, too, being pulled by a force of gravity much stronger than I am accustomed to.

"Be careful!" I scream.

He doesn't respond. He continues descending and I follow.

Along smoothly-worn stone steps, we are pulled away from the blinding light into a dark chamber smelling of damp, fecund soil. The chamber has a hard, cold rock floor and a low, rough, cave-like ceiling. The air is cool and disturbingly still.

Two bats flap noisily past our faces, and I gasp and shriek. The sound echoes in the large space we are occupying.

"God!" I say. "What're we supposed to do now?"

John looks around in astonishment.

"There's one thing for sure, Lin," he says, his voice echoing deeply, "you gotta *keep calm*. I've learned me lesson more than once in circumstances like this! There's a lesson in *everything*— give yerself the chance to figure out what it is. You can only do that if you keep yer head."

He looks at me harshly and continues, "I told you about this! Now you see what I mean. It's good for you. Life ain't just a bowl of cheerios, ya know."

"You're right, but I was hoping to avoid scary times like this."

Our mumbled voices echo against great walls of stone.

"And spoil a good opportunity?"

"Well, can I help it if I'm chicken?" I sigh.

"I, too, was such a god-damned chicken it wasn't even funny! I sympathize with you. It's part of earth's conditioning. But I've had the opportunity to get over it since I came Here."

"Does that mean you're going to lead the way?"

"Do you want me to?"

"You're damned right I do!"

"Okay. No problem! Let's keep movin'."

He looks more serious than I would have expected, and I wonder if there is danger ahead.

"Are these the challenges which face you in Arcadia? It was looking so easy! Where's our merry meadow when we need it?"

"Linda—forget the merry meadow right now!" John snaps. "It's a matter of integrity that you don't run away when something like this comes to meet you! It's a matter of probing for the meaning behind the event—what does it want to *tell* you? Those voices were answering a need in both of us to communicate better with our shadow side. And the nature forces are so bloody aware that both you and I are often lacking in that area! We were attracted to the oak circle because we need to take part in the Blueprint Rituals."

"Blueprint Rituals?"

"Yeah. You realize Arcadia is keeping the original nature rites alive and well, don't you? The turn and step of every dance; the word and note of every song and prayer; the shape and color of every painting, image or construction invented in nature's guise . . ."

"Thank goodness! It's unbearable that most of the ways of primitive man have been replaced by empty, passionless activities! It's disastrous how respect and appreciation for the basic principles of life have been forgotten . . ."

"Maybe it'll console you to know the blueprint for all of that is alive and well in Arcadia. The Eternal Plan will be sustained forever—somewhere."

"Somewhere . . . does this mean not on planet earth?"

"That depends on whether or not earthlings get their bloody act together."

"Speaking of getting an act together, what are we doing here
... standing barefooted under the cold ground having a
philosophical conversation? Are we going further or not?"

My four-dimensional consciousness has decreased, although
I don't feel particularly normal. But at this point, what's
normal?

Advancing further into the dark, we discover a large, standing
stone reaching above our heads. It is covered with elaborate,
spiraled markings and engenders an atmosphere of mysterious
power.

"These things are incredible," John says as he touches the
spirals. "They're like God's own fingerprints."

I am reluctant to touch it. After my ordeal with the voices and
the trap door, I don't want to encourage more secret forces
which I'm not sure I can deal with.

John steps aside and continues, undaunted. Because the glaring
light coming from outside is steadily dwindling, I'm wondering
how we're going to see anything. I remember horror films I saw
as a child that left me with recurring nightmares. I thought I had
been a victim of someone's poor taste. However, at this moment
I realize those youthful fears have new meaning and purpose
which had escaped me.

I think, too, about the initiations of Egyptian priests and
priestesses in which the entrant was forced to lie in a coffin-like
container for days in total blackness and isolation. This was
done to achieve proper links to higher spiritual guidance—a feat
which would either strengthen or destroy the seeker, and deem
him or her fit or unfit to be keeper of the higher knowledge.

"Things could be worse," I think to myself. I consider what
John told me about daring to face whatever comes along my
path and trying not to run away from the menacing, dreadful
things in life. Surely there is wisdom in this. I recall my solitary
visit to the cemetery in Liverpool and how, at a certain moment,
I needed to run out in disgust. What might have happened if I'd
stuck around? Would I have discovered something important to
John or me?

We proceed quietly through the chamber, and it seems my
eyes are capable of seeing in the dark.

"Just like a cat!"

"Yeah, thatsa girl!" John answers wryly.

We arrive at a door. It is heavy and wooden with rusty, iron latticework. Propped next to it are two slightly-bowed walking sticks.

"My Lord," I say, sucking in my breath.

"Yes. You've got it precisely."

John inspects one of the thick, gnarled sticks and leans it back against the wall. Reaching for the rusty iron latch on the door, he lifts it and pushes.

"Help me if you can," he grunts.

"Okay."

There is a grating noise of wood on stone as we push the heavy door open. My cat-like eyes search frantically for safe images. It smells musty and old. On the floor in front of us are two pairs of strange leather slippers embroidered with golden thread, their toes pointing upward. Like the walking sticks, they seem to have been placed here especially for John and me.

"Put these on," he says, his voice continuing to echo.

"Are these magic flying shoes like Dorothy received from the good witch of the North?" I ask, my voice bouncing off the walls.

"Perhaps something along those lines," John chortles.

I wipe the dust from my feet and put on the slippers, which fit perfectly. John does the same.

We notice a massive, roughly-hewn wooden table with six crudely-matched chairs. Draped over the two nearest chairs are familiar linen capes.

"Hey! How convenient!" I exclaim. "We can use those right now." I rush to retrieve the handsome cloak which I had last seen at the beach. I hug it and drape it over my shoulders.

Fingering the soft material, I say, "This is getting to be an old favorite."

"Aye, it is," John replies happily, putting his cloak on too.

With my exceptional vision, I discern objects on the table. Most striking is a large white candle in a beautifully-engraved golden holder. Next to it is a small metal box which John picks up and opens.

"This is ta light the candle with," he whispers. "Lemme see . . . ya hafta go like this . . ."

He strikes two unidentifiable objects—perhaps flint—together, and suddenly the candle has a vigorous flame which is an unexpected luxury to my light-starved eyes.

"This is fantastic!" I say. "Everything looks so different!"

The room has instantly acquired a safe, soothing ambience.

I gasp. "Look! The walls! They're covered with spirals, too!"

Indeed, the stone walls of this second large room are elaborately adorned with the same puzzling spirals on every visible surface.

"What do the engravings mean?" I ask.

"The spiral is an ancient symbol for eternal Life. It carries with it the never-ending movement of the path of individual existence."

"They're stunning," I sigh.

Our attention is drawn to other objects on the table: a large silver chalice, a crystal ball resting upon a wooden stand, a small Celtic cross carved out of wood and two peculiar spiraling bracelets in the form of snakes. They are made of shimmering gold, with jewels for eyes and tails.

"Look at these!" I say, pointing to the identical bracelets.

"Two again. Methinks we're supposed to put them on."

"Do you think it's okay? I've never worn anything like this before—they're gorgeous!"

"Count yer blessings while ye may."

John picks up one of the bracelets, and with some difficulty, slips his left wrist through the coil. It is wrapped around his lower arm with the head pointing upward.

"Am I not luv'ly?" John spoofs.

"Yes, you are! Why am I afraid of everything—where's my passion for adventure?"

"Right on."

I gingerly pick up the other bracelet, examine it for a moment and put it on. It's easier for me to get my wrist through, but I need to push it higher on my arm to keep it from falling off.

"Most esteemed Arcadian!" I say, bowing to John in my splendid new outfit of embroidered slippers with pointed toes, luxurious golden-brown cape and golden snake bracelet.

"Most revered earthling!" John retorts, bowing toward me with an outfit that mirrors mine.

"As above, so below . . ." I say proudly.

"Aye, truly!"

In the flickering candlelight, I see a big, black, furry spider walking along the edge of the table. I shriek.

"Let's go further!" John gasps, and we move swiftly away from the table's end. He picks up the lighted candle from the right side of the table. I move to the left, both of us keeping more than an arm's length from the horrible creature.

"I agree with you, Linda. I wouldn't mind bein' in our sunny meadow sipping a beer, listenin' to the birds, havin' a good, old-fashioned chat!"

"That's kind of you to acknowledge."

"Yeah, but see that door over there?" He points to the other side of the table.

"Yes?"

"Well . . . we may think it fine to mosey out of here and make our way to the meadow, but I'm *sure* that's not what we're supposed to do."

"Oh? What are we *supposed* to do?"

He points dramatically to the second door.

"We've fuckin' well gotta go through *that* door."

"What if I don't want to?" I say soberly, suddenly drained of energy.

"I don't think it matters. Out of valuable experience, I'd say we're intended to go through that door—otherwise we might miss a big chance."

"Chance for what?" I glance at the spider resting comfortably on the crystal ball.

"The chance to learn something important about ourselves."

"Does it really work that way?"

"It does Here—in Arcadia—and it usually works that way on earth, too . . . although it's not always as obvious as it is Here.

I mean, on earth it can be even more difficult to be sure of which decisions to make, because the consequences can be so final."

John glances warily at the spider.

"But right now," I say, "you're sure we have to keep searching this creepy place . . . because we might discover information important to us, important for our growth."

"Right."

"Okay. I'm prepared. But you have to open the next door yourself."

Gripping the candlestick, John moves in the direction of the second door, which is decorated with elaborate iron lattice-work.

I notice how anxious he is and suspect he knows something I don't. Placing the candle in one hand, he rotates a rusty iron knob. There is a grating noise as the door scrapes along the hard stone floor. We peer into yet another mysterious compartment.

A huge rat scurries past our feet through the open door, causing an eerie, screeching echo. I instinctively grab John's arm and feel him trembling violently. The flickering candle flame throws shadows on several long, heavy objects. Cautiously standing outside the door, we try to determine what is there.

There are no playful slippers, no capes, no walking sticks. Instead, there's a nauseating, acrid odor of old mold and dust mixed with dank air. I shudder, feeling repulsed.

"Go in, John."

"Okay . . . but yer comin' with me."

We step inside and the blaze of the candle discloses details of the room. Two long, wooden objects lean at an angle against a spiral-covered wall. They look like long, thin boxes. I have chills running up my back and arms and wonder if I'm going to be sick. I've never seen John look so uncomfortable, either. He is white, like a ghost.

Stepping closer, our flame begins to illuminate the contents of the wooden boxes. The shocking sight causes me to recoil in revulsion. John bellows, "*God, no!*" and covers his face and moans.

Staring at us from the boxes are two hideously shriveled and decayed duplicates of John and myself—down to the smallest details! The capes are so aged, they are nearly disintegrated. The hair and skulls are like mummies.

"Let's get out of here!" I wail, my face twisted in disgust.

"No!" John cries. "We can't! We have to go through to completion—there's no other way!"

His face is contorted with anguish. With violently trembling hands, he lifts the candle, forcing himself to inspect the grisly display.

"It's gotta be faced, Linda! This is another part of the Cycle of Life! We have to participate *consciously* in our own metamorphosis, otherwise . . ."

"Otherwise?"

"We'll continue living in fear, over and over . . . generating more of it on earth, as we pass through each human Expression!"

"But what can we do?" I mutter through icy-cold fingers plastered against my mouth.

"You've gotta repeat certain *words* with me . . ."

Pale and drawn, John is standing straighter now, holding the flame resolutely in front of him. Closing his eyes, he speaks in a strong, determined voice:

"May the Love of the God and the Goddess surround us,

  May the Love of the God and the Goddess flow deep within us,

  May the Love of the God and the Goddess make us free!

  May we be free to know ourselves,

  May we be free to love!"

He begins to look stronger and is regaining his color. He asks me to repeat these words with him, which I do. The prayer continues:

"May the Light of the Christfire surround us,

  May the Light of the Christfire burn bright within us,

  May the Light of the Christfire make us free!

  May we be free to love ourselves,

  May we be free to know!"

While repeating this together, a mysterious aura of light begins to appear before us. John carries on:

"May the Wisdom of the Higher Self and Teachers surround us,

May the Wisdom of the Higher Self and Teachers live within us,

May this Wisdom make us free!

May we be free to help ourselves,

May we be free to grow!"

As we repeat this part of the prayer, our voices steadily become stronger and more confident. The aura of illumination intensifies, and John places the candle on the floor in front of the horrifying shapes.

In an enormous effulgence, the figure of an old man dressed in a long, white gown slowly appears. A white cloth is folded flat across his forehead and hanging down behind his shoulders. Three short, thick, black lines joined together at the top by another such line, are embroidered on the fabric.

"Hail, Pendragon!" John responds, incredibly consoled.

"Hail wise spirits!" answers the man in the strange white scarf and wide-sleeved gown. A large, circular brooch of dried flowers pressed under glass is pinned on his chest.

"You have come to cleanse, I see!" he says, inspecting us cheerfully.

"Yes, Pendragon, we have! We implore you to help us," replies John humbly.

The man in white looks at us supportively.

"I suggest these archetypal forms be led into dissolution by the eternal flame, and I shall assist you. Please step over here!"

The Pendragon points to his left and John and I move there, getting further from the coffins with their appalling contents. He raises his arms and hands and proclaims loudly:

"May darkness and light abide in peace!

May the cycle of death and rebirth be rightly honored!

May the violet flame of transformation make itself known!

May the beauty of dawn unfold in the hearts of its seekers!

May there be peace in the Universe!"

To our amazement, the boxes and their dreadful contents burst into columns of fire. At first the flames are a dazzling, golden-white; then, they slowly change into a luminous, light-violet color. In shock, we observe our gruesome doubles disappear into an inferno of purplish iridescence.

The chamber now appears to be empty and is lit by an astonishing glow. Our friend, the Pendragon, nods.

"We thank you for yer help, sir," John says, the color back in his face.

"Yes, I can't tell you how much we appreciate it," I add, finally able to relax.

"Let us go now, wise spirits, for the moment is right."

Placing his hands on our shoulders, the Pendragon exits the chamber with us. I have an innate trust in him. He exudes a warm luminescence. Returning to the second room, it appears the same, except the black spider is nowhere to be found.

I am shocked to see the first chamber has transformed. It is filled with a white light like an ethereal mist. It can't be the first chamber, I silently reason, because there is no stairway to lead us out! I start to panic. I can't tell if John has noticed. He seems overwhelmed by the bright light and his face reveals an enthusiastic rosiness.

"I have a gift to bestow upon this Arcadian soul of the Nine Cycle, Blue-Green Ray," the Pendragon announces proudly.

"Really?" John questions naively.

"Take this and bear it honorably," says the man in white, presenting John with an exquisite, gleaming sword which materializes out of the Light.

"From now on it shall be invisible and become part of your cosmic destiny—the ability to nurture higher intelligence with inventiveness of spirit. Take it in the name of Love. May there be peace in the Universe!"

The Pendragon slips the shimmering sword into a colorfully-embroidered sheath and fastens it beneath John's cloak. I can still see it and am curious when it will become invisible.

"My most revered high teacher, Pendragon, I thank you with all my soul for this gift. May there be peace in the Universe!" John says proudly.

The two men embrace and I feel honored to be part of their ceremony.

The Pendragon faces me and declares, "Earthling . . . indeed you are a brave soul to venture so far. We welcome you Here! You bridge the gap between two worlds—you are sorely needed! The visitation of earthlings to Arcadia is one of the finest events that comes to pass. May there be more of these sojourns!"

"I am honored to make your acquaintance, sir. I hope I'll be fortunate enough to meet with you again."

My manner of speech sounds odd, and I find myself bowing to this man as if I'm used to such things.

"It is possible to meet with me whenever you choose," says the Pendragon. "You only need to speak my name."

"That's easy enough," I chuckle softly, somewhat embarrassed.

"Let us go above to the Sacred Oaks where a dance and feast await."

Relieved, I see he is leading us to a door on the other side of the chamber. I wonder if it will lead us back the way we came—to the room with the standing stone, more spirals, and the trap door. John is beaming and appears oblivious to where we are going.

Indeed, as the door opens, I behold the large stone standing reassuringly in the center of the first chamber. The Pendragon and John make motions indicating that I take the lead. Passing through the doorway, I see the walking sticks resting against the wall.

"Here, kid . . . take this!" John says, offering me one of the thick, knobby staffs—keeping the other for himself.

This room is large and spacious and makes me remarkably happy. Our surroundings are illuminated by our teacher. Passing the standing stone on my way to the staircase, I finger it lovingly.

We approach the deeply-worn staircase.

"Be my guest," says the Pendragon, pointing toward it.

Looking up, I see the trap door is closed and become agitated.

"Don't worry, earthling, it is easy to open."

I move hastily up the stairs, pushing against the door with both hands. It opens without effort.

A large bonfire blazes nearby, and it is nighttime. Shimmering moonlight floods the turf, and many people dressed in white clothes are moving about in small groups.

"Are ya goin' out or not?" John bellows.

"Yes . . . of course! I'm going!"

I step into a deliciously fragrant, cool evening. A sea of moonlight drenches my entire being. John and the Pendragon are standing next to me, gazing about with satisfaction.

~6~
Night Dance

In the bracing moonlight, I wiggle my toes inside my pointed slippers, shove the snake bracelet up my arm and adjust my cape. Delighting in the warmth from the crackling bonfire nearby, I inhale deeply the aroma of dampness and smoke. The graceful, white-robed figures are forming a circle around us, and I gaze at them with fascination.

What must they think—three figures emerging from subterranean quarters, standing like hubs in the center of their ceremonial wheel? They are dancing now—men and women of all ages. Some smile at us shyly for an instant, then shift their focus elsewhere.

Staring at John's open cape, I realize his new sword has become invisible. Next to him stands the Pendragon, strong and imposing. The moonlight, combined with the bonfire's glow, creates such brightness and casts numerous shadows, it seems to be nearly daytime. John and I watch, spellbound, leaning on our walking sticks.

"Dig this!" John leans over and whispers to me, "Isn't it like the good old days?"

"I have a strong desire to join them."

"Well, let's do it, then . . . it's okay. They'll accept us, although they're from a different cycle group than mine."

"Is it really okay?"

"Sure! Give 'er a go, dear . . . but let's leave these here fer now."

We let our walking sticks fall to the ground.

"Ease into line over there."

I follow him to the circle, and the dancers make an opening for us. They start to sing as they move, and we attempt to follow their simple, rhythmic steps. Immediately, we become part of the dance and listen with wonder to their slow, enchanting song:

"Lau-li, lau-li,

Ma-pa-da la-ma soo-ma,

Lau do-mi soo-ma pa,

Lau-li, lau-li . . ."

In unison, we swing our arms up and slowly down. The dance steps are incessant. John and I listen as the white-robed people continue to chant their haunting melody. I am falling into a hypnotic reverie, as if reliving a forgotten dream. Somewhere, part of me is being reborn, and John is going through the same process.

From the circle, we see the Pendragon staring into the fire. I perceive he is standing at the spot where the magic stone is lying—next to the trap door leading into that buried world from which we have recently surfaced.

Were we actually part of this captivating ritual? Were these people celebrating our successful emergence from the dark chambers of death and fear? I glance at John with a questioning look. He nods; and in an instant, I understand everything. This dance is a continuation of the ritual we began after entering the circle of oaks. Indeed, the celebration is being completed after our triumphant journey out of darkness.

The dancing has stopped and the figures are milling about, speaking in a baffling, exotic tongue. Individuals here are either pure blond or dark-haired—some are attractive, others not at all. They seem meek and introverted, radiating friendliness; yet I'm beginning to sense why they are not part of John's group. Is it because they're so mild?

"D'ya like it?" John asks.

"It's wonderful!"

He leads me to the fire, and we stare into it—speechless. The Pendragon has disappeared. The luscious smell of roasting meat fills our nostrils; we see wild boar being cooked over the open fire.

"I wonder if those are the ones that frightened us when we first came here," I cackle.

"I'm surprised they're blessing, then eating, those animals," John replies. "I haven't seen this for a long time."

"You mean most Arcadians are vegetarians?"

"Very often, yes. But, don't forget, it's not what you do—it's how you do it. These folks have prayed, celebrated and thanked the spirit of the animal they are eating. They're making it a pure and symbolic act. So, if yer hungry, you may be their guest."

"Are you going to eat it?"

"Yeah, I'm gonna be part of *their* ceremony . . . and *ours* too! We have a lot to celebrate, don't we? I've got me invisible sword . . ."

"Congratulations, John."

". . . and yer getting *another* new child! Congratulations yerself!"

I blush. "News certainly travels fast in your world! Were you aware of it all along?"

"Of course! This is one of the most important events to celebrate Here . . . when a soul decides to Express itself again on earth—or on any other planet, fer that matter."

"It's amazing," I say, still gazing into the fire, "because back on earth—just now, between Good Friday and Easter—we've been having a full moon. And I've just discovered that I am again with child! These earthly events coincide with our emergence from the underground chambers and the moon we're witnessing Here."

"The original theme of Christ's death and resurrection is gonna play an increased role in earth's metamorphosis, ya know. At least part of yer experience goin' underground with me is connected with a voyage you've made into the depths of yer own terrestrial womb."

I look at him. "You know, I'm often confused about which world I'm really in! I seem to live in a double world . . . where spirit and matter are interchangeable."

"Don't you see, Linda, yer bein' a mother on earth is one of the primary factors keeping you well-grounded there? It's not true for everybody; but in the Expression you're in now, there's nothing more common nor extraordinary than to bear and raise children . . . earth's love and fruit."

The bright flames frolic over John's face, and I know he is happy. Suddenly, we are distracted by children playing nearby and babies held in their mothers' arms. They, too, are dressed in modest white garments and have joined their parents for this part of the celebration. Unlike their elders, they're noisy and outgoing.

"Well, look at that!" John exclaims. "They sure are rowdy little buggers!"

"Has it been long since you've seen children, then?" I ask, amused.

"Not long enough!" he answers, lowering his voice. "But I realize it's gotta do with me own painful launchings into my last preposterous Expression."

"Maybe you should go easier on yourself, John."

He nods with an ironic smile.

"Anyway," I say, "I want to ask you more about Expressions sometime—if we ever get back to our meadow."

"If? It's gonna happen soon, I promise!"

"At night?"

"You wait an' see. Meanwhile, let's eat, drink and be hairy."

A man dressed in white brings us a wooden plate filled with savory roasted meat and a large tankard of wine.

John gives the wine to me and toasts: "To yer awaited baby, and the success of yer story."

I take a drink—it's mead, a delicious wine of fermented honey. Now it's my turn to toast John: "To your new sword, your growth and the success of your story." I look into John's eyes and give him the tankard.

He grins and drinks. With our fingers we eat pieces of the succulent pork which has the taste of wild herbs, soil and smoke. Far away, an owl hoots. We hear children playing and the unobtrusive muttering and occasional bantering of the simple folk surrounding us. The position of the moon has changed. It's slowly sinking toward the horizon.

"I guess we won't be seeing the Pendragon again for awhile," John says solemnly.

"I noticed he was gone. What a fantastic guy! It would have been less pleasant without him."

"That's how it is with high teachers . . . they're *there* when you need 'em."

Suddenly, a crack of thunder stuns us, followed by a few drops of rain.

"Let's dash over there," John says, pointing to one of the oaks near the stone gateway.

"Hey, I finally get to use the hood on my cape," I declare, lifting it over my head as we run.

As we approach one of the trees, there is a brilliant flash of lightning nearby, followed by a terrifying crack of thunder.

"Isn't it dangerous to stand under trees with this lightning?" I shout.

"Not now—my sword will serve as a rebuff."

"That's handy!"

John sprints ahead, and I follow. We reach a tree just in time—torrents of rain are plummeting around us. The gentle people and children have gone; and to our dismay, the bonfire is rapidly extinguishing. Soon we are standing alone in the oak grove, surrounded by darkness, listening to a heavy downpour.

"They're all gone!" I wail.

"They do tend to do that—appear and disappear in an instant," John retorts satirically.

"I'm getting wet in spite of this tree," I say.

I reach up to touch the dampness forming on my hood. John hasn't been using his and has wet hair, but doesn't seem to mind.

"What's our next plan of action?" I inquire politely.

"Just wait. Yer gonna see real soon."

"Okay."

Wet and cold, I lean against the massive oak and try to be patient. John stands with his arms folded, staring across the circle of trees, as if concentrating on something. I fall into another reverie.

Then I notice a scant cast of orange and a hint of pink lighting the sky. Slowly, the faint glow unfolds through the trees until a slice of fire begins to emerge, and I catch my first glimpse of dawn.

"God Almighty, John!"

"Aye, that's for sure!" he answers proudly.

We watch this continuous eruption of awesome, orange-pink daylight.

"This must be a good day for traveling," I speak at last.

"Precisely my sentiments. Don't forget yer stick, dear."

"Thanks! I would've forgotten it. They must be lying near where the bonfire was."

We step onto the wet turf and look around in the half-light of the new morning. The thick grass has been flattened in most places and there is a large, wet pile of black rubble where the bonfire had been. Near it is the chiseled stone which is again resting on top of the wooden trap door. Nearby, our walking sticks form a cross on the grass.

"It may seem sentimental, but I'm pleased we didn't forget these," I say, picking one of them up.

"That may be . . . but I suspect they'll come in handy later on."

He picks up the other stick, stroking its knobby smoothness.

"By the way, what's it feel like having your invisible sword around your waist?"

"Exceptionally good . . . as if I'm stronger inside. It's hard to explain."

With scraggly hair, scruffy beard and his outfit, he looks like the type of person I saw in Haight-Ashbury in the 1960s.

"You look great! You really do!" I exclaim.

"Why thank you!" he jests in a deep voice, taking a bow. "Methinks it is time to take another stroll toward the meadow. Don't you agree?"

"Yes! Let's go."

Traveling toward the rising sun, we enter a large, open area which is teeming with birdsong. The wetness and the strange shimmer of dawn make everything look surreal. I have yet to become accustomed to the new consciousness I've acquired since our ritual. I assume it's part of my intensifying experience in Arcadia: colors are more varied and dynamic now, light produces unusual contrasts and the sounds and smells of nature are stirring the deepest core of my being. I assume this is part of the normal state of consciousness experienced Here.

"Is it always so psychedelic?" I ask.

"Hah! That awakens many memories . . . but yer right. It *is* psychedelic here. Once ya get used to it, it's hard ta recall how it was the other way."

"Having limited perception, you mean?"

"Aye."

We explore this open, grassy area which I recognize as the place where our journey began. Sunlight is beginning to beam its full radiance directly into our faces, and my entire body becomes brightened with contentment.

I am startled to see John's physical appearance has altered. His cape is gone, and he's wearing—I assume as a prank—a white tee-shirt with "Arcadia" printed in gold letters on the front. He is neat, cleanshaven and appears older. His glasses are gone, making his prominent nose seem thinner and indented on the sides. With the sun illuminating him and his hands placed together to greet it in prayer, he looks ethereal.

I've been so engrossed in his activities and new appearance, I failed to notice my cape is missing and my green jumpsuit is now a brilliant marine-blue. Our novel bracelets are gone, but we're still wearing the slippers.

"We still have them!" I yell foolishly.

Soon I recognize the idyllic stream which was flowing through the meadow before. I know its final destination is a joyous reunion with the Mystical Ocean. Taking a running leap near a large birch tree, we cross the stream, gripping our sticks and laughing as we frighten an unsuspecting raccoon.

The temperature continues to rise, and I realize we are headed for the spot where John and I embarked with Basil so long ago—a large oak tree on the other side of this meadow. A deer appears, a large buck which bounds away. A scarlet tanager flits in front of us, then disappears.

Our feet are leading us to the right spot. There—under the shade of a big tree—are two familiar tarpaulin lounge chairs and a small wooden table. There is something shiny and metallic on the table which I can't identify. John is looking extremely pleased with himself; as we approach, I see the object is a large tray with a silver dome. Next to it is an earthen pitcher, two glasses and two large linen napkins.

"How d'ya like it? Breakfast in the great out-of-doors!" John hums as he walks to the table.

"Care to join me, milady?"

"Breakfast in heaven!" I say. "And I always thought breakfast in bed was the ultimate."

He removes the dome from the tray, mimicking a deep inhalation of appetizing aromas.

"Fruit," he declares, "every kind of fruit imaginable! Care for some freshly-squeezed orange juice?"

Carefully pouring a glass of juice, he offers it to me. The flavor is marvelously fresh and pure.

"Ahhh . . ." John sighs, finishing his glass, then handing me a napkin.

"Have some of the most tantalizing fruits in the universe. Is milady pleased?"

"This is wonderful!" I say, inspecting the exotic fruit—some familiar and some strange.

"The possibilities are endless, my dear."

"Before we eat, don't you think we should bless it—like those funny people did? Their ceremony stands out in my mind. And the food was so distinctive!"

"Yer right! Blessing one's nourishment makes all the difference. Okay, I've got a simple one for you then:

Luv'ly is this food!
Thanks be to the love that made it,
Thanks be to the health that grades it,
Amen."

"That's easy enough," I say, and repeat after him.

Feasting on the remarkable fruit, it's the nicest breakfast I ever had.

PART V

Trip to
the Mountain

~1~
Family Ties

As the bubbling call of a meadowlark reverberates nearby, I place my napkin on the table.

"There's something I want to ask," I say, sinking back in my chair.

"Shoot."

"When are you coming back to earth?"

John doesn't answer for a moment.

"Well, this particular Johnny Lennon ain't ever comin' back!" he clowns, pointing to himself. "But, may I take a rain check? There's so much I need ta do Here. I'm not in any hurry, actually."

He looks at me, making a silly face and fingering his walking stick.

"I appreciate you telling me this," I reply. "I've become curious about when you might choose your next Expression. It may not be wise, however, to discuss these things. The privacy you give yourself next time around will be extremely important."

John nods, but doesn't speak. He takes his slippers off and rubs his feet.

"How's it going with your sword, by the way? You're not sitting on it, are you?"

"Oh, no . . . great! I forgot I had it on!" He shoots a hand to his side and fingers its imperceptible contours.

"Would you tell me more about the Expressions we've had together?"

"What d'ya wanna know?"

"So many things have happened to me since our initial visit Here . . . I need to sort them out."

"Fer instance?"

"For instance—when I saw you as my mother in Greece—among other things. I've received so many impressions which I keep mulling over and . . . I need to tie the loose ends together. Is that okay?"

"Of course it's okay, silly! I'm not the Pope."

"But to imagine," I say, "you were once my mother! When I saw that under hypnosis, it was ridiculously real. I was forced to go to war and didn't see you again. What happened after that?"

"When you left for war, I knew we'd never see each other again! Mother's intuition, ya know. You were my favorite child, although a mother isn't supposed to love one kid more than another. I suffered deep agony from losing you that way. It was real heavy."

He looks at me and smiles apologetically.

"What was the purpose of this hardship? I mean, before this, we had been fondest of cousins in the Temple of Delphi."

John remains serious. "I was learning ta receive love and let go of it at the same time, and you were learning to accept life for what it is. More important in the end—we both realized how much we cared about each other. Things had always gone so well before, we were startin' to take each other for granted. In the early days of Atlantis, fer instance, you were my father. We developed a psychic bond and weren't entirely conscious of the love that was there. We were working in a functional way, and emotional life wasn't important. I learned yer trade of guiding and helping folks and took over yer role after you died. But I was so aware of spirit, it was as if you were physically with me. It's strange how the world has changed."

"The funny part is how real it is when you relate these things. It gives me the shivers."

"And, if we wanted to," I continue after a few moments, "could we find that father and son wandering in Arcadia?"

"Aye. Maybe we will, you can never tell."

"The story could be endless."

"Or incredibly long."

"So far I've got Atlantis, Greece, the British Isles, the rest of Europe and America in which I've had earthly Expressions with you . . ."

"Right!"

"Are there more?"

"There are more," he hesitates, "but the teachers say you've got enough information to work with already. And you needn't get fanatical, dear! It's all gotta do with the proper timing of things—that's crucial."

"I agree with the teachers. If we sum up the experiences we've shared in other lives, it's striking that they represent close family ties—my son, my mother, cousin, brother, a treasured nanny—with one exception—a musical colleague."

"Yeah, even the nanny, Gracie, got the chance ta smother you with motherly affection to make up for her loss in Greece! Except for the musician—although he, too, served as a family role-model for me—you can see they've represented domestic nourishment. You understand how much *that* has meant to me."

I nod. "In the last songs you wrote, you seemed to be singing mainly about the importance of family. That impressed me . . . I guess because your last family was broken up. What is the other side learning from this?"

John looks at the ground, thinking for a moment.

"My family is learning a lotta things! But most importantly, they're learning to trust themselves and the universe—and to become stronger and more self-reliant. I think they're doin' a good job."

He smiles and blinks. It touches me to see how much older he looks, as he might have appeared in his fifties.

"Anyway," I say, "it's hilarious to remember when I was afraid I was misusing the name of a deceased Beatle."

"Hah! That's a good one—you were only lookin' on the surface then." He whistles. "Hey, you forgot one thing . . ."

"What?"

"After yer last Expression—after *you* died—you were one of me guardians when I was a kid."

"Oh, right! I wanted to ask you about that. Did I stop helping you when I was born into my present life?"

"Yes and no. In some ways, you did stop being my guardian because you were establishing another Expression on earth. But in other ways, part of your soul essence remained in touch with me for the rest of my life. It's complex how these realities function simultaneously."

I become lost in reflection.

"I suppose that's why I could perceive you so easily when you died . . . yet didn't comprehend why."

"Right. Because the soul remains *whole*, like the center of a flower. That's the part of us which can't be defined by time, space, personality or gender. The infinite number of petals—those are the myriad Expressions. They're part of the blossom, you understand. When you return to Arcadia—or any other place of learning—you see that each metaphorical flower is the Expression of the total soul consciousness. You know the John Lennon yer lookin' at now is just one petal . . . and all of these petals—these separate body-personalities which have ever been Expressed—exist somewhere Here."

"Even future lives?"

"Well, yeah . . . but I was hoping you weren't going ta ask about that! It's gettin' too heavy fer now."

"Oh, sorry. But let me ask you this . . . do you sometimes all get together and have a party?"

"Basically, we do all the time!" John beams. "By the way, this new kid of yers—I'm not supposed to say if it's a boy or a girl—is a real gem! I know this soul, ya see."

"Oh really?"

"No, O'Reilly . . ."

"John!"

He laughs. "This new baby is an old friend of mine . . . and, of course, yours too! It's an old, seasoned Arcadian in every sense of the word."

"That wouldn't surprise me in the least. Its father and I were shocked when we discovered what had happened! There's so much we want to learn about this person. He or she is extraordinarily strong and bright," I say, patting my belly cheerfully.

"I can tell you a few things," John volunteers. "The personality has tremendous humor, and is creative as well as precise and contemplative. The child will bring you great joy," he adds affectionately.

"Thanks for the scoop—perhaps you'd enjoy being one of its guardians?"

"I wasn't sure I should mention it, but that's something the kid and I have already agreed on."

"How nice!" I cry, leaping up to hug him. "I'm sure the baby will be wiser for it."

"If the child doesn't go actin' crazy—or grow up wantin' ta be a rock 'n roll star."

"If my baby is crazy like you—or even wants to be a rock 'n roll star—more power to the kid," I exclaim, returning to my chair.

"May I quote you—in about fifteen years?"

"Of course. It's a deal."

He leans over, offers his hand and we shake. The meadowlark calls again, and I am charged with a new surge of inspiration.

"There's something else you need ta know about yer new kid. The child you are carrying is yer soul mate," John says candidly.

"But I thought Aart was my soul mate."

"It's confusing, I realize, but Aart is yer *twin soul*, and that's a different breed of tiger."

I look at him, perplexed. "What's the difference?"

Playing with a large red apple, he clears his throat. "There's this other tale I've been meaning ta tell you, but never got the chance."

"Well, go ahead!"

The corners of his mouth curve slightly upward, and he stares into the branches of the oak tree.

"Once upon a time when the universe was still young, after Mr. God and Mrs. Goddess witnessed the gruesome dismemberment of their children into polar opposites, they thought they'd seen it all! For eons they watched anxiously, wringing their hands and pulling their hair—but this didn't keep the crazy Twosomes from their next uncivilized skirmish.

On good days, when they were in harmony, and two parts of the whole could be seen romping and tittering in the blaze of the mighty sun, the supreme progenitors could forget the stark realities. But, give 'em a few bad stretches—a couple billion bloodcurdling screams and three sleepless nights—and they were again on the royal skids.

After one particularly grievous night, when the old folks had had enough, Mrs. Goddess speculated to her husband over breakfast, 'Maybe we're making them work too hard with all this learning business.'

'Why not give 'em an alternative?' he answered brightly.

'Whadaya mean?' she asked.

'I mean, when one twin soul needs a vacation from the other, why not give 'em another sort of playmate. Someone who's not going to stir things up! Someone who's there to help and make peace! These sleepless nights are killin' me . . .'

'But the twins wouldn't be learning anything that way!' Mrs. Goddess objected heartily.

'All work and no play makes Adam a dull boy. Do you want to get some rest or not?'

'Yes!' Mrs. Goddess cried into her apron.

'Okay! We'll provide each twin soul with a soul mate—an additional someone who's there to comfort and make peace.'

'Where will we *get* them? And what about the population explosion?'

'They already exist, dear—an' have their own twin ta boot.'

Mrs. Goddess paused, slowly stirring her coffee.

'I believe this is one of the best ideas you've had since sound! But how can these *mates* be matched up?'

'It's not beyond our capabilities, I'm sure,' Mr. God said smugly, picking up his newspaper.

They succeeded in this momentous undertaking, of course. Not only did each twin get its essential allotment of peace and comfort, but they seemed ta understand better while learning—proving a friend in deed is not always a playboy bunny."

~2~
Periwinkle

Gazing over the meadow, I realize it is summertime. On the tree above us, the leaves are thicker than before and provide more shade.

"Isn't it novel to be married to my twin soul . . . and have a soul mate as my child?" I ask.

"Yes, yer a lucky woman!" John says. "Some folks go through entire Expressions without meeting either of 'em!"

"Aart and I work hard on our relationship . . . but as you said, we realize how much we can learn. That always seems to be in the back of our minds when we're going through classic conflicts. It took time to come to this measure of realization, though—sometimes we still need to remind each other."

"Meeting a twin soul means not only bliss, but agonizing, hard work. Not everybody is up to that! Some folks opt for the soul mate routine because they need a rest. An' who can blame them?"

"Doesn't a person learn anything with a soul mate?"

"Of course they learn, but by helping—not by confronting. And ultimately, a relationship with a soul mate helps one to communicate better with his or her twin—the other half waiting for them. Harmony with the twin needs ta be *earned*, while the instant harmony shared with a soul mate is a divine consolation prize—which not all folks are lucky enough ta receive."

"And do all roads have to lead to Rome? I mean, why couldn't we make it easier on ourselves by hanging out with our soul mate, and forget about the twin?"

"Because, dear, the laws of the universe won't allow it! Each soul longs for wholeness. An' harmonious reunion with yer twin soul represents the highest possible attainment of God and Goddess consciousness that exists."

"What happens to polarity at this point, then?"

"It cooperates with itself! It merges into a oneness of being where its elements are no longer separable."

I stop to consider this, then continue, "So, it would be normal for a person to meet their twin soul in a particular Expression—but not their soul mate as well, right?"

"Yeah! There are all sorts of possibilities. Not everybody is gonna have a twin as a lover, either . . . it could be their mother or father, sister or brother . . ."

"Child . . . or best friend."

"Aye. But the sure sign of bein' with yer twin soul is the depth of the duality experienced—the 'heaven and hell' syndrome."

"I know it well."

"So do I! And like us, more souls will be daring ta meet their physical twin—and trying to do so more often as the earth matures . . . especially as partners. It's a matter of having to get back ta the garden."

"Of Eden?"

"Something of that nature. The garden represents a level of existence at peace with duality. Planet earth has become beautifully specialized in this duality business . . . that's why it's one of the better places ta learn."

"Where does duality come from?"

"It started with Mr. God and Mrs. Goddess. But it became more conspicuous when they decided to have children. If they hadn't done that, there wouldn't have been anyone to complain . . ."

Looking at John's face, I wonder if he is serious—I'm not sure anymore.

"I'd better give my mortal brains a break for awhile," I say, suddenly tired.

"I've warned you before—earthlings aren't supposed to think so much. It's too confusing for them."

"I'm going to lay my mortal head back . . . and take a well-deserved mid-morning siesta . . ."

"A wise move, indeed. I'll join you."

When I awaken, it is hot and sultry. With his head fallen to one side, John is snoring. The twittering of birds serves as a tranquil backdrop. Scanning the meadow, I wonder if I'll catch sight of a deer or other wild creature.

"Clover, thistle, figwort, heather, heliotrope, evening primrose, waterlily, wild rose, violet, morning glory, forget-me-not, snapdragon, honeysuckle, bluebell, sunflower, iris, cattail, lupin, lily, periwinkle, wild blackberry, wild strawberry, wild mint . . ."

John is talking in his sleep.

"What's that?" I say gently.

He snorts, jerking awake.

"Oh! Good morning! Guess I was dreamin' again."

"You were naming all sorts of plants and flowers."

"Right! There's this great spot between the meadow an' the foothills. We're gonna pass through it as soon as we're outta here."

"And when might that be?" I ask enthusiastically.

"Any time ya want. Right now, as far as I'm concerned! There's still so much left to do," John says, suddenly leaning over to fasten the crested slippers to his feet. "C'mon . . . follow me!"

He jumps up energetically and grabs his walking stick. I follow, picking my stick off the ground and looking furtively— one last time, I presume—at the lounge chairs and little table piled with fruit.

John is marching toward where the sun came up, into the open meadow sprinkled with clover and attended by large, zealous bumble bees. I observe new kinds of trees—larch, maple, yew and another sort I can't identify.

My four-dimensional consciousness has become a way of life by now; sometimes I forget I have it. John is silent and preoccupied, yet I don't mind because it gives me the opportunity to inspect the surroundings.

We arrive at a thicket lined with birch trees.

"Right," John mumbles, forging ahead through some flowering underbrush. I stalk after him.

Soon we are standing in a sunlit beech forest where the air is moist and sweet.

"This is what I was tellin' you about," John sighs proudly.

"It's beautiful! Look at the flowers!"

"There's lots more and various kinds, but we'd have ta spend ages huntin' if you wanted to see everything. This grove connects with our stream, and somewhere there's this outrageous pond."

"I could stay here forever," I say, breathing deeply. I step ahead to admire towering stalks of bluebells.

"That's the danger, kid—we've still got some work ta do! But, don't ferget—you can come here whenever you want."

"I won't forget."

Traipsing along, we stop occasionally to appreciate a plant, flower or tiny creature.

I hear the sound of rushing water.

"There's our stream again," John announces. "We're gonna follow it toward the foothills."

We approach a cascading stream lined with giant ferns. There is a refreshing coolness on my skin. We lean across a large rock, dipping our hands into the clear, cold water for a drink. Retrieving our sticks, we continue on with the din of rushing water crashing in our ears.

Soon the terrain becomes slightly graded, rockier and nearly impenetrable. We need to watch every step to avoid stumbling. The stream diverges sharply, and we head further up the grade for easier hiking. With the sound of the water steadily diminishing, the woods begin to thin out and we find ourselves standing in an expanse of open, yellow hills dotted with volcanic rock and tiny scrub oaks.

"This sure is different!" I exclaim. "Hey, look over there! A little boy!" I point to a small child skipping through the golden grass.

"Yeah, that's me in my last Expression," John nearly whispers. "You can see how delighted I am—'cause me folks aren't far away."

"But I don't see them."

"Yer not supposed to," he answers, leaning on his walking stick.

"This was before they broke up. They were never so happy together as I'm makin' 'em out ta be *Here* . . . nor was I so loved or safe! But it's part of this great process I'm goin' through—ta heal the wounds."

"Looks like fun, anyway."

"I finally managed to make it that way. You see, I'm recreating these experiences as I would have *liked* them to be . . . just like reshooting the scenes of a movie! Of course, I needed the other experience in order to Express the personality of John Winston Lennon, planet earth, 1940! An' one Past-Mode dimension of me exists in that small boy. I can communicate with him and heal him . . . if only I have enough guts to confront him."

"Are you saying we can reconstruct our past on earth?"

"In one sense, no—the history books can't be changed. They've been molded in time. But in other dimensions, yes! Outside of time, Past, Present and Future Modes are all one. In a definite sense, then, we *can* heal the past because it's part of our present and future. See what I mean?"

"My brains don't get it . . . but somewhere inside I sense what you mean."

"That's one reason you can travel Here so easily. Nobody's brains will *ever* get it."

We walk closer to the boy, but he doesn't notice us—as if we are invisible.

"Hey! I see you over there," I say, motioning, "but you keep changing as you move."

I frown in puzzlement, for the young man's hair is growing longer, then shorter . . . now he has a beard, now a mustache and goatee, now he's clean-shaven. His clothes continuously reshape themselves in an endless variety of color and style.

"That's me after my boyhood days," John chuckles, "when I was a teenager, and afterward, when I was a Beatle."

"I was busy experimenting with my *outward* identity. Who was I to the outside world? When I died, I still didn't have an answer. This has been a major area of learning in my Nine Cycle . . . and in some of the other sub-groups, too."

"It feels so large and spacy."

"Well, that's because I'm gettin' to see myself from a much broader perspective."

He looks at me intently. "Ya see, we've got endless reels of movies which we carry around as souls, even after death. These movies aren't physical, of course, but they exist, nonetheless."

"And you get to review the movies of yourself—not only from your last earthly Expression—but the others, too?"

"Right. After death, we get that chance—but only if we've got the guts, mind you! We can look at our so-called past and our so-called mistakes, although you realize by now there really is no such thing."

"Yes . . . you and Basil have made that very explicit."

"Well, it's one hell of an important message. Every mistake is a priceless opportunity to learn something new. That's essential to the movie-viewing—ta be able to perceive it in such a way. If we weren't so filled with pride and bigheadedness, we would be oh-so-happy with our mistakes, dearie—but that's a difficult area for most souls ta deal with! And on earth, it's even harder to realize because illusions can be more powerful."

I stop in my tracks. "What is illusion, anyway?"

"It's seeing yerself separate from yer own creation," John answers, looking at the young man in the distance. "But, now it's time ta go further. You up to it?"

"I've never felt better."

~3~
God or Mommy

The yellow hills are temperate and inviting. Beyond them are blue mountains. John is singing an unfamiliar song, slapping his leg as he walks. It's a catchy tune, and I start to hum along:

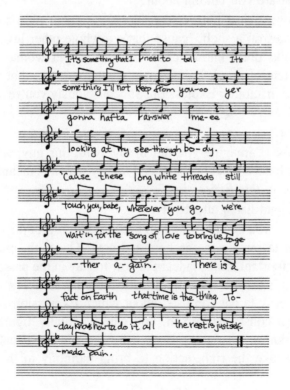

We're hiking through parched hills at a steady pace. I'm not the slightest bit tired, as if I possess an unknown, superhuman strength.

"An' because earthlings are caught in the mold of time, there's nothing more important to them than learning to exist in the present," John declares, as if he's been talking all along.

"It's the only state of consciousness which can connect them with their natural strength . . . and that of the planet. It's where each person's sacred spotlight shines. Present Mode is where it's at, literally."

He looks at me rather seriously and I nod.

"Closely connected with this is the fact that each Expression is centered around a given base," he continues. "Often this is the family circle, although it isn't a prerequisite. And this base needs ta be intelligently focused in Present Mode, otherwise a terrible confusion can raise its flabby head."

"What are you talking about?"

"Okay . . . just put yer considerations about twin souls and soul mates on a shelf, 'cause that's a whole other level which most folks don't know about. Go back to yer woman-on-the-street state of mind. Pretend you meet some guy that was yer husband in another Expression. Subconsciously you're aware of this."

"Okay."

"Well . . . imagine you fall in love with this guy, when you already have a great husband and family which is meant for yer learning in *this Expression*."

I nod and listen attentively.

"So . . . you get all fucked up because you forgot it's essential for you ta remain in the here-and-now! On earth, one of the most important things ta learn is how to stay in the present time. So, what's the meaning of this little morality tale? The message is: It's easy ta get confused about which Expression yer in! If you're a conscious person, you can eventually figure it out. You'll know what's appropriate for yer present situation and how to take the right action to bring harmony to the greater whole."

"I guess this is why delving into the past can be risky."

"Aye, but at the same time, it helps ta see the entire picture more clearly . . . as you've been able to do with me," he says, jabbing his walking stick firmly into the ground. "It's a matter of using great wisdom."

"I'm not sure everybody has that."

"I'm not either. And, besides, the example I gave you can easily bring confusion in its reverse form."

"How's that?"

"A person can end up marrying somebody they knew in a Past Expression—which is terribly common, mind you—because that person seems familiar. They recognize and feel something for each other, not understanding why. It may be that meetin' up with this old companion is meant to be part of a reconciliation or brief reunion . . . and is *not* meant to be a long-term relationship. Get it?"

"Only too well, I think."

"I can use my marriage to Cynthia as a good example. We'd known and loved each other in other Expressions and had important things to learn as a couple. But—like with the Beatles— we stopped learnin' and growin' together. Our time was up, and that was it! We were standing in each other's way and holding on to something we had ta let go of, however painful that might be. This kinda thing happens as often as the other way around. Ain't life complicated?"

I roll my eyes.

"So, there are always key questions comin' up which take lotsa wisdom ta deal with: Do both parties have important things ta iron out together? Are they supposed to work things out—or let go and move on to a more appropriate relationship focused in the present?"

"And how are people to know this?" I object. "Luckily, I can answer many of these questions myself because I have specific tools to work with. How can the woman-on-the-street discover the truth for herself?"

"Yer forgetting one important thing, dear. It's why souls go to earth in the first place—ta learn how! Of course, one of the most helpful discoveries is that they have spiritual guardianship anytime they want it. You know, like Call-A-Guardian, 24-hour-a-day Service . . ."

I barely smile. "I know. But what about the lost children resulting from broken marriages. Don't you think it's tragic?"

"It is tragic, sure, and don't forget, I know all about that! We need those hardships in order ta grow, painful as they may be," John says, tramping at a lively pace through the yellow grass. "Basically, life on earth is first learnin' ta accept the events that occur, and second, learnin' to take responsibility for making desired improvements."

"And what about large-scale suffering and catastrophe of the masses—the torment of children and the helpless?"

"In this case, the great illusion is they're only victims of earth's hardness and cruelty. If you look at the previous Expressions of these individuals, you would see why they need these terrible lessons—for spiritual purposes."

"But, John . . . it's easy for a person to sit back and smugly say this when he or she isn't personally suffering."

"Another classic argument! Yeah—it's easy to be smug! And I warn against it! But I adhere to the basic fact that all human consciousness is striving toward two basic aims: to accept life for what it is and to learn how to change."

He heaves a sigh and continues, "I haven't had a conversation like this since Huey Newton. But I sure as hell said different things back then . . ."

I won't relent. "What about helping to improve other peoples' lives? What about the poor and starving? We shouldn't try to take away the problems of others; but surely we need to be sensitive to the needs of those around us! Otherwise, we're not being human."

"Of course! People have gotta use their brains! But yer getting heavy into morals, principles and mind-tripping now. You won't get to the real point this way," John says flatly.

"It would be nice to know what 'the real point' is."

"It's spiritual clarity—gained by knowledge and honesty."

"And what about your old favorite—love?"

"I need to update one of me favorite sayings: Love ain't all you need! You also need spiritual clarity and respect for each other's freedom."

"It wouldn't do your song much good, John."

"No, but ultimately it's the same, dear. Because *real love* contains the other principles—whether on earth, in Arcadia or any other place."

"I'm delighted to hear it—that was always one of my favorite songs."

He looks at me with a vague smile. "And, in our lives, both you and I have needed ta learn how to be more honest with ourselves and with those around us—in spite of the pain it might cause. It shows great respect to let other people learn their own lessons and have their own problems without doin' it for them—thereby trying to play God or Mommy."

"You're right," I say, suddenly aware of a tightness in my body, "I've been afraid of hurting others . . . at my own expense."

"Well, dearie, you and I still have a helluva lot in common."

As he speaks, my attention is seized by a curious sight ahead of us. It is a low structure, totally incongruous to its surroundings. I don't mention it, wondering if John is intending to surprise me. We come closer to it with every step.

"Ever been in a Buddhist temple?" he asks indifferently.

"No, never. Is that what I'm seeing?"

"You've got it! Wanna go inside?"

"Sure! If you think it's okay."

"To hell with what *I* think! What do *you* think?"

I smile tensely. "It's something I've always wanted to do. I'd like to go in."

"Okay. So would I!"

We move closer to the wooden structure. It looks bizarre in these open, flaxen hills. Soon we are standing in front of it. John clasps his hands together for a moment and bows before entering the door, which is ornamented with weathered-looking brass. I do the same.

Once inside, I observe the large, spacious room filled with Asiatic-looking men in saffron robes. They are sitting cross-legged in meditation and take no heed of us.

"We won't stay long," John whispers. "But I thought you might enjoy it here—it's one of me favorite places."

"The incense makes me feel weird!"

"Yeah, it's powerful stuff. It can send yer four-dimensional consciousness flying," he chuckles.

We sit down on the matted floor and close our eyes. Instantly I see the enormous image of Buddha smiling at me.

"It shows great respect to allow other people to learn their own lessons and have their own problems without playing God or Mommy," the Buddha articulates in John's voice.

"Is that the meaning of Zen?" I ask in my thoughts.

"Whatever," he laughs. I shake my head and open my eyes. John has opened his, too, and is looking at me wisely. As he looks away, I close my eyes again.

"You can't rectify all the misery in the world," the Buddha continues, this time in a deep, booming voice.

It seems I can *see* John's thought-forms: He is standing with a group of men and women near a great body of water. He's receiving a blessing from a man in a toga. At John's side is a lion. I rub my eyes and open them.

As I do this, the room is filled with deep, guttural intonations. The voices of the worshippers in the room join to produce a stream of sound-force which unifies the thoughts dancing in my mind. The images and ideas spinning inside me have become motionless, like dead leaves after a storm. Eventually the sound dies too, and we wait, frozen in place, for what seems like hours. John nods, and we quietly leave.

Once outside, the air is hot but not oppressive. I absorb the golden glow of the hills and their wonderful smell of dried grass. We do not speak. I follow John in the direction of the mountains, which are slowly turning from blue to purple.

A raven flies overhead like a large, black dot. It circles and lands on John's right shoulder, as if returning to its master. He greets the bird without losing a step or a swing of his walking stick.

"It's helping us ta find our way," John says.

"Where are we going?"

"To the place of the wild swans."

We walk uphill for many miles as the sun begins to set behind us. The landscape has become rockier, much of it the same volcanic material we've been seeing all along. The raven has taken flight several times, yet reappears to roost on John's shoulder each time.

I see large, white, flying objects in the sky, and soon realize they are swans. John is watching them, too.

"We're almost there," he says happily. "Just a little further."

He motions toward the soaring creatures. Going around the bend of one more hill, I suck in my breath as my eyes behold awesome, white stone structures resembling Greek temples. They are nestled at the foot of the mountains and cast bronzed shadows from the fading sun.

~4~
The Trumpeting of Swans

Approaching the classic structures, we come to stand upon a carpet of lush grass. Next to us is an elder tree laden with ripe berries. Beyond glistens an oblong pond with circles of blooming rose bushes on the opposite side. Gazing into it, we see fish with scales like silver and gold.

"Look over there," John says, pointing into the dimming sky. Rising from the mountains is a silver moon, round and large. A pair of swans sail directly above us and make a spectacular landing on the water.

"Where is everybody?" John exclaims.

"Is there supposed to be somebody?"

"They were expecting us," he answers, preoccupied.

Immediately appearing on the steps of the nearest temple is a group of women varying in age. They wear robes of unusual pastel tints and smile and gesture as if we are familiar. They utter no sound.

"What do they want?" I ask John, amused.

"Yer supposed ta go with them, dear . . . I hadn't told you."

"Go with them? What are *you* going to do?"

"Oh, I'll be sleeping in the men's quarters. They're old-fashioned here!" he snickers. "Enjoy yerself. Toodle-oo!"

With these words, he waves goodbye and saunters toward another section of the complex. For a moment I feel lost. One of the young women approaches and puts her arm in mine. We join the group walking through stone corridors and enter a hallway lined with ferns and exotic flowers. Outside, beyond large archways, another pool shimmers in the twilight.

Not a sound escapes our lips, except for the occasional tittering of a few younger girls. Grinning appreciatively, I'm charged with curiosity about where they are taking me and where I will be sleeping this night.

We enter an indoor bathing area which is wonderfully steamy and scented with lavender. They offer coarse linen towels, a pale, corn-yellow robe and matching slippers. Undressing, I notice my body is covered with dust. A servant takes away my slippers, jumpsuit and walking stick. I wonder if I'll see them again.

Relaxing deeply in a hot mineral bath, I soak in luxury. The tension in my body swiftly melts away, and I realize I am exhausted—and hungry. The maidens glance at me politely, and the younger ones continue to giggle. The woman who escorted me earlier comes closer and makes gestures of putting food into her mouth and chewing. She laughs and points to a door on the other side of the room. I nod enthusiastically, and we swim toward the azure-blue steps of the pool.

After everyone has dried and dressed, we pass through a doorway into another long corridor filled with flowering plants. We come to a small kitchen where I am given a bowl of cooked rice and steamed vegetables. The women of silence watch patiently as I eat.

Finally, I am led to a tiny, candle-lit chamber with a narrow bed and a window overlooking the inner pool. Next to the bed is a small table with a jug of water and a bowl; underneath the bed is a large chamber pot! It's dark outside, except for the flush of the moon reflecting in the pool. With the chirp of crickets singing softly in my ears, I crawl into the hard bed, blow out the candle and immediately fall asleep.

I'm awakened in the early morning by the trumpeting of swans. What were those peculiar dreams? I recall grotesque, archetypal objects resembling musical instruments. There had been a magnificent harp. I feel like I've been chewed up by the gods and spit out in a new form.

There is a gentle tapping at the door.

"Yes?" I say.

My woman-friend enters carrying a steaming hot mug of tea and a small platter of fruit. She grins, showing her handsome teeth, and indicates I should enjoy my meal. I thank her, and she departs.

While eating breakfast, I notice my clothes and pointed slippers have been cleaned and returned. After throwing cold water on my face, I put them on.

I feel marvelous—like new. My walking stick stands in the corner by the door. I grab it, humming, and peer into the corridor. I don't see a soul, but manage to find my way outside.

Soon I'm standing alone in the cool, invigorating, pinkish atmosphere of dawn. Returning to the fish in the pond, I greet them and the swans gathered there. I spy a pair of black swans! Moving to the other side, I explore the rose garden which fills my entire being with happiness.

Across the pond, I see John waving from the steps of the nearby complex.

"Good mornin'! How's it goin'?" he says softly, joining me in the garden.

"Good morning! I've never felt happier. You certainly know how to pick your lodgings! It's as if I've been on a month's vacation. Where are the people?"

His animated features inspect me.

"I guess they're at work."

"What do they do here? It's an amazing place."

"These are healing temples, my dear, have you forgotten?"

"You mean . . . our healing temples?"

"I thought you'd remember. Of course, these are a composite of many . . ."

I look at him and shake my head.

"I wish I had known that last night! But can't we say goodbye to them? I don't know how the men are, but the women are incredibly kind. Do they work together here?"

"You can answer that yerself, kid. Don't you remember?"

He gives me a playful push with the end of his walking stick, and I pretend to be upset. "Well, we have to thank them and say goodbye! But I don't want to disturb anyone."

With these words, we notice a small group of people clustered in front of the temples. Among them is the woman who served as my guide. The men are also dressed in robes of varying pastel colors. Moving briskly forward, John and I motion to them and they gesture back.

"Thank you for your wonderful hospitality," I say quietly, approaching my friend. She comes forward, embraces me and places a stunning necklace of amber beads around my neck. It glitters like liquid sunlight.

"Thank you!" I exclaim, dumbfounded.

John waves goodbye with both hands, and I imitate him. The whole group is smiling and waving in the same funny way. We depart, gesturing one last time before moving out of their sight around the bend of a parched hill.

Clasping the necklace, I express my excitement. "What a gift! Why do you suppose they gave me *this*?"

"It's gonna help you carry the Light," John answers cheerfully. "It's also a protective talisman for the remainder of our journey. Wear it with pride—as I do my invisible sword."

"Look! Inside these beads are crystallized insects . . ."

"Aye! Caught in the act of taking life's breath."

~5~
Mashoe

Blinding shafts of sunlight are peeping out from above the mountaintop as we find ourselves standing in a rocky area adjacent to the mountain.

"Yer gonna need every bit a that superb rest you had last night! Ready ta climb?"

"I'm ready!"

"Our first stop will be on the plateau."

"What's there?"

"Oh, it's better to wait and see. Meanwhile, I'm lookin' for a path which'll make it easier for us ta get there."

"Thank goodness. I was wondering about this mountain climbing, to be honest."

John dashes ahead, around a pile of boulders.

"Okay, I've found it!" he shouts. "This way!"

I join him, and our steep climb up a narrow, rugged footpath commences.

"Tell me if it's too much fer you," he says, turning his head.

"I'll do my best."

"Yer not afraid of heights, I hope?"

"Sometimes. But this trail seems solid enough."

"It's fascinating. These elevations can finish off a lotta folks."

"Well, if vertigo starts to haunt me, I'll let you know."

We wend our way skyward in the splendour of the morning. The view is exhilarating—we are even able to see the Mystical Ocean, which makes my chest ache. I don't know if this comes from the cherished memories or my burning lungs.

At last, approaching a broadening in the path, John looks for a place to sit down.

"Quite a climb, eh?" he puffs.

"It reminds me of Switzerland—where I first saw you in the form you're in now," I gasp.

He sits on a cushion of soft vegetation, and I plop down next to him.

"That was an important walk! Although, you were hard to convince in those days. You've come a long way, luckily."

"Yes, look at me! A fearless pioneer in your veiled, abstract world," I say, squeezing the amber beads with both hands. "Nothing could make me ignore it, now."

We pause to catch our breath.

"You've told me so much," I continue, "and my burning questions have begun to smolder. But you must have other earthly Expressions which are important to relate. Am I right?"

"You are."

He waits, contemplating.

"The two most interesting ones are the Shakespearean actor and the Italian opera singer. Those probably had the most direct influence on my ability to write good music and lyrics."

"I figured you had something like that in your past history . . ."

"Of course, we can't forget the troubadour, the devilish old chap."

"Were you really one of those, too?"

He nods with a smirk.

"It sounds romantic. Wouldn't it be fun to live another Expression like that?"

"I'd love to . . . if modern-day earthlings could forget about ticketing and possessing everything they get their hands on!"

"Do you think they will?"

"I don't know. It might ruin their whole trip of being able to brag once they return Here. 'I survived planet earth!' could be scrawled on their tee-shirts. It would set them apart from the other souls who never risked it themselves."

"Are there many who haven't done that?"

"More than you think. If all the souls who wanted to Express on planet earth were allowed to, it would be like trying to fit an elephant into a thimble."

"You mean, not everyone can gain admission?"

"No! And there are few people on earth who realize what a privilege it is to be there. Talk about ignorance and lack of gratitude. C'mon . . ."

We stand and resume our climb. I become jittery when the path gets narrow along a precipitous edge, which happens frequently. At these moments, I stare with total concentration at my feet, not daring to admire the breathtaking view.

I seem to know more and more of what John is thinking about; but perhaps it is the other way around. For instance, in my mind I see Basil laboring with an object resembling a pole when John turns and asks, "How'd ya like to see old Basil again?"

"I'd like that! It's been a long time since I saw him in Arcadia."

"He's a busy man. But guess what? We're gonna see him on the plateau . . . which isn't far away."

I put my hand to my forehead. "There's an odd pressure in my head. I'm so giddy."

"It's part of the whole setup here, Linda. No one can climb this high and not feel entirely transformed."

We approach a wider trail which is less steep. Advancing further, we are suddenly standing on a broad plateau, filled with bushes, trees and open plain.

"Hey! There's a whole different world here!" I shout.

"Right . . . and see that fellow over there?" John says, pointing to our left.

"It's Basil! What's he doing?"

"Tending his garden."

Walking toward the vast, open fields, we observe Basil toiling with a large hoe.

"He's been working on this garden as long as I've known him," John muses. "Every seed symbolizes the creative force being planted in individuals on earth. Many thousands are being helped by him—directly or indirectly. As the seeds grow into plants Here, they symbolize the potential realities which manifest themselves in human beings."

"He's a hard-working man," I say, "a man of the soil. How does he manage to achieve such a good integration between the forces of heaven and earth?"

"He's had numerous Native American Expressions. I didn't find it unusual."

"Yes, it's logical." I stop to think. "But . . . doesn't he see us here? Why hasn't he come to talk with us."

"Oh, he can't see us right now. He's in another environment which we're not allowed to share—like the little boy you saw in the foothills. We're lucky we can watch."

"Now I understand. A long time ago, when I first received Basil's help, he told me he and I had shared Expressions as Native Americans," I boast. "See the corn growing at the far end? It's lovely . . ."

John nods. "Basil said it helps send the Corn Goddess to earth. She has somethin' ta do with the original use of sun energy, remember? The yellow cast of the sun affects a human being's solar plexus area, and the Corn Goddess speaks to that. She speaks of creativity in union with universal guidance."

"No wonder Basil has helped so much," I whisper.

"I wanted ta show you this, but actually, we've got an appointment."

"Oh! How exciting. We've never had one of those."

"Yer gonna attend a meeting of the Group of Seven with me."

"Sounds exclusive. What was it now . . . the Green Ray or something like that?"

"Green Wave. The Group of Seven is the smallest of my Green Wave topic groups, okay?"

"Sure! I forgot the details. And I'm allowed to attend a meeting with you?"

"Right! You'll be pleased. It's novel, of course, to have an earthling join us."

"What does everyone else think?"

"They were intrigued. They said maybe we had a great deal to learn from it. But they'll hafta adjust their life-wheels. Some of 'em haven't had direct contact with an incarnate soul for an earth's age."

"Well, it sounds good. I'm ready when you are."

We leave Basil's garden, going toward an open plain.

"Mashoe is here somewhere," says John looking in all directions.

"Who's that?"

"He's our group lion."

"Not dangerous?"

"Oh, God, no. He wouldn't hurt a ratatouille."

"What's his importance?"

"It began as a joke, but now he's become indispensable to us—for the present—*now* in Arcadia, meaning the environment we are constructing."

A lion is bounding across the plateau toward us. If John hadn't told me he was tame, I might think he was attacking us.

"Thata boy. Good Mashoe."

The lion stops a few meters away and then sidles up to us, looking wary.

"He'll have to get used to you," John laughs, grabbing the animal by it's enormous mane and patting its posterior.

The thing is gargantuan; I've never stood next to a lion.

"And maybe," I say, "I'll have to get used to him."

John doesn't seem to hear.

"As I told you before, the cycle group which a soul is in stays the same for a series of Expressions," he tells me, still patting the lion. "But under the umbrella of each are the theme and topic groups which vary according to individual needs. When you first came to visit me in Arcadia, my smallest topic group—the Green Wave Sub—was comprised of different individuals than it is now—except for one. This was because of my own development. When you first got Here, me own father,

Freddie, was part of this motley gang, but we have since parted ways. Souls keep switching not only their themes and topics of learning, but the smaller groups within."

"It sounds complex. Basically you're saying your theme and topic groups can be assorted colors—and within each color, there are shifting groups."

"Exactly. It's not the easiest thing to describe."

"Do you know when you will meet someone again?"

"Not really. It's intuition. I've yet to be in a sub-group with me mother, fer instance. But I have a basic trust that we'll end up in one eventually. We're both part of the Nine Cycle . . . see?"

"Are you limited to meeting only those souls who are included within your own cycle group?"

"We're limited in the sense that we learn mostly from members of our own cycle. Otherwise, we can have contact with any soul we please."

"Who decides this?"

"Nobody decides—it's natural law. Souls learn in their own unique tempo, and learning transforms energy. Simultaneously, energy bodies attract and repel, seeking their own kind—their own reverberation. When there has been enough learning and exchange, all groups reorganize spontaneously."

The lion, Mashoe, is staring at me.

"What if he doesn't appreciate earthlings?" I ask nervously.

"No problem. I know he likes you. And now we're off to our meeting."

With Mashoe beside us, we tramp across the plain until we come to a sparsely-wooded area.

Suddenly, from behind a tree, an elderly black man appears. He is tall and dressed in an elaborate tribal costume.

"Hallo! Oneye-ooh!" John calls out.

The man looks like a chieftain and emanates greatness. He raises one hand in salutation and answers John in words unintelligible to me, although I know exactly what he is saying. "Hail worthy friend! Fine to meet you on the pathway to our teachers."

I accept this new telepathic ability as being entirely natural. Furthermore, I wonder how I'd functioned without it.

"Oneye-ooh was once a man of wide influence in his community," John informs me. "I've learned crucial things from him."

The three of us travel silently through the woods, Mashoe at our side.

"Do you ever have arguments?" I ask. "Is it always so friendly?"

"Not always! It depends on the subject. Once I had to fight this royal warrior," John says, inspecting Oneye-ooh with obvious admiration. "It wasn't easy, was it?" he asks sincerely.

Oneye-ooh nods cordially.

"Who won?" I interrupt.

"Who do you think?" John laughs.

I don't answer because Oneye-ooh is telling a story. Ambling along a broad and well-worn path, he relates how John had once become temperamental and needed to learn a lesson. Oneye-ooh could have destroyed him, he confides, but instead chose to teach him about introspection and self-control. I ask the old man if he succeeded and he answers with a parable-like saying: "If you trust your helpers on the way to the mountain, you will surely succeed."

Without warning, an attractive blond woman appears directly in front of us. I get a vivid picture of her having been a prostitute in the California Gold Rush days. She has a sexual presence which is spellbinding, yet this is distinctively combined with an air of intellectual refinement.

"Donna Dee! How good ta see yer pretty head," John calls gleefully.

"How are y'all?" she answers in a husky voice, exuding ardor and charm. "An' ah thought ah might be late! Hi there."

Donna Dee gives me a special nod, and I offer my hand.

"Nice ta meet you!" She answers genuinely.

Mashoe wanders up to her and sniffs.

"This should be a good one," she says to no one in particular and I assume she is referring to the upcoming gathering of the Group of Seven.

Donna Dee seems familiar. I observe her with fascination. At this moment, a short, stout, middle-aged individual takes shape with bright, curly red hair, several chins and rosy-red cheeks.

"Tubber!" The others cry out.

He is indisputably Irish.

"Thought I would join ye lads . . . and lassies! Excuse me madams!" He bows ostentatiously, ". . . before the show begins!"

As he turns to bow, I notice a penny whistle sticking out of his back pocket. Studying him closely, I realize he was once an innkeeper and someone always willing to entertain.

Oneye-ooh inspects the party with an amiable expression and Mashoe persists in making his rounds, even approaching to sniff at me.

John struts proudly through the woods with his merry kin, and I follow along like a newly-initiated apostle.

"Four down, three ta go . . ." he bellows.

Looking to my side, I see Donna Dee hoisting her long skirts while Tubber labors to keep up.

"Why, Woo-Ling!" I hear in John's Liverpudlian accent, "how you've changed!"

Standing next to John is a matronly Chinese woman in a beautiful silk pantsuit. She bows, then greets the group in her own language. She is saying, "May our road to the Mysterious Ones be blessed."

Woo-Ling personifies refinement, proper conduct and worthy ideals. She has borne many children and was once married to a tailor in the emperor's court. She is afraid of no one and will easily voice her opinion if vexed.

I am shaken from my intense character study of Woo-Ling by the sight of a teenage Native American girl standing next to her. She is shy and restrained, with long, black hair and bad skin. I sense she once had an Expression on a reservation in the American Southwest, but chose to end it prematurely by her own hand.

"An' here we have Mary Wilkens—originally called Mary Wild Dog 'til her parents died and she tried to get work outside the reservation," Donna Dee volunteers, stroking the girl's head.

"Nice to meet you," I respond, offering my hand.

She takes it, and the corners of her mouth turn slightly upward, but she says nothing. There is a curious strength in her handshake that startles me.

By now I am dazed by the new faces and personalities. For the first time, I feel lost in the crowd. John is more aloof and, in spite of my impressive new telepathy and clairvoyance, I don't know what to do with myself.

I think of the Buddha I saw in the foothills.

"Hold onto Life instead of people," he's telling me. "If you hold onto Life, the people will always be there."

"Where have I heard that before?" I wonder.

"It doesn't matter," the Buddha replies, "just do it."

"Okay! I'll try."

As I'm occupied with these thoughts, the strangest-looking character I've seen in Arcadia appears and approaches us.

~6~
Archimedros

He—or she—is extremely tall and dressed in a silvery costume which extends upward covering the head. Peering at us is a face with large round eyes, which look both male and female.

"Well, well . . . our token Andromedean! I wondered if you were gonna show up . . ." John chides.

Instantly, I get the message that this is an androgyne from another constellation! My heartbeat quickens as Shehe advances in our direction. I'm becoming emotional and wonder what is going on.

The creature is speaking to us in a language which resembles the music of panpipes. Who can explain the sensation of deep love I now feel? As Shehe speaks, its eyes reveal a peculiar, melancholic kindness.

"My dearest friends! Let us go at once to the place of our teachers!" Shehe proclaims in its amazing musical vernacular.

"Workers of the universe, ignite!" John throws in. Then, leaning over toward me, he whispers, "This is our astonishing colleague. Shehe has had a number of Expressions in the constellation Andromeda, and I'm just beginning ta comprehend the deeper sense of its reality. Talk about another kinda place! There's this certain intensity of love comin' from parts of that constellation which simply boggles the spirit. It's like a fire consuming everything in its wake."

"I don't know what to think! I only know it hurts."

"The love?"

"Yes!"

"Shehe definitely adds a distinctive element to our group," John mutters.

I gawk at the silvery figure with bewilderment, but Shehe doesn't seem to mind. I don't know what has come over me. It's as if I've fallen desperately in love, but obviously it's more.

Passing through the forest, everyone is conversing in a cacophony of sound. I assume they are catching up on the latest experiences and events. Mashoe is at Mary Wilkens' side as she earnestly confides in Tubber, the rotund Irishman. He responds sympathetically, occasionally patting her on the shoulder. Woo-Ling, Oneye-ooh and the Andromedean are chuckling and gesturing to one another. Donna Dee and John are discussing the pros and cons of Expressing in modern times on planet earth.

I would like to talk to the Andromedean, but lack courage. Perhaps if I didn't care so much . . .

We arrive at an open area next to a towering, leafy tree with thick, lofty branches. This is the Learning Tree which Julia mentioned so long ago! Obviously it is a familiar meeting place, and the groups continue their discourses as if waiting for something to happen. I try to remain objective and patient.

Suddenly there is absolute silence. Nobody is talking or looking at each other, as if by common agreement. Each individual directs his or her concentration inward, and the atmosphere becomes contemplative and serene.

Tubber removes the penny whistle from his pocket and starts to play a slow, poignant air. Oneye-ooh beats softly on a drum in accompaniment, and Mary Wilkens is shaking her rattle. Donna Dee begins to vocalize in a low, enchanting hum while John sings harmonizing notes. Woo-Ling is playing an ancient Chinese zither as the Andromedean recites its traditional poetry in the language of panpipes. And Mashoe and I join in utter stupefaction.

Somehow it works. They are producing the most glorious sounds—definitely other-worldly. Combined with the giddiness in my head, I feel intoxicated. Mashoe gives me a knowing glance.

The Group of Seven are blending their individual sensibilities into a collective awareness which will establish a new environment. The lion and I are allowed to join because we are their guests, however silent or unimportant we may be.

Thunder resounds in the skies, and our surroundings take on new form. The ground starts to rumble and becomes greener. To my amazement, a vast lake appears on the opposite side of the Learning Tree, producing a new sensation of freedom and openness.

The last tones of music are gently ebbing, and its creators are standing around wearing proud grins. All attention focuses on a small white figure moving toward us on the shore of the shining lake.

He is an old and shriveled little man wearing a Greek or Roman tunic. He appears so old that I wonder how he gets around. Suddenly he is transformed into a younger version of himself; by the time he has reached us, he looks about sixty-five. He is carrying a load of papers and books under one arm, and a crown of olive leaves is perched on his head.

"What a character!" I think, and he winks at me. How embarrassing that everyone can read each other's thoughts!

"This is someone who doesn't take life too seriously," I muse.

He announces, "First, one good dash around the lake, and we'll commence!"

Of course he's joking, since I see no one moving. Oneye-ooh, Tubber and Woo-Ling would not manage well, to say nothing of Shehe, who has probably never dashed in its life.

Archimedros is the little man's name. Like the Pendragon, he is a high teacher here to address us.

"So, at last you've shown up to give us a lecture about early Greek religious cods," John jests.

Woo-Ling tries not to laugh, and the others are plainly enjoying themselves. Even Shehe looks less forlorn.

"First I'm going to return your papers from the last session," Archimedros says informally in Greek. "As you will see, I was hard on you. But, of course, that's why you are here."

The papers are passed around, and for a moment there is complete stillness among the Group of Seven. I look at John's paper, and it is filled with colorful, incomprehensible scribbles. Oneye-ooh is pressing his paper to his chest—with eyes closed, while Shehe explores its test with an open palm. Others seem to be reading theirs.

"Thank you for your commentary," Archimedros responds casually. "Consider these principles for the coming Eighth-Cycle of Bloom, and we'll work afterward on integration."

Mashoe is sleeping beside the mammoth trunk of the Learning Tree. My giddiness has lessened, but I have odd itching sensations in my life-wheels, particularly those in my solar plexus and forehead. Everyone is sitting on the soft grass, including Archimedros who, carefully tucking his tunic between his legs, prepares to speak.

"Consider the worship of nature on planet earth as the original human doctrine. Consider what has gone wrong with this doctrine and what caused it to occur. Consider how the first Greek poets worshipped nature and assumed it was God. Yet their God existed in all forms on earth, including mythical characters who represented all shades of light and dark and all stages of good and evil—though it wasn't until later that Greeks would come to label these terms as such. These early myths preached no morals because no one took it upon themselves to judge. Life could simply be what it was—experience! This left it up to small groups and individuals to make decisions according to their innate common sense. Where did this practicality come from? It came from the human ability to trust nature in all her pain and complexities. It was the absence of intellectual judgement—the absence of an absolute truth presided over by a stern, reproachful father-god. In the earliest mythology, Zeus was subject, as was everyone, to the powers of Ananke—'what has to be . . .' "

I watch the Group of Seven observing Archimedros. He goes on to mention the primitive Greek instinct for logic and unity and how well it blended with the inventive freedom abounding in mythology.

"These are but a few of the many pages of human history which have been carefully stored in the Arcadian Eternal Plan's timeless vaults, along with the Blueprint Rituals, which are being gradually resurrected by soul-starved earthlings."

Without thinking, I raise my arm.

"Yes, esteemed earthling?" Archimedros says eagerly, adjusting the folds of his tunic.

"Well, I wanted to ask about this separation-from-nature business. Has it gone this way on other planets?"

"A good question. It has, to varying degrees. But nowhere in the universe has separation been so radical as on earth."

I look at him, swallowing hard. "Why is that?"

"Because earth is one of the foremost planets of contrast. It is a costly kind of instruction, but if understood properly, can provide deep and lasting rewards."

"Thank you, sir," I reply.

"What about the later Greek philosophers?" John interjects. "Didn't they contribute largely to the elimination of nature worship in the Western world?"

"Correct. It was the philosopher's—notably Plato's—concept of the sovereign One-God which later helped to alter earth's original spiritual tenets and prepare it for organized religion. Next question?" says Archimedros, pointing to Donna Dee.

"Speaking of the masculine One-God, what about the enfranchisement of the female principle on earth?" she asks.

"Yes! The new, enlightened, male earthling will learn to love and appreciate the female principle living inside of him. This female principle can release him from a long and terrible term of bondage."

"And what about the male principle? Is it not of equal value?" Oneye-ooh objects.

Archimedros smiles benignly. "The male principle is of no less value, of course! Each new, enlightened, female earthling will learn to love and appreciate the male principle living inside her, which can release her from a long and terrible term of bondage."

He chuckles and continues. "The simple point is, dear ones, the male and female principles cannot exist without each other—not only between people, but within the psyche of one individual. The cosmic joke is that so many humans have tried for so long to live without a logical consolidation of the two! Now it is all coming out in the wash, so to speak," he says, continuing to beam.

"As an androgyne, I wish to comment," sings Shehe cheerfully. "Where I come from, most citizens have forgotten that the male and female principle *can* be separated."

"May I ask you something?" I articulate carefully, hoping it'll understand.

Shehe nods appreciatively.

"I don't mean to be offensive, but . . . is it any fun that way?"

"Fun is relative!" the voice of panpipes answers mirthfully as Shehe's splendid, round face challenges me in wonder and amusement.

"What about the importance of family?" Mary Wilkens inquires.

"We have them, but acquiring offspring is a different procedure . . ."

"Before we get too far off track," Woo-Ling interrupts, "I desire to ask a question of our honorable teacher. Is it not important to emphasize that the primitive Greek mind was entirely different than that of his classical descendants? Is it not the same story for nearly every society that has resided on earth—of how, imminently, intellect replaces instinct, and men end up dominating their women?"

"How can you say that?" Tubber objects vehemently. "My wife dominated me for over forty years!"

The assembly falls into a hubbub of verbal exchange until Archimedros restores order.

"My good scholars! Please accept disparate views as part of the one unfailing whole! Keep in mind the principle of integration—of all levels of experience and Expression."

Something small and hard hits me on the head. Glancing upward, I see an old, disheveled woman roosting in the branches of the Learning Tree. She is waving at me.

~7~
Naya

Little stones are being thrown at me! I pretend for a moment I haven't seen her. Archimedros is concluding his animated talk, and everyone else is oblivious to our new visitor. Then she does it again—tiny pebbles are hitting my head.

"If you don't mind," I say loudly, standing up and looking at her.

Archimedros and the Group of Seven glower at me in unison.

"Who is *that*?" I demand.

"Who is *who*?" Archimedros questions politely.

"Look!" I cry, pointing into the lofty branches. But there's no one there.

"If you could be more patient, my good earthling, our meeting will be finished in a twinkling," he says with a lighthearted tone.

I sit again, feeling foolish. Soon everyone is standing and chattering, and it seems the meeting is coming to an end. John approaches me.

"What possessed you? Rants in yer pants?"

"How embarrassing! But, really . . . there was an old woman in the tree throwing stones at me!"

"Yeah, you do look a bit stoned. What shall we do about it?"

"Dammit, believe me . . ."

As I say this, John turns and greets an old, toothless woman dressed in animal skins. "Naya! What a privilege! Yer just in time to meet my earthling friend . . . Linda, meet one of my favorite high teachers."

Confounded, I offer my hand and notice how homely she is.

"Nice to meet you," I say, trying not to sound artificial.

"It's good to drop in, now and again, to other folks' meetings," Naya utters innocently in an unfamiliar language.

She once had black hair. Now it is heavily streaked with grey and hangs unkempt on her shoulders. Her large face—sagging, wrinkled and toothless—stares at me in delight.

"Yes, I could say the same thing," I respond, warming up to her a bit. Then, deciding to be honest I ask, "Was there some objective to the pebble tossing?"

Touching a hairy hand to my amber necklace, she says, "Child, it's time to go to the top."

"The top of what?"

"Of the mountain, of course. Your loyal ally here," she points to John, "is ready to make the journey. Do you dare accompany us?"

I look at John probingly. "Well, if it's allowed . . . there isn't anything I'd rather do."

"If he has brought you this far . . . there must be a purpose," she replies.

"Naya is an excellent climber, ya know . . . one of the best," John says consolingly. "But first, let's say goodbye ta the others."

He steers me to Archimedros, who is chatting with Woo-Ling and Tubber. We stand, waiting, which gives me the chance to view the teacher's remarkable blue-green eyes; they are the color of the Mediterranean. Continuing to inspect him, I reflect on the attributes of water; I'm sure he has plenty to teach about human emotions.

"It's a rare moment when an incarnate soul is allowed to come Here," he exclaims happily to us. "This place used to be thick with them—but generations have changed! Now we're lucky if we get one embodied priestess, shaman or witch doctor passing through here in the course of an entire evaluation period."

"I'm honored . . . not only to be part of this, but to have met you, Mr. Archimedros."

"Oh, call me Archie."

"Well, thank you! Sorry I interrupted the last part of your meeting—it wasn't my intention."

"Naya does enjoy her flashy entrances," John says supportively.

"Yes, forget it happened, okay? Now, I want to wish both of you all the luck . . ."

It's as if I hear him saying, "You're going to need it."

John is humming to himself, giving the impression all is right with the universe. We say goodbye to the rest of the group, and I thank them for allowing me to share these moments.

"It has been a most intriguing experience," Woo-Ling proclaims cordially. The others agree.

"It gave me ideas for my next Expression," Mary Wilkens says optimistically. "Thank you for coming."

"What did I tell you?" John pipes up. "Consciousness Conveyance is alive and well! I knew it was an excellent idea. 'Til next time, folks."

He waves enthusiastically, then we pick up our walking sticks and look for Naya. She is waiting patiently, sitting on the ground with legs crossed, leaning against the Learning Tree. She's stroking Mashoe, who is awake and alert.

"Ready, my worthies?"

She stands with difficulty, causing me to doubt her ability to take us up the mountain.

"We've never been more ready," John answers staunchly, "eh earthling?"

"He's right, we never have been."

"See ya around, fella," John says, approaching Mashoe and slapping him firmly on the back.

Archimedros and the others wave goodbye, and Naya leads us toward the shining lake. Beyond it are the mountain peaks, crowned with snow.

Arriving at the lakeshore, we walk three-abreast on the firm sand.

"Don't forget to trust, earthling!" Naya cackles in her curious vernacular. "It goes by itself."

"I know," I answer sadly, "it's a matter of allowing it."

John doesn't seem to hear us. He's unusually quiet—ogling the mountain peaks.

We walk for miles beside the shining lake. Naya plods along like an aged lioness, and John's attention is somewhere in the clouds.

At last we reach the other side of the lake and are ready to ascend. The path Naya has chosen is narrow, steep and formidable. With John between us, she leads the way. I'm astonished at her strength and stamina.

"They don't make 'em like that anymore," I reflect.

John remains withdrawn and contemplative. Glancing down the sunny precipice, I realize I could easily plummet over the edge without anyone taking notice. Yet the view is superb. As my walking stick digs fiercely into the dirt, I notice that the funny, pointed slippers on my feet have become old and worn.

Eventually a cold, blustery wind comes up, making me shudder. Naya has acquired several extra animal skins on her burly frame, making her resemble a miniature abominable snow-woman. I feel a velvety-soft warmth covering my shoulders and know it's my trusty cape. I caress its downy edges with relief and rub it lovingly against my cold face. I recognize its scent—slightly musty with a hint of the sea, flowers, herbs and rain. I won't forget this smell, not in a hundred Expressions.

My reminiscing has made me lightheaded, and I snap out of it in panic, fearing a loss of equilibrium. John has his cape on now and is moving with a steady gait up the narrow trail, not once looking back. It's as if I'm not there. For the first time, I am angry with him.

"What does he expect? That I am his servant—following him like a flunky?"

"Embrace Life instead of people," echoes through my dazed head. Despite this, a devastating sense of loneliness engulfs me. I'm not sure I want to continue. *Why should I? What's the whole point anyway?*

My years of arduous work on earth race through my mind, making my eyes burn and shoulders ache. *What is the point? Is it really worth the pain?*

The sharp, cold wind increases. I toil upward in despair, disoriented and not knowing what to do.

The wind is dying, and being replaced by a mist which rapidly encloses us. The sensational view has vanished behind a thick, impenetrable fog. I trudge ahead. I can't see John a few meters ahead of me! I'm incapacitated by fear. I must heed my step! It's the only thing I've got left.

In this mood of survival, my sensibilities are becoming toughened and resigned. My body has adjusted to the demands, and adrenaline is pulsing resolutely through it. I lumber on.

Fear is gone now, replaced by composed sadness. There is no room for rationality, only resourcefulness. I am going to make it to the top of this mountain, even if it destroys me. But what mountain wants to destroy any being, even in Arcadia?

"I am not a victim," I mutter through clenched teeth.

My hand seizes the amber necklace. It feels sunny and comforting, linking me with the generous people who gave me food and shelter. I remember the tranquillity of the rose gardens and the wild swans gliding on the water.

We keep hiking. At certain moments when the fog has thinned, I see John and Naya ahead of me. Not once do they look back.

~8~
The Gate

The air has become colder. But with the lavish comfort of my cape, I'm not cold; instead, my feet are hot, my cheeks are blazing.

The fog begins to lift. I see John and Naya in front of me and directly ahead of them, through patches of vanishing fog, I see banks of immaculately-white snow. I see it stretching far and wide as the mist disappears.

We are no longer scaling a precipitous alpine trail. We have reached the great summit of the mountain, and my feet hardly know how to cope with their new horizontal stance.

Reflecting off the snow, blinding sunshine assaults my eyes. Naya stops and pivots to face us for the first time since starting. John turns around too, looking strangely exuberant; they examine me probingly.

"You are to be commended for your endurance," Naya remarks in her curious, guttural sing-song voice. She displays a toothless grin.

John has been 'mum' for such a long time that I'm shocked to hear him speak.

"Lo, though I walk up the mountain of the phantom of death, I shall fear no evil . . . ."

"Does that mean you had the same terrifying ordeal I did?' I sigh.

"Let's put it this way . . . I've had easier trips," he answers reservedly.

I'm intrigued with the expression on his face. It shows an odd sort of elation, but also bears a tinge of grief. With silvery locks and crinkles around his eyes, he looks older and wiser than I've ever seen him. But this does not seem to hinder his childish mirth.

"Naya will be leading us to The Gate," he says, giving me a meaningful stare.

I realize I already know about The Gate. There's not much I need to ask John, as if we've entered a sphere of perception which requires no explanations.

Naya steps between John and me and takes our arms in hers. She directs us along a narrow passage in the brilliant snow.

"You are filled with grace," she intones.

Suddenly she has the face of a baby—toothless and unblemished—and is being entirely supported by our arms. The many animal skins are wrapped around her like swaddling clothes.

Looming above us like a mirage is a gateway of shimmering light surrounded by exquisite rainbow hues.

"My task has been completed," Naya croons. "Go in safety with The Unfailing One."

With these words, her body shrinks to the size of a baby, and I am cradling her in my arms. John looks at me with gleaming eyes.

"Don't worry, dear, she'll be fostered by the Ancient Mother."

Images of my new baby son on earth sparkle through my mind.

"I was going to say I have enough responsibility at home."

"You may deliver her to me as a gift," a gentle voice murmurs, "to bless your sacred entrance through The Gate."

There, standing before us in resplendent glory, is an angel—wings and all.

"Please be my guests," it beseeches. "Do step through!"

Bracing ourselves, John and I cross the threshold to witness a veritable paradise. My breath is taken away, its pristine beauty surpasses any environment I have witnessed in Arcadia.

Passing the sleeping infant into the arms of the angel, I hear the sound of a horn being blown, followed by the tinkling of distant bells.

"Felicitations upon your safe arrival!" the angel proclaims. "May the strength and joy of The Unfailing One be with you."

Leading us through verdant pastures and ripening orchards, the angel sings in a joyful voice. There are no words to the song, but I know it's about bliss—the bliss of freedom.

"That's Gabriel for you," John says, picking a ripe apple off a tree and taking a bite. "Want one?"

"How could I not?"

He plucks another bright red apple and hands it to me. Sinking my teeth into the firmness of its flesh, I taste the sweetness of all creation.

Cradling baby Naya, the angel leads us into a world of majestic waterfalls where the sun shines like gold through mists of rainbow light. Stepping on wet, glistening stones, we cross to mossy banks and lounge in contentment.

"The good news is," Gabriel says, carefully cradling the sleeping infant, "the gate to paradise is open to everyone. The bad news is, few know how to find it!"

The refreshing vapors from the nearest waterfall waft delicately across our faces.

"I have more good news," John adds with reassuring conviction, "those who *truly* desire to find it will succeed."

Eventually I dare to speak. "Finally, a real angel! I was starting to give up hope I'd ever have the satisfaction of meeting one."

"Well, a true rendering of heaven wouldn't be complete without 'em," John says, tossing his apple core into a swirling eddy. "Not seeing an angel in heaven would be like not seeing the pitcher at a baseball game."

Gabriel nods, pleased. He fixes his animated eyes on me.

"We will be going forthwith to a place where the reality of all schools and all worlds may join together," he says in delighted tones. "It's the only place in Arcadia where this can happen—are you willing?"

"Yes! Please take us there," I answer, looking ecstatically at John. I can tell by his face this will not be his first visit, yet I detect in him an exhilaration equal to mine.

Scaling steep banks, we enter a sunny glen filled with rare flowers, treating our nostrils to unusual, exquisite fragrances. Wild canaries flit about, serenading us with their enraptured melodies.

At the far end of the glen, we reach flat, open countryside. Patches of lovely white heather grow everywhere and the scent gladdens our spirits even more. With one free arm, Gabriel points proudly to the horizon. There, dancing and flickering—as if a living creature—is a fire of unbelievable intensity. An immense, white, bowl-shaped foundation jutting close to the ground houses the flames. There are tiny shapes walking to and fro.

The sky has become a vibrant, marine-blue. Around the leaping flames a light-violet tint hovers in the atmosphere. A feeling has arisen in me which is similar to the one I felt when in the presence of Shehe, the Andromedean. This time it is stronger, however, making me wonder if I can bear it.

I recall the dream I had on the tenth anniversary of John Lennon's death: I had been awakened by this same euphoric sensation. In the dream, I'd been helping John cleanse his past. Afterward, this amazing, burgeoning love for the whole world, the entire universe, was being aptly related by John's phrase, "all you need is love."

"Ah, the Christfire burns brighter than ever!" John exults.

"Because your eyes have become keener," Gabriel answers.

Turning to me he adds, "We call it the 'Christfire,' and although it may have different names in countless places, lo, it is the same."

John's face has become solemn. "All the great teachers on earth have been illuminated by it—the Great Fire of Love and Forgiveness. It is the eternal flame which will consume everything in its wake, if the heart is prepared."

"Is that the pain I feel?"

"Yes! That's part of it—the great pain of happiness. For many souls it is practically unbearable, so they do their best to forget about it."

"But why did I feel it so profoundly in the presence of Shehe? I don't understand."

"Because," John explains, "there are folks who have taken the Christfire into their hearts more successfully than earthlings—up 'til now, anyway. It's a well-known fact here in our Infinite Dwelling . . . but there are so many things you couldn't possibly know yet, dear!"

"And this little one goes off to her Ancient Mother," Gabriel blithely reports, rustling his wings and admiring the sleeping baby in his arms.

"In the name of the God and Goddess One, the Christfire and the Higher Self, I wish you the fondest adieu!"

Gabriel swings around and moves, half-walking and half-flying, in the direction of the glen.

I am standing next to John, amazed. Besides the nearly-intolerable pain I encounter, I'm afraid. I know we will go closer to the mighty flames, but I doubt I'm ready for it. A tremendous desire rages in me to escape to the glen, the waterfalls, the orchards and the green fields. I give John a despairing glance.

"Don't be such a scaredy-cat," he chides. "Look!"

I am compelled to watch the fire. In doing so—by not trying to resist—I feel much better. The ache in my chest is decreasing, as is the fear. I take a deep breath.

"Are you up ta meeting it face-to-face?" John asks kindly.

"I don't know if I'm up to it, but I'm going to anyway."

Traveling between large patches of heather, I begin to realize that the many figures traveling to and fro from the Great Fire are not adults—they are children! The closer we get, the more I see what they are doing.

Each child approaches the edge of a vast, golden circle which encompasses the bowl-shaped foundation holding the flames. Apparently, this is the border over which no child dares cross for fear of getting burned. Some youngsters don't even get *that* close and hang back timidly.

The most striking thing about the whole scene is how, once facing the fire, each child is standing. In an endearing manner, he or she is leaning toward the Light—with arms extending behind and head uplifted—receiving it into his or her heart with complete surrender. I see the expression on each child's face: each is radiant and blissful, conveying a sense of timelessness and perfect serenity.

I realize the appearance of each youth alters—representing itself in new ways. Each child acquires a distinct face, hairstyle, clothes and characteristics, such as he or she would if progressing through centuries at a time of earthly lives. Other children resemble Shehe and are changing in strange ways. Their outward appearance alters only slightly, yet the colors surrounding them change—giving me an odd tingling sensation.

My stomach drops when I realize John and I are *no longer adults*. John has turned into a little school boy wearing a sweater and tie, his hair brushed neatly back. He is grinning at me sheepishly. Looking down, I view thick, auburn braids, a light-blue dress, and patent-leather shoes with white socks. Staring at him naively, I feel the freckles burning on my face.

~9~
Christfire

"I've been here before," the boy boasts.

"I have too, but I'd forgotten," I answer shyly.

"I'm waitin' fer me mum an' dad," he continues, fidgeting with his tie, which appears too tight.

"When are they coming?"

"Oh, they'll be here soon, they told me so!"

"*Then* what are you going to do?"

"We're goin' home and have a good laugh."

"My grandmother told me about this place, once," I declare, scrutinizing the heather.

"Wha'd she say?" The boy stops pulling on his tie and wrinkles his nose at me.

"That everybody carries secrets in their heart. Then she said, 'The truth which abides in us will be with us forever.' "

"Behold, I make all things new . . ." little John proclaims, giggling, then runs away with his arms out-stretched as if he's going to fly.

Dashing to the edge of the golden border, he bravely faces the flames with his chest protruding and his head proudly held up. I am awestruck as countless young personalities begin to display themselves before me.

Among them is a boy who is almost naked, wearing only a loincloth. He is transformed into a girl dressed in furs. I wonder how it would be to wear those clothes—it must tickle horribly!

Soon John's small frame has changed into a boy wearing a white tunic. In my mind, I see him standing next to blue pools while his father, Ra Na the Atlantean, talks with him about nature spirits.

A Greek boy has appeared who will work in a temple with his female cousin when he gets older. I try to recall his name, and as I do, a dark-skinned girl in Egyptian finery takes his place. It's impossible to keep up!

A Druid child in rough vestments has arrived, and another takes his place—I know they were born in a land which is later called the British Isles. Then a Japanese boy appears in elegant silk apparel.

It is stunning to witness how each of these innumerable children dares, at one moment or another, to lean toward the Light and receive it with complete surrender.

When a small gentleman playing the violin—once named Wolfgang—shows himself in a powdered wig, I am filled with ecstasy. His music, although not truly formed, has a curious, rousing quality which reminds me of the angel's song.

A boy named Robert comes into view. He loves to play in the green fields near London, daydreaming of drawings, music and rhymes.

At last I am standing face-to-face with a winsome black girl. With braids piled on her head, and wearing a big, white apron, she frolics as she works. With arms extended and head uplifted, Gracie receives the Light into her courageous heart.

The brazen schoolboy in sweater and tie returns to ogle my freckles, and I let out a deep sigh.

"I told you they'd come for me!" he shouts.

"Who?"

"Me *mum and dad*, silly! We had a jolly time like they promised!"

As he is saying this, I feel myself embarking on the same journey of metamorphosis as all the other children who come here. John is watching, but I can't see or hear him anymore. It's as if I'm in one of those nature films in which flowers are budding and blossoming instantaneously or a caterpillar endlessly transmutes into a butterfly.

It goes too fast for rational comprehension, yet is not the least bit confusing. My state-of-mind is as simple as the flower or the butterfly itself. Like them, I am in a reality where past, present and future are woven into one unfailing whole.

I am startled by the light-violet flames which incessantly lick at me and the other children without harming us. I sense these purplish flames are helping to propel us into our divine dance of change, encouraging us to more readily release our burdens of suffering. Miraculously, each child is rendered capable of carrying the good news of these workings into all dimensions of space and time.

My auburn braids and blue dress have reappeared.

"You looked funny," the little boy says thoughtfully. I'm not able to answer him. He scampers away with arms outstretched as if he really is going to fly.

"Come with me!" he squeals.

I run after him, frantically fluttering my arms. We begin to sail like birds into the marine-blue sky. Hovering above the unfathomable blaze, it looks like the sun itself.

"You see," the boy reveals, "Christfire was the first child of Mr. God and Mrs. Goddess. Only the love between 'em could have made it like *this*."

"How can I feel so free?"

" 'Cause love *is* free an' always has been! The fire is inside us . . . burnin' away the pain."

Sailing higher, we see the orb of the Great Fire expanding into the whole of paradise, ringed with magnificent rainbow luminescence. I hear an unusual sound—the rush of wings. Flocks of angels pass, moving undisturbed to their next appointments.

I see little John gazing open-mouthed at paradise. Looking quickly, I watch it grow into the blue pearl—our beloved planet earth! The finest nuances of color sharpen our vision, producing a clarity and brilliance beyond comparison. Amidst an impenetrable silence, this fragile vessel is floating in a sea of creation.

It is piercingly beautiful—so touchingly alone! Upon it is everything dear to us. It is our home, our sacred refuge.

Hovering like astronauts in the blackness of space, we embrace this perfectly round spaceship with our entire being. It embraces us back—our dazzling mother of material form! When we stand and breathe upon her again, her scent will be unspeakably sweet and intoxicating.

The boy and I behold the moon, rising and setting.

He points into the hidden darkness of the universe at the shining stars. Entire constellations are beckoning, daring us to fathom them, and the boy makes a promise. We'll go to those stars sometime—to those faraway beacons of Life.

Epilogue

I'm back in the meadow—with a lion at my side. He has been a faithful companion and is sleeping peacefully after our long journey. A neatly folded, golden-brown cape is lying on the ground, as well as worn and dusty slippers, and a walking stick. Their job is done. My weary, bare feet nestle into the soft ground for comfort. The handsome amber beads still hang securely around my neck.

My surroundings are delightfully warm and sunny—gentle with bird song. A brook is flowing nearby and I can smell the moist, green grass and fresh air. The sky is spacious and blue with a few puffy clouds hanging lazily about. Everywhere around me beautiful wild flowers reach out with a myriad of color. I am sitting under the shade of a large, stately oak, and—as I gaze into the distance—I notice those familiar trees, still whispering secrets to one another.

After our fantastic episodes in paradise and outer space, John and I gradually found our way back to The Gate. Traveling through the snow and down the crest of the mountain, we were children no more. Going back to the plateau, John's Group of Seven was congregating again by the lake, and he invited me to join them. Mashoe bolted toward us to sniff his long-lost friends, and I wondered how I could have thought him dangerous.

Naya had been there, too—a funny old lady sitting in the branches of the Learning Tree trying to distract us. This time I managed to ignore her, for I was enthralled by Archimedros' yarns of bygone Greece and its special bond with the universe.

During our descent to the plateau, John and I celebrated the spectacular success of Consciousness Conveyance. My apprenticeship was over; now he pronounced us colleagues in spirit. We agreed to keep the two-way path clear for mutual growth, happiness and continuing dialogue.

We had lengthy discussions about the Christfire and its uncanny genius for setting things straight.

"Behold, I make all things new," he kept on repeating, as if I could have forgotten!

At a distinct moment, I knew I must go. I parted from John on the plateau, and he asked Mashoe to be my protector and guide for the remainder of my journey through Arcadia.

Of course, I visited Basil's garden on the way out. He congratulated me on my stamina and said I made a good astronaut. I agreed—I could honestly admit both heaven and earth are my home.

Reclining in my lounge chair, I slowly turn my face to catch a few delicate, glorious sunrays. A fly buzzes around my ears, then darts away, and I linger, doing absolutely nothing. Gradually, I get the urge to return to my study in our house in the Dutch town where the weather, surprisingly enough, has been improving. Nearly six earth years have passed since I first permitted myself to travel to this place, to come into contact with my colleague in spirit, John Lennon.

★　　★　　★

Between voyages to Arcadia, I knew I needed to make another trip to Liverpool. But I didn't know what I was supposed to do there. I decided to do what any Beatlemaniac would do: surrender myself to the tourist trade. In one day, I visited Penny Lane, Strawberry Field, Menlove Avenue, St. Peter's Church and the old homes of the Fab Four. At each of these places, I experienced a distinct awareness that I'd been there before.

The next day, I backtracked alone to the suburbs of Woolton and Allerton—to the mundane world where John Lennon had grown up—wanting to absorb its intangible impressions. I had always known, since my trip the year before, that John could experience this through me. It was something I had learned to accept during my apprenticeship with him; we needed each other to encounter the Other World. This time I was more alert to it than ever.

Wandering in the rain, I was coming into contact with two disparate moods—one depressed and melancholic; the other joyous and free. A painful sense of duality was brooding inside me, and not all of it was mine. Much of it was John's, and together we were trying to mend the rift between doubt and certainty.

John's mending had to do with his past here, while mine mirrored his in present-time. In one way, I was totally convinced he was living through me. In another, I feared I had gone off the deep end—that this whole Lennon project was going to be my downfall. Pondering these stark contrasts brought even more confusion.

"All artists doubt," I can hear John announcing, as if resolving his own dilemma, "if they're any good, that is! If they're making something unique, doubting makes them stronger."

"You must be right. You once said my doubts made me more open."

"Aye, yer constant skepticism *did* make it easy fer me ta get through! So, I guess we should be celebrating good old-fashioned doubt—and be thankful for it's bold perseverance."

"Okay—let's do that."

I was pleased to be leaving Woolton on the upbeat—not only for myself, but for John, too. Following in the footsteps of his obsessive interest in death, I knew I had to return to the graveyard in Allerton I had left so abruptly the year before. I hadn't solved the mystery of that visit and was determined to complete my obscure mission. Why hadn't John led me to his mother's grave? I'd heard that Julia was, indeed, buried there. What was the meaning of my encounter with the other gravesite—the one belonging to a man named George Stanley?

After having gone home the first year, I read that Julia's father had been named George Stanley, but died much later than his namesake. A psychic friend told me that the George buried at the gravesite I visited had been a distant relative of John's; that his spirit was in distress, and I was supposed to help!

Having relocated the familiar Celtic cross, I deciphered the letters on Mr. Stanley's gravestone and noticed he had died in his mid-forties. Buried next to him was his wife who had passed away seventeen years later. Now I understood why he needed help. His spirit, anguished by leaving the physical world so prematurely, had remained earth-bound. Placing a tiny piece of amber at the base of the rosebush growing at his grave, I said a prayer for him. I could almost hear the rush of angel wings as Mr. Stanley was delivered into the Light.

But what about Julia? Why hadn't I been led to her grave? Under the large oak sheltering the Stanley gravesite and me from the pouring rain, I ventured to ask John about it.

"Me mum an' I still have a lot ta work out," I hear him saying candidly. "It's not yer place ta help us now, even though we need it and you are willing."

I left the cemetery full of respect for life's mysterious workings. Finally, events were making sense. As I waited to catch my train, I was seized with the realization that the cold I'd had was gone—no runny nose, no sore throat, no cough. I considered it a minor miracle; the power of healing apparently knows no bounds.

I had nothing material to show for my journey to Liverpool, yet I felt rich. Not only had I acquired unforgettable memories, but John had shared with me more elements of his unforgettable past; and for this, I felt honored.

★   ★   ★

On the morning of October 9th, John Lennon's fifty-second birthday, our children laughed as we sang to him. Little did they realize how sincere their parents really were.

"This is a great way to end, John. I suppose you organized it this way."

"Me? I thought *you* had."

"Well, I guess it's one more example of co-creation. How's it feel to be fifty-two?"

"Great. I can have my cake and eat it too! It makes me think of great, great uncle George."

"You mean . . ."

"Yeah, that poor, earth-bound chap who was finally rescued by a prayer. You don't know how happy you've made him! I saw him the other day—larking about with his wife, Ada—and all he could say was, 'I'm free!' "

"That's wonderful—though it did take awhile to figure out."

"It's not always easy. But, like Einstein said, 'everybody's got relatives,' " John says, smiling.

"Before this is over," he continues, "I want to remind folks of the importance of listening . . . and of saying hello to those who've passed over. Don't be afraid! It'll probably turn out different than you think."

"But shouldn't people be careful? Like with George—he didn't know how to let go."

"Right, because Ada didn't either! There's a fine line between loving someone and holding onto them. There needs ta be subtle understanding and respect, on both sides. And human beings will keep wondering, 'What is real? What is unreal?' One day they'll find their own answer."

"I guess this is goodbye, then?"

"I was never any good at saying goodbye! But now I want to say it to all the people John Lennon ever loved who are still walking the earth. I'm sorry for lots of things I did—but I'm glad for just as many. On a larger scale, there is no goodbye. We all shine on . . . the story is never-ending."